TESTS THAT TEACH

Analogies

Which pair of words a[re related in the]
same way as the words [...]

DIPSOMANIAC : TEETOT[ALER]

a. opponent : foe

b. billionaire : pauper

c. instructor : faculty

d. [...]

e. obstructionist : delay

Thinking with your new words

Which of the following creatures is least *photophobic*?

a. bees   b. bedbugs   c. earthworms

Someone who has *agoraphobia* would be least comfortable in _____ space.

a. an enclosed   b. an open   c. a shady

Building additional words

Complete the unfinished word by adding one of the following as a suffix:

PHOBIA	MANIA	PHILE
PHOBE	MANIAC	PHILIC
PHOBIC		

A Franco_____ has an extreme aversion to the French.

A Xeno_____ admires foreigners and foreign culture.

Signet

A World of Reference at Your Fingertips

THE NEW ROBERT'S RULES OF ORDER (2ND EDITION)
MARY A. DE VRIES
Long considered the bible of parliamentary procedures, this
new edition updates the archaic prose of the original into
easy-to-follow, contemporary English while maintaining the
work's original order and content.

**THE NEW AMERICAN ROGET'S COLLEGE THESAURUS IN
DICTIONARY FORM (REVISED & COMPLETELY UPDATED)**
PHILIP D. MOREHEAD, ED.
• First full revision since the original 1958 publication
• More than 20,000 new words and phrases
• 1,500 additional entries
• Synonyms and antonyms for each word listed
• New feature: famous quotes and phrases

**THE NEW AMERICAN WEBSTER HANDY
COLLEGE DICTIONARY (4TH EDITION)**
PHILIP D. MOREHEAD, ED.
The essential dictionary for every school, college, office, and
home. Inside this bestseller you'll find more features than in
any other pocket dictionary.

**Available wherever books are sold or at
penguin.com**

SIGNET
Published by New American Library, a division of
Penguin Group (USA) Inc., 375 Hudson Street,
New York, New York 10014, USA
Penguin Group (Canada), 90 Eglinton Avenue East, Suite 700, Toronto,
Ontario M4P 2Y3, Canada (a division of Pearson Penguin Canada Inc.)
Penguin Books Ltd., 80 Strand, London WC2R 0RL, England
Penguin Ireland, 25 St. Stephen's Green, Dublin 2,
Ireland (a division of Penguin Books Ltd.)
Penguin Group (Australia), 250 Camberwell Road, Camberwell, Victoria 3124,
Australia (a division of Pearson Australia Group Pty. Ltd.)
Penguin Books India Pvt. Ltd., 11 Community Centre, Panchsheel Park,
New Delhi - 110 017, India
Penguin Group (NZ), 67 Apollo Drive, Rosedale, North Shore 0632,
New Zealand (a division of Pearson New Zealand Ltd.)
Penguin Books (South Africa) (Pty.) Ltd., 24 Sturdee Avenue,
Rosebank, Johannesburg 2196, South Africa

Penguin Books Ltd., Registered Offices:
80 Strand, London WC2R 0RL, England

Published by Signet, an imprint of New American Library, a division of Penguin Group (USA) Inc. This is an authorized reprint of an edition published by Amsco School Publications, Inc. For information address Amsco School Publications, Inc., 315 Hudson Street, New York, New York 10013.

First Signet Printing, September 1997
20 19 18 17 16 15 14 13 12 11 10

 REGISTERED TRADEMARK—MARCA REGISTRADA

Printed in the United States of America

PUBLISHER'S NOTE
The publisher does not have any control over and does not assume any responsibility for author or third-party Web sites or their content.

If you purchased this book without a cover you should be aware that this book is stolen property. It was reported as "unsold and destroyed" to the publisher and neither the author nor the publisher has received any payment for this "stripped book."

The scanning, uploading, and distribution of this book via the Internet or via any other means without the permission of the publisher is illegal and punishable by law. Please purchase only authorized electronic editions, and do not participate in or encourage electronic piracy of copyrighted materials. Your support of the author's rights is appreciated.

THE JOY OF
VOCABULARY

SECOND EDITION

HAROLD LEVINE
Chairman Emeritus of English,
Benjamin Cardozo High School, New York

NORMAN LEVINE
Associate Professor of English,
City College of the City University of New York

ROBERT T. LEVINE
Professor of English,
North Carolina A & T State University

A SIGNET BOOK

PREFACE

The Joy of Vocabulary is intended for people who love words and delight in making choice additions to their vocabulary, or for those who feel they need a superior vocabulary to help them distinguish themselves in their chosen professions. This book provides materials and procedures to enable them to build that superior vocabulary pleasurably.

For this second edition, each chapter has been carefully reviewed and, where appropriate, revised and enriched. Altogether, some seventy-five words and expressions have been added. A new chapter—Chapter 26—deals with expressions English has adopted from other languages.

Thumb through *Joy,* noting the following:

- The variety of the lesson words (look at chapter titles)
- The previews allowing you instantly to see what you may already know about the lesson words
- The model sentences showing how to use each lesson word or expression
- The lessons on getting the meaning of an unfamiliar word from its context—or from its component parts
- The fun and challenge of the numerous exercises
- The skills of critical thinking, close reading, and concise writing taught in the exercises
- And the enlightening and entertaining examples

Imagine the powerful boost to your vocabulary that *The Joy of Vocabulary* can give as you pursue success in your academic, business, or professional world.

We hope you enjoy this book as much as we enjoyed putting it together.

CONTENTS

1

Number Words

What is a *fortnight*?

Once you realize that *fortnight* is a contraction of the Old English words for "fourteen" and "nights," you will not forget the meaning of this word.

By the way, doesn't it seem odd that time should be measured in *nights* rather than *days*? The fact is that, according to the Roman historian Tacitus, reckoning time in *nights* was an ancient custom of the Germanic tribes, which included, among others, the Angles and the Saxons.

A word about these Angles and Saxons: About the year 450, they invaded England, and they dominated the country until 1066. Their language, known to scholars as "Old English" or "Anglo-Saxon," was the earliest form of English.

We cannot, of course, say that *night* is *day*, but we can say that a fort*night* is fourteen *days*, or two weeks.

A. Preview

Complete each sentence below with a number, like *seven* or *1492*, as in the following sample:

Sample:

Johann Sebastian Bach (1685–1750) became a *sexagenarian* in 1745, and Ludwig van Beethoven (1770–1827) would have been one, too, had he lived another _____three_____ years.

Note, too, that each sentence contains one or more italic words, like *sexagenarian*, that you may or may not know. We shall pay special attention to these italic words shortly. In the meantime, answer each question to the best of your ability.

2 THE JOY OF VOCABULARY

1. If you own a cat, a dog, and two parrots, you have
   _____ *quadrupeds*.
2. Participants in a *decathlon* compete not just in the
   broad jump, high jump, and discus throw, but also in
   _____ additional track-and-field events.
3. After the *tithe* was collected, the French peasant who had
   harvested thirty bushels of wheat had only
   _____ of them left.
4. Harvard University, established in _____,
   had its *tercentennial* in 1936.
5. The United States, founded in 1776, celebrated its *centennial* in 1876, its *sesquicentennial* in _____,
   and its *bicentennial* in _____.
6. Among the winners of the Nobel Peace Prize were Martin
   Luther King, Jr., in 1964, and Desmond Tutu in
   _____, two *decades* later.
7. Anna Mary (Grandma) Moses (1860–1961) became
   a *sexagenarian* in 1920, a *septuagenarian* in
   _____, an *octogarian* in _____, a
   nonagenarian in _____, and a *centenarian* in
   _____.
8. The client waiting for Sherlock Holmes on
   July 15 had seen him a *fortnight* earlier, on July
   _____.
9. According to the Bible, Methuselah, grandfather of Noah,
   lived to the age of 969, just _____ years
   shy of a *millennium*.
10. Since the Olympics are a *quadrennial* event, contestants
    dissatisfied with their performance must wait
    _____ years for another chance.
11. A search of the suspect's van yielded three shotguns and a
    brace of pistols, or a total of _____ weapons.
12. The epidemic *decimated* the community; at least
    _____ in ten perished.
13. Divers working at five *fathoms* are _____
    feet below the surface.
14. When you buy twelve ears of corn, the seller often throws
    in _____ more without charge, so that you
    come home with a *baker's dozen*.
15. Having already won _____ games, the
    rookie pitcher needs one more win to end the season with
    a *score* of victories.

16. A *dichotomy* has developed within the club; there are now _____ factions.
17. A member of a *triumvirate* shares power and responsibility with _____ corulers.
18. Because it has _____ sides, the building that houses the Department of Defense is called the *Pentagon*.
19. If A gets 20 votes, B 15, and C 10, no one has a majority, but A has a *plurality* of _____.
20. The dues that used to be $5 a year are now $_____; the cost of membership has *trebled*.

B. Details About the Number Words

WORD	MEANING
baker's dozen *n* 'bāk-ərz'dəz-ᵊn	thirteen (Bakers, for fair measure, used to add a roll to each dozen sold.)

We now have twelve in our group, and if you join us we'll be a baker's dozen.

| **bicentennial** *n* ˌbī-sen-'te-nē-əl | 200th anniversary |

Louisiana, which became a state in 1812, will be observing its bicentennial *in 2012.*

| **brace** *n* 'brās | two of a kind; pair; couple |

A search of the suspect's van yielded three shotguns and a brace *of pistols, or a total of five weapons.*

| **centenarian** *n* ˌsen-tə-'ner-ē-ən | one who is 100 or older |

Irving Berlin (1888–1989) became a centenarian *in 1988.*

| **centennial** *n* sen-'te-nē-əl | 100th anniversary |

The Republic of Mexico, founded in 1824, observed its centennial *in 1924.*

WORD	MEANING

decade *n*
'de-,kād

period of ten years

There are ten decades *in a century.*

---

decathlon *n*
di-'kath-lən

track-and-field contest consisting of ten events

Every entrant in a decathlon *competes in ten track-and-field events.*

---

decimate *v*
'de-sə-,māt

destroy ten percent or more or a large portion of

In the 14th-century, Europe was decimated *by the bubonic plague.*

---

dichotomy *n*
dī-'kä-tə-mē

division in two; split

A dichotomy *on the issue of gun control threatened party unity.*

---

fathom *n*
'fa-<u>th</u>əm

measure of water depth equaling six feet

At least sixty feet of line is needed to touch bottom if the depth is ten fathoms.

---

fortnight *n*
'fort-,nīt

period of fourteen days; two weeks

We spent a fortnight *visiting our English cousins last summer.*

---

millennium *n*
mə-'le-nē-əm

1000 years; 1000th anniversary

Many redwood trees are more than a millennium *old.*

---

nonagenarian *n*
,nō-nə-jə-'ner-ē-ən

person in his or her nineties

Pablo Picasso (1881–1973) achieved the status of nonagenarian *in 1971.*

---

octogenarian *n*
,äk-tə-jə-'ner-ē-ən

person in his or her eighties

If she had lived two more years, Eleanor Roosevelt (1884–1962) would have been an octogenarian.

WORD	MEANING
pentagon *n* 'pen-tə-ˌgän	plane figure of five sides and five angles

In a regular pentagon, *all five sides are of equal length.*

| **plurality** *n*
plù-'ra-lə-tē | victor's margin over the runner-up when no candidate has a majority of the votes |

If A gets 20 votes, B 15, and C 10, A is the winner by a plurality *of 5.*

| **quadrennial** *n*
kwä-'dre-nē-əl | occurring or being done every four years |

Our Presidential elections are a quadrennial *event.*

| **quadruped** *n*
'kwä-drə-ˌped | four-footed animal |

The elephant was the most popular quadruped *in the circus.*

| **score** *n*
'skòr | group of twenty; twenty |

The legislator had spent a score *of years in the House, having been elected to ten consecutive terms.*

| **septuagenarian** *n*
(ˌ)sep-ˌtü-ə-jə-ˌner-ē-ən | person in his or her seventies |

At threescore and ten, one becomes a septuagenarian.

| **sesquicentennial** *n*
ˌses-kwi-sen-'te-nē-əl | 150th anniversary |

The Alaska purchase of 1867 will have its sesquicentennial *in 2017.*

| **sexagenarian** *n*
ˌsek-sə-jə-ˌner-ē-ən | person in his or her sixties |

In five years, one who has just become a sexagenarian *will be 65.*

| **tercentennial** *n*
ˌter-(ˌ)sen-'te-nē-əl | 300th anniversary |

Our 1776 Declaration of Independence will have its tercentennial *in 2076.*

WORD	MEANING
tithe *n* 'tī th	one-tenth; tenth part of a person's income paid as a contribution or tax to support a religious establishment

In France, before 1789, everyone except the nobles and clergy was required to pay tithes.

treble *v* 'tre-bəl	multiply by three; triple

If you invest $100, you have to get back $300 to treble *your investment.*

triumvirate *n* trī-'əm-və-rət	ruling body of three; troika

A member of a triumvirate *shares responsibility and power with two corulers.*

C. Thinking with Your New Words

Answer briefly.

1. A fortnightly magazine is dated May 1. What will be the date of the next issue? _____

2. Stella got 19 votes, Marie 12, and Eduardo 10. What was Stella's plurality? _____

3. The price of an item has trebled. It used to be $2.25. How much is it now? _____

4. What is the smallest number of complaints you must have received to be able to say truthfully that you have had more than a score? _____

5. Dalton has been with the company eight years, Lopez three, Martin two, Romano seven, and Axelrod seven. How many have given a decade of service?

_____

6. To what earlier date in our history was Lincoln referring when he began his 1863 *Gettysburg Address* with the words "Forescore and seven years ago"? _____

7. How many presidential elections normally occur in a score of years in a country like ours, where such elections are quadrennial? _____

8. If each side of a pentagonal field is 120 feet, how many feet of fencing would be needed to enclose the field? _____

9. Suppose you were a farmer in the Middle Ages. How many head of cattle would you be required to pay as a tithe if your herd had increased by twenty during the year?

_____

10. What year will be the millennium of the 1066 invasion of England by Norman-French forces led by William the Conqueror? _____

D. Concise Writing

Express the thought of each sentence in *no more than four words,* as in 1, below.

1. There are not too many people alive in this world who have reached the age of 100.
   There are few centenarians.

2. When is the 150th anniversary of the admission of the State of Nevada to the Union?

3. Is it true that the people who live next door to you are in their eighties?

4. Donald had a total of four votes more than the total number of votes cast for the runner up.

5. Most of the people who are between the ages of seventy and up to, but not including, eighty are retired.

E. Analogies

Write the *letter* of the pair of words related to each other in the same way as the words in the capitalized pair. The first three entries have been made and explained to assist you.

1. WEEK : FORTNIGHT
a. month : year
b. second : minute
c. inch : foot
d. pint : quart
e. slice : pie

Answer ___d___

Explanation: A WEEK is half a FORTNIGHT; a *pint* is half a *quart*.

2. DICHOTOMY : DISSENSION
a. pollution : environment
b. laryngitis : throat
c. page : book
d. bus : terminal
e. infection : fever

Answer ___e___

Explanation: DICHOTOMY may cause DISSENSION; *infection* may cause *fever*.

3. HORSE : QUADRUPED
a. cotton : fiber
b. fish : water
c. spider : victim
d. nylon : silk
e. cereal : oatmeal

Answer ___a___

Explanation: A HORSE is classified as a QUADRUPED; *cotton* is classified as a *fiber*.
Note: Choice *e* is incorrect because it is in the wrong order. If it were "oatmeal : cereal," it would qualify as a correct answer.

4. CENTURY : MILLENNIUM
a. penny : coin
b. dime : dollar
c. fog : visibility
d. jury : verdict
e. foot : yard

Answer _____

5. EPIDEMIC : DECIMATION
a. negligence : accident
b. starvation : famine
c. smoke : fire
d. oak : tree
e. foundation : building

Answer _____

6. BICENTENNIAL : ANNIVERSARY
a. summit : mountain
b. ocean : river
c. chisel : tool
d. hand : friendship
e. vehicle : bicycle

Answer _____

7. POLE VAULTING : DECATHLON
a. goalpost : football   d. calf-roping : rodeo
b. arena : bullfight   e. rink : ice hockey
c. bull pen : baseball   **Answer** _____

8. NONAGENARIAN : LONGEVITY
a. truant : attendance   d. chatterbox : silence
b. zealot : enthusiasm   e. child : experience
c. spendthrift : foresight   **Answer** _____

9. TITHE : FRACTION
a. toe : heel   d. flower : lily
b. thumb : finger   e. punch : fist
c. favoritism : resentment   **Answer** _____

10. THREESCORE : DOZEN
a. gold : silver   d. finger : hand
b. quarter : nickel   e. fathom : foot
c. penny : copper   **Answer** _____

Phobia, Mania, and Phile Words

Phobia (Phobe, Phobic). A *phobia* is an "abnormal fear, dislike, or hatred." *Acrophobia* is an "abnormal fear of being in high places." *Anglophobia* is an "abnormal dislike of England or the English." If you have such a dislike, you are an *Anglophobe*. Plants that require shade are described as *photophobic*—literally, "light-hating."

Mania (Maniac). A *mania*, on the other hand, is an "exaggerated enthusiasm, craze, or mad impulse." The exaggerated adoration of the Beatles, a rock music group extremely popular in the 1960s, was described as *Beatlemania*. An exaggerated devotion to England or the English is known as *Anglomania*. If you have such devotion, you are an *Anglomaniac*.

Phile (Philic). *Phile* is a root meaning "lover or admirer." An *audiophile* is "someone who admires, or is enthusiastic about, high-fidelity sound reproduction." An *Anglophile* is an "admirer of England or the English." Plants that thrive in the sun are described as *photophilic*—literally, "light-loving."

A. Preview

Here are some words for your *phobia*, *mania*, and *phile* vocabulary:

acrophobia	bibliophile	kleptomaniac	photophilic
agoraphobia	bibliophobe	mania	photophobia
audiophile	claustrophobia	megalomania	photophobic
balletomania	dipsomaniac	monomania	pyromaniac
bibliomania	hemophiliac	phobia	xenophobia

Complete each statement or question below by adding the most appropriate word from the above list.

1. Roses are _____: they love sunlight.
2. Some immigrants have been encountering instances of _____.
3. "What Shall We Do with the Drunken Sailor?" is a song about a(n) _____.
4. My cousin is a hi-fi audio enthusiast. Are you a(n) _____, too?
5. From the summit I admired the view, but Ruby would not look down, and became terrified. This was my first hint of her _____.
6. Lynne has an abnormal fear of drafts. Do you know anyone else with such a(n) _____?
7. Some bidders would have given anything to acquire the rare book, but I did not share their _____.
8. I really like books. You may say I am a(n) _____.
9. The woods abound in _____ plants that thrive in dense shade.
10. Those who suffer from _____ often prefer to remain indoors.
11. In his fantasies, Don Quixote did grandiose deeds, like fighting giants or rescuing a princess. He was afflicted with _____.
12. Fred's _____ dates from a childhood prank in which a playmate locked him in a closet.
13. Coming out of a movie theater in daylight, many of us experience _____ until our eyes become accustomed again to the light.
14. Captain Ahab would have been perfectly sane if not for his _____ for pursuing the white whale Moby Dick.
15. The suspect pleaded insanity, but the evidence showed he was an arsonist, not a(n) _____.
16. It is impossible to see the visiting dance company perform unless you ordered a ticket six months ago. There is _____ in this town.
17. I have a friend with a(n) _____ for running who does ten miles a day, rain or shine.
18. Even a minor wound can cause a(n) _____ to bleed excessively.
19. A court-appointed psychiatrist found that the well-to-do person charged with shoplifting was a(n) _____.

20. Students who used to hate books have been helped by skilled teachers to overcome their _____.

B. Details About *Phobia, Mania,* and *Phile* Words

WORD	MEANING
acrophobia *n* ˌa-krə-ˈfō-bē-ə	abnormal fear of being in high places

Sufferers from acrophobia *are not enthusiastic about mountain climbing.*

| **agoraphobia** *n* ˌa-g(ə)rə-ˈfō-bē-ə | abnormal fear of being in crowds, public places, or open areas |

One who has agoraphobia *tends to feel more at ease indoors.*

| **audiophile** *n* ˌȯ-dē-ō-ˌfīl | one especially interested in high-fidelity sound reproduction |

My cousin is a hi-fi audio enthusiast. Are you an audiophile, *too?*

| **balletomania** *n* ba-ˌle-tə-ˈmā-nē-ə | extreme enthusiasm for the ballet |

Enthusiasm for the ballet keeps growing; at times it approaches balletomania.

| **bibliomania** *n* ˌbib-lē-ə-ˈmā-nē-ə | craze for acquiring books, especially rare ones |

Some bidders would have given anything to acquire the rare book, but I did not share their bibliomania.

| **bibliophile** *n* ˈbi-blē-ə-ˌfīl | person who loves or collects books |

Many a bibliophile *enjoys acquiring rare old books.*

WORD	MEANING

bibliophobe *n*
'bi-blē-ə-,fōb

person with *bibliophobia* (hatred, fear, or mistrust of books)

With teacher help, some former bibliophobes *have gotten to like books.*

claustrophobia *n*
,klȯ-strə-'fō-bē-ə

dread of being in closed or narrow spaces

Fred's claustrophobia *dates from the time he was trapped in an elevator.*

dipsomaniac *n*
,dip-sə-'mā-nē-,ak

person with an uncontrollable craving for alcoholic beverages

The driver in the fatal crash was a dipsomaniac.

hemophiliac *n*
,hē-mə-'fi-lē-,ak

person afflicted with *hemophilia,* a tendency to bleed excessive from minor injuries; bleeder

A mere scratch can be a life-threatening emergency for a hemophiliac.

kleptomaniac *n*
,klep-tə-'mā-nē-,ak

one who has a persistent neurotic impulse to steal, though not in need

The well-to-do shoplifter may be a kleptomaniac.

mania *n*
'mā-nē-ə

exaggerated enthusiasm; craze; mad impulse

I have a friend with a mania *for running who does ten miles a day, rain or shine.*

megalomania *n*
,me-gə-lō-'mā-nē-ə

mental disorder characterized by fantasies of grandeur, power, wealth, etc.

In his fantasies, Don Quixote did grandiose deeds, like fighting giants or rescuing a princess. He was afflicted with megalomania.

WORD	MEANING
monomania *n* ˌmä-nə-ˈmā-nē-ə	derangement of the mind on one subject only

Captain Ahab's monomania *for revenge on Moby Dick is proof of his insanity.*

| **phobia** *n*
ˈfō-bē-ə | abnormal and persistent fear, dislike, or hatred |

Some grown-ups have yet to overcome their childhood phobia *of the dark.*

| **photophilic** *adj*
ˌfō-tōˈfil-ik | light-loving; requiring abundant light |

Roses are photophilic: *they love sunlight.*

| **photophobia** *n*
ˌfō-tə-ˈfō-bē-ə | painful sensitivity to light |

Coming out of a movie theater in daylight, many of us experience photophobia *until our eyes become accustomed again to the light.*

| **photophobic** *adj*
ˌfō-tə-ˌfō-bik | shunning light; light-hating |

Photophobic plants, like pachysandra, grow best in the shade.

| **pyromaniac** *n*
ˌpī-rō-ˈmā-nē-ˌak | person having an insane impulse to start fires |

Pyromaniacs are a menace because they feel compelled to set fires.

| **xenophobia** *n*
ˈze-nə-ˈfō-bē-ə | unreasonable fear or hatred of foreigners or strangers |

Tourists tend to boycott countries where xenophobia *is prevalent.*

C. Building Additional Words

Complete the unfinished word by adding one of the following as a suffix:

phobia	mania	phile
phobe	maniac	philic
phobic		

Sample:

A xeno<u>phobe</u>_____ has an intense dislike of foreigners and strange customs.

1. A mono_____ is deranged on one subject only.
2. If you are particularly fond of Chinese customs and traditions, you are a Sino_____.
3. An abnormal or unreasoning fear of fire can be summed up in one word: pyro_____.
4. A Franco_____ has an extreme aversion to the French.
5. A Hispano_____ is an admirer of Spanish culture.
6. The reporter's stories were Anglo_____; they showed partiality to the English.
7. Those rulers who believed they were invincible and set out to conquer the world were clearly megalo_____s.
8. Though he had been a Germano_____, Winston Churchill favored close ties with West Germany after the defeat of the Nazis.
9. Is there a cure for klepto_____?
10. A xeno_____ admires foreigners and foreign culture.
11. Anyone working in a small windowless room is likely to get a claustro_____ feeling.
12. Alcoholics Anonymous has been doing its utmost to combat dipso_____.
13. Hemo_____ bacteria thrive in a medium that contains blood.
14. When a democratic government was installed in the U.S.S.R., there was a worldwide lessening of Russo_____.
15. Italo_____s admire the achievements, customs, and traditions of the Italian people.

D. Thinking with Your New Words

Write the letter of the correct choice. The first answer has been entered as a sample.

1. It would be most dangerous to employ a dip-   b
   somaniac as a (a) bartender (b) bus driver (c)
   gardener.
2. A Hispanophile would have an understand-
   able preference for visiting (a) Brazil (b)
   Mexico (c) Canada.   _____
3. Which of the following creatures are least
   photophobic? (a) bees (b) bedbugs (c)
   earthworms   _____
4. You are least likely to encounter a bibliophobe in a (a) restaurant (b) motion picture
   theater (c) bookshop.   _____
5. Americans sometimes encounter xenophobia
   when they travel in (a) New England (b) the
   South (c) Europe.   _____
6. If you had acrophobia, you would probably
   feel most secure (a) on a diving board (b) at
   the beach (c) on a cliff.   _____
7. Which of the following is least likely to
   appeal to a person afflicted with claustrophobia? (a) hiking (b) outdoor dining (c) cave
   exploration   _____
8. Someone who has agoraphobia would be least
   comfortable in (a) an enclosed (b) an open (c)
   a shady place.   _____
9. Photophobic individuals do not enjoy (a)
   deep-sea diving (b) reading (c) sunbathing.   _____
10. An audiophile is particularly sensitive to (a)
    extreme heat (b) sound distortion (c) inade-
    quate lighting.   _____

E. Analogies

Write the *letter* of the pair of words related to each other in
the same way as the words in the capitalized pair. To assist
you, the first two entries have been made and explained.

1. DIPSOMANIAC : TEETOTALER
   a. opponent : foe   d. conductor : orchestra
   b. billionaire : pauper   e. obstructionist : delay
   c. instructor : faculty   **Answer** __b__

Explanation: A DIPSOMANIAC is the opposite of a TEETOTALER; a *billionaire* is the opposite of a *pauper*.

2. BIBLIOPHOBE : BOOKS
a. athlete : sports
b. nurse : health
c. democrat : tyranny
d. prisoner : liberty
e. performer : applause

Answer __c__

Explanation: A BIBLIOPHOBE dislikes BOOKS; a *democrat* dislikes *tyranny*.

3. XENOPHOBE : FOREIGN
a. kitten : milk
b. Anglomaniac : English
c. miser : expensive
d. guest : hospitable
e. bibliophile : books

Answer _____

4. BALLETOMANIA : CRAZE
a. injustice : rebellion
b. merit : fault
c. inmate : confinement
d. magazine : periodical
e. jealousy : friction

Answer _____

5. PYROMANIAC : FIRES
a. spendthrift : self-control
b. author : critics
c. speeder : crashes
d. tenant : housing
e. orphan : parents

Answer _____

6. MANIA : INDIFFERENCE
a. arthritis : handicap
b. overconfidence : defeat
c. smoking : addiction
d. doubt : certainty
e. enthusiasm : zeal

Answer _____

7. PHOBIA : ANXIETY
a. overwork : fatigue
b. spinach : vegetable
c. exercise : moderation
d. period : punctuation
e. cowardice : bravery

Answer _____

8. AGORAPHOBIA : CROWD
a. hemophilia : scratch
b. megalomania : power
c. claustrophobia : sunlight
d. dipsomania : alcohol
e. kleptomania : illness

Answer _____

"One" and "Many" Words

By "one" words, we mean words beginning with the ancient Greek prefix *mono* or the Latin prefix *uni,* both meaning "one."

*Mono*culture, for example, is the use of land for the growing of only *one* crop.

A *uni*directional wheel is a wheel that turns in only *one* direction.

By "many" words, we mean words beginning with the ancient Greek prefix *poly* or the Latin prefix *multi,* both meaning "many."

A *poly*syllabic word consists of *many* syllables.

A *multi*nuclear cell contains *many* nuclei.

A. Preview

Complete each partially spelled word below by adding *mono, uni* or *un, multi,* or *poly.*

Samples:

Though Henry VIII had six wives, he was a
_____ mono gamist because he was married to only one of them at a time.

"Cat" is a _____ mono syllabic word; "hippopotamus" is _____ poly syllabic.

A _____ uni corn is a mythical animal with the body of a horse and a single horn in the middle of its forehead.

Under the Moors, medieval Spain's chief city, Cordoba, was _____ multi cultural; it had a harmonious African-European population of Moslems, Christians, and Jews.

1. A _____gamist is a person who is married to several mates at the same time.
2. Every word in "the house that Jack built" is _____ syllabic.
3. A _____national corporation has branches in two or more countries.
4. It is _____tonous to listen to anyone who speaks in one unvarying tone.
5. A _____math is someone who is learned in many subjects.
6. Potatoes usually are not _____form; they vary in size and shape.
7. The loser had ads in only one of the media, newspapers, while the winner was running a _____media campaign of TV, radio, and newspaper commercials.
8. A _____lateral treaty is many-sided and involves more than two countries.
9. The Greeks and Romans were _____theistic: they worshiped many gods.
10. A _____graph is a scholarly treatise on one particular subject.
11. A _____lateral opinion does not represent the thinking of the entire group: it is one-sided.
12. A conversation in which one person does all the talking is really a _____logue.
13. Rensselaer _____technic Institute, which granted the first U.S. engineering degrees, provides instruction in many areas of science and technology.
14. Anyone who understands and speaks several languages is a _____glot.
15. Some legislatures are _____cameral; they consist of only one house.
16. Some problems are difficult because they contain many aspects: they are _____faceted.
17. _____sex clothes and haircuts offer one and the same style for males and females.
18. A _____rail is a railroad whose cars are suspended from a single rail.
19. Everyone had one and the same opinion; the vote was _____animous.
20. Anything that is the only one of its kind is _____que.

B. Details About *Mono, Uni, Multi,* and *Poly* Words

WORD	MEANING
monograph *n* 'mä-nə-ˌgraf	learned treatise on a particular subject; scholarly article

In 1905, Albert Einstein published his first monograph *on the theory of relativity.*

monologue or **monolog** *n* 'mä-nᵊl-ˌȯg	lengthy talk by one person

The next scene is a monologue *since one actor does all the talking.*

monorail *n* 'mä-nə-ˌrāl	railway whose cars are supported on or under a single rail

Monorails *provide transportation over short distances in several cities.*

monosyllabic *adj* ˌmä-nə-sə-'la-bik	having only one syllable (*ant* **polysyllabic,** having two or more syllables)

All the words in "all dressed up and no place to go" are monosyllabic.

monotonous *adj* mə-'nä-tᵊn-əs	tiresome because of lack of variety

The same menu was followed each day; the meals became monotonous.

multicultural *adj* ˌməl-tē-'kəlch-rəl	reflecting many different cultures

In a multicultural *city, one sees churches, mosques, and synagogues, and hears many foreign tongues.*

multifaceted *adj* ˌməl-tə-'fas-ə-təd	having many facets or aspects

Labor disputes are usually multifaceted; *they involve wages, health benefits, working conditions, and many related matters.*

WORD	MEANING
multilateral *adj* ,məl-ti-'la-tə-rəl	having many sides; participated in by more than two participants (*ant* **unilateral,** one-sided)

In 1911, a multilateral *agreement was signed by Great Britain, Japan, Russia, and the U.S. on the hunting of seals.*

| **multimedia** *adj*
,məl-tə-'mē-dē-ə | involving a combination of media, such as TV, radio, and newspapers |

Companies that use TV and radio ads are multimedia *advertisers.*

| **multinational** *adj*
,məl-tə-'nash-nəl | having subsidiaries or operations in several countries |

We deal with a multinational *bank that has offices in the world's leading cities.*

| **polygamist** *n*
pə-'li-gə-məst | person married to two or more mates at the same time (*ant* **monogamist,** person with only one spouse at a time) |

It was his third marriage, and not having been divorced from his first two wives, he was in fact a polygamist.

| **polyglot** *n*
'pä-lē-,glät | person who speaks or writes several languages |

Our guide was a polyglot *who spoke English, Spanish, Creole, and Chinese.*

| **polymath** *n*
'pä-lē-,math | person of great and diversified learning |

My knowledge is not encyclopedic. I am not a polymath.

| **polytechnic** *adj*
,pä-lē-'tek-nik | providing instruction in many technical arts and applied sciences |

Degrees in engineering, applied physics, and industrial technology can be earned at polytechnic *institutes.*

WORD	MEANING
polytheistic adj ˌpä-lē-thē-ˈis-tik	believing in more than one god (*ant* **monotheistic**, believing in only one god)

When the Hebrews first adopted the concept of one God, most of the other religions were polytheistic.

unanimous adj yu̇-ˈna-nə-məs	being of one and the same opinion; showing complete agreement

On the matter of raising the dues, we were not unanimous; *one member dissented.*

unicameral adj ˌyü-ni-ˈkam-(ə)-rəl	consisting of or having one legislative chamber

The Swedish legislature is unicameral, *consisting solely of the Riksdag.*

uniform adj ˈyü-nə-ˌfȯrm	always the same; not varying in form, degree, or manner

The construction has not been of uniform *quality; most of it is good, but some of it is poor.*

unique adj yu̇-ˈnēk	being the only one of its kind; highly unusual

Donna's straight-A average is remarkable but not unique; *two others in the graduating class have the same average.*

unisex adj ˈyü-nə-ˌseks	not distinguishable as male or female; designed for both sexes

The unisex *clothes of the peasants working in the fields made it difficult to tell whether a particular individual was a man or a woman.*

C. Building Additional Words

Complete the unfinished word by adding one of the following as a prefix:

mono *or* mon	multi
uni	poly

Sample:

_____ Mono gamy is the practice of being married to only one person at a time.

1. To be in perfect _____ son, we must act together as one.
2. When you have several million dollars, you will be a _____ millionaire.
3. A _____ clinic is a clinic or hospital treating many kinds of diseases.
4. If you can speak or use only one language, you are _____ lingual.
5. An exhibit is _____ chromatic if it uses various or changing colors.
6. This is a _____ racial city; members of several races live here.
7. _____ gamy is the practice of being married to two or more spouses at the same time.
8. You need excellent balance to ride the trick one-wheeled vehicle called a _____ cycle.
9. _____ theism is belief in one God.
10. An eyeglass for one eye only is known as a _____ ocle.

D. Thinking with Your New Words

First read all of the following statements. Then answer each question below.

Statements

Just before his death in A.D. 337, the Roman Emperor Constantine became a Christian.

Louise, a member of the Entertainment Committee, hired a band without consulting the other members of the committee.

Mitchell used his acreage solely to grow corn.

Henrietta would have preferred something more feminine than the coveralls required on her assembly-line job.

Davis spoke nearly an hour; no one else said anything.

Before moving to the Netherlands, Raquel knew only English.

Mario had a fine command of Italian, Russian, French, German, and English.

Edna was a walking encyclopedia. She had extensive knowledge of a wide variety of subjects.

Smith was no talker; about all he was ever heard to say was "yeh," "naw," and "gosh."

Koji started in the New York office, was transferred to Athens, and later took charge of the Singapore branch.

Questions

Answer by inserting the most appropriate name from the statements above. The first answer has been inserted as a sample.

1.	Who used to be monolingual?	Raquel
2.	Who acted unilaterally?	
3.	Who worked for a multinational corporation?	
4.	Who had a monosyllabic vocabulary?	
5.	Who was a polymath?	
6.	Who abandoned polytheism?	
7.	Who practiced monoculture?	
8.	Who disliked unisex attire?	
9.	Who was a polyglot?	
10.	Who delivered a monologue?	

E. Analogies

Write the *letter* of the pair of words related to each other in the same way as the words in the capitalized pair. To assist you, the first two entries have been made and explained.

1. MONORAIL : TRANSPORTATION

   a. locomotive : track
   b. cart : horse
   c. elevator : grain
   d. ambulance : hospital
   e. encyclopedia : information

   Answer __e__

Explanation: A MONORAIL provides TRANSPORTATION; an *encyclopedia* provides *information.*

2. MULTIMILLIONAIRE : WEALTH
a. kleptomaniac : guilt   *d.* hunter : prey
b. investigator : evidence *e.* photocopy : uniqueness
c. genius : intelligence   **Answer** _c_

Explanation: A MULTIMILLIONAIRE has a great deal of WEALTH; a *genius* has a great deal of *intelligence.*

3. UNIFORM : VARY
a. irritating: annoy   *d.* temporary : endure
b. tiresome : bore   *e.* promising : encourage
c. informative : enlighten   **Answer** _____

4. DOOR : PRIVACY
a. desk : furniture   *d.* monologue : variety
b. dampness : mildew   *e.* window : ventilation
c. rug : wool   **Answer** _____

5. EMPEROR : POWER
a. miser : generosity   *d.* vandal : damage
b. victim : assistance   *e.* polyglot : translation
c. zealot : enthusiasm   **Answer** _____

6. LISTENER : MONOTONY
a. parent : disobedience   *d.* customer : courtesy
b. reader : suspense   *e.* song : repetition
c. cousin : relative   **Answer** _____

7. LAMP : ILLUMINATION
a. house : shelter   *d.* heat : furnace
b. refrigerator : electricity *e.* precipitation : hail
c. unicycle : skill   **Answer** _____

8. EXECUTIVE : RESPONSIBILITY
a. prisoner : freedom   *d.* prestige : champion
b. beginner : guidance   *e.* polymath : learning
c. mathematician : numbers   **Answer** _____

4

"Over" and "Under" Words

By "over" words, we mean words beginning with the Greek prefix *hyper* or the Latin prefix *super,* both meaning "over," "above," or "excessively."

A *hyper*acid stomach, for example, is one that produces too much acid, *over* or *above* the amount needed for normal digestion.

A *super*structure is all of a building *over* or *above* the foundation.

By "under" words, we mean words beginning with the Greek prefix *hypo* or the Latin prefix *sub,* both meaning "under" or "below."

A *hypo*acid stomach produces too little acid, *under* or *below* the amount needed for normal digestion.

A *sub*structure is an *under*structure or foundation of a building.

A. Preview

Complete each statement or question below by inserting the most appropriate word from the following list:

hyperacidity	hypodermic	subaqueous	supererogatory
hyperactive	hypoglycemic	subcutaneous	superficial
hypercritical	hyposensitize	sublethal	supernatural
hypersensitive	hypotension	submarginal	supernumerary
hypertension	hypothermia	subservient	supersonic

1. Lori's feelings are easily hurt; she is
_____.

2. The medical term for abnormally high blood pressure is
_____.

3. The prime minister who differed with the monarch's

views was ousted and replaced by someone more
_____.

4. A plane flying above 750 miles an hour (the speed of sound) is moving at a _____ speed.

5. The medical term for abnormally low blood pressure is
_____.

6. The injury is quite _____: the underlying tissues have not been damaged.

7. The indiscriminate taking of antacids to relieve _____ can lead to serious consequences.

8. You always find fault with others and never say a good word about anyone. Why are you so _____?

9. The would-be suicide had taken a _____ dose and was therefore able to recover.

10. With the temperatures mostly below freezing, the poorly clad troops began to suffer from _____.

11. Professional divers have been able to photograph a variety of _____ animals and plants.

12. Addicts may contract AIDS if they inject drugs with an unclean _____.

13. Bloodless and fleshless beings, like ghosts and spirits, belong to the _____ world, not the real world.

14. Since I am not in charge, it would be _____ for me to give orders.

15. A first-degree burn reddens only the outer layer of the skin, with no _____ damage.

16. If the only tooth you have ever lost was a _____ one, you still have a complete set of teeth.

17. Patients whose blood sugar level is abnormally high are hyperglycemic, and those whose level is abnormally low are _____.

18. Let me warn you not to believe all of the stories the child has been telling; he has a _____ imagination.

19. Future increases in silver prices may make it economically feasible to reopen mines now considered
_____.

20. The patient received treatment to _____ her to the pollen causing her allergic reaction.

B. Details About *Hyper, Hypo, Super,* and *Sub* Words

WORD	MEANING
hyperacidity *n* ,hī-pər-ə-'si-də-tē	excessive acidity, especially in the stomach

The indiscriminate taking of antacids to relieve hyperacidity *can lead to serious consequences.*

hyperactive *adj* ,hī-pər-'ak-tiv	excessively active

Let me warn you not to believe all the stories the child has been telling; she has a hyperactive *imagination.*

hypercritical *adj* ,hī-pər-'kri-ti-kəl	excessively fault-finding; captious

You always find fault with others and never say a good word about anyone. Why are you so hypercritical?

hypersensitive *adj* ,hī-pər-'sen-sə-tiv	abnormally sensitive

Lori's feelings are easily hurt; she is hypersensitive.

hypertension *n* ,hī-pər-'ten(t)-shən	abnormally high blood pressure

Hypertension *is quite common. Almost every one of us knows someone who has high blood pressure.*

hypodermic *n* ,hī-pə-'dər-mik	small syringe with a hollow needle for making injections beneath the skin

Addicts may contract AIDS if they inject drugs with an unclean hypodermic.

hypoglycemic *adj* ,hī-pō-,glī-'sē-mik	afflicted with *hypoglycemia* (an abnormally low concentration of sugar in the blood)

Patients whose blood sugar level is abnormally high are hyperglycemic, *and those whose level is abnormally low are* hypoglycemic.

WORD	MEANING

hyposensitize *v* — make less sensitive
ˌhī-pō-'sen-sə-ˌtīz

The patient received treatment to hyposensitize *her to the pollen causing her allergic reaction.*

hypotension *n* — abnormally low blood pressure
ˌhī-pō-'ten(t)-shən

Do you have hypotension? *My blood pressure, too, is abnormally low.*

hypothermia *n* — subnormal body temperature
ˌhī-pō-'thər-mē-ə

With the temperatures mostly below normal, the poorly clad troops began to suffer from hypothermia.

subaqueous *adj* — underwater
ˌsəb-'ā-kwē-əs

Professional divers have been able to photograph a variety of subaqueous *animals and plants.*

subcutaneous *adj* — being, living, or introduced
ˌsəb-kyù-'tā-nē-əs — beneath the skin

A first-degree burn reddens only the outer layer of the skin, with no subcutaneous *damage.*

sublethal *adj* — not quite *lethal* (death-
ˌsəb-'lē-thəl — causing); insufficient to
cause death

The would-be suicide had taken a sublethal *dose and was therefore able to recover.*

submarginal *adj* — below minimum standards;
ˌsəb-'märj-nəl — inadequate for some end;
unproductive

Future increases in silver prices may make it economically feasible to reopen mines now considered submarginal.

WORD	MEANING
subservient *adj* səb-'sər-vē-ənt	useful in an "under," or subordinate, capacity; excessively submissive

The minister who differed with the monarch's views was ousted and replaced by someone more subservient.

| **supererogatory** *adj*
,sü-pə-ri-'rä-gə-,tōr-ē | beyond the requirements of duty; performed to an extent not demanded |

Since I am not in charge, it would be supererogatory of me to give orders.

| **superficial** *adj*
,sü-pər-'fi-shəl | over or on the surface only; not profound or thorough |

The injury is quite superficial: the underlying tissues have not been damaged.

| **supernatural** *adj*
,sü-pər-'na-chə-rəl | beyond what is natural or observable; not explainable by the laws of nature |

Bloodless and fleshless beings, like ghosts and spirits, belong to the supernatural world, not the real world.

| **supernumerary** *adj*
,sü-pər-'nü-mə-,rer-ē | exceeding the standard or prescribed number; extra |

If the only tooth you have ever lost was a supernumerary one, you still have a complete set of teeth.

| **supersonic** *adj*
,sü-pər-'sä-nik | having a speed beyond that of sound |

A plane flying above 750 miles an hour (the speed of sound) is moving at a supersonic speed.

C. Building Additional Words

Complete the unfinished word by adding one of the following as a prefix:

hyper   hypo   super   sub

Sample:

> After World War II, the U.S. and the U.S.S.R. were the
> leading _____super____powers.

1. Our fuel resources have been increased by
   _____oceanic oil discoveries.
2. The concrete foundation is in place, and the carpenters are
   now beginning on the _____structure.
3. With the help of their physicians, _____tensive
   patients have been able to reduce their blood pressure.
4. Deficient production of hormones by the thyroid gland is a
   condition known as _____thyroidism.
5. A 300,000-ton _____tanker can transport an
   immense quantity of oil.
6. _____allergenic cosmetics are for persons
   allergic to ingredients in ordinary cosmetics.
7. _____microscopic substances are too tiny to be
   observed with an optical microscope.
8. Excessive intake of vitamins may cause _____
   vitaminosis.
9. It was impossible to hear what they were saying because
   they conversed in _____audible tones.
10. When you said you have a "million" golf balls at home,
    you were using a figure of speech known as overstate-
    ment, or _____bole.

D. Thinking with Your New Words

First read all of the following statements. Then answer each
question below.

Statements

Bill has no authority to tell you when to go to lunch; he is
not the office manager.

Hamlet, in an unforgettable scene, has a conversation with
the ghost of his murdered father.

Tests show that Kathy's blood sugar is abnormally low.

The club bats .272 and fields .914. Ralph's achievements in
these areas are .249 and .700, respectively.

Though some of the shop procedures seem wasteful to him, Fred never challenges them, but does as he is told.

Pearson, an elderly tenant, is unable to keep warm. There has been no heat or hot water in his apartment for four days.

Helen says there are tons of food in the refrigerator, so please do not bring anything to eat.

Andy was hired as an extra; he appears on stage in a crowd, or as a passerby.

Richard often complains of acid indigestion.

Everyone praised my paper except Edith, who said I had not dotted two *i*'s and crossed one *t*.

Questions

1. Who appears to be fond of hyperbole? _____
2. Who encounters a supernatural agent? _____
3. Who is hypercritical? _____
4. Who is supererogatory? _____
5. Who is a supernumerary employee? _____
6. Who is subservient? _____
7. Who appears to be hypoglycemic? _____
8. Who may be coming down with hypothermia? _____
9. Who is a submarginal performer? _____
10. Who seems to be afflicted with hyperacidity? _____

E. Analogies

Enter the *letter* of the pair of words related to each other in the same way as the words in the capitalized pair. Several hints are provided.

1. SUBSERVIENT : SUBMISSIVE
a. easygoing : strict
b. neurotic : stable
c. wavering : confident
d. irresponsible : trustworthy
e. painstaking : careful

Answer _____

Hint: A SUBSERVIENT person is very SUBMISSIVE.

2. HYPERTENSIVE : BLOOD PRESSURE
a. xenophobic : strangers
b. overoptimistic : expectations
c. hypoglycemic : blood sugar
d. reckless : caution
e. malnourished : vitality

Answer _____

3. UNDERSTATEMENT : HYPERBOLE
a. origin : source
b. irregularity : uniformity
c. score : twenty
d. plurality : majority
e. result : outcome

Answer _____

4. SUPERFICIAL : DEPTH
a. alluring : charm
b. multilateral : sides
c. significant : meaning
d. perilous : risk
e. unattractive : appeal

Answer _____

Hint: Something that is SUPERFICIAL lacks DEPTH.

5. MUTTER : SUBAUDIBLE
a. whisper : loud
b. grieve : gleeful
c. shout : low
d. moan : complaining
e. gargle : pleasant

Answer _____

Hint: A person who MUTTERS makes SUBAUDIBLE sounds.

6. SUBMICROSCOPIC : MINUTE
a. astronomical : large
b. inconsequential : necessary
c. puny : noteworthy
d. colossal : undersized
e. overshadowed : conspicuous

Answer _____

7. CAPTIOUS : PLEASE
a. stubborn : dissuade
b. attentive : instruct
c. timid : worry
d. accessible : reach
e. hypersensitive : offend

Answer _____

Hint: A CAPTIOUS person is hard to PLEASE.

8. HYPOSENSITIZE : SENSITIVE
a. enlighten : knowledgeable   d. demote : important
b. congratulate : proud   e. educate: independent
c. liberate : free   **Answer** _____

Hint: To HYPOSENSITIZE someone is to make that person less SENSITIVE.

5

New Words from Opposites in the Context

When we meet a new word, it is rarely by itself. Most of the time it is used with other words. These other words are its *context*.

The context often can help you get the meaning of a word you do not know. For example, if *bagatelle* is unfamiliar to you, you should be able to get its meaning from the following context:

A forged signature is no mere *bagatelle*. It is a serious matter.

Obviously, two ideas are being *contrasted* in the above context: (1) a *bagatelle* and (2) a *serious matter*.

Since the two are *opposites*, if we know one we can tell the meaning of the other.

A *bagatelle* is the *opposite* of a *serious matter*: *bagatelle* means a "trifling matter," or "trifle."

A. Preview

Write the meaning of the italicized word. In each case you will find a clue to its meaning in an *opposite* or *contrasting expression* in the context.

Sample:

The friendship between Canada and the United States is not of a *transitory* nature: it has endured for generations.

Transitory means <u>temporary</u>.

1. My friend's mother says little, but his father is particularly *garrulous* and engages me in hour-long conversations.

   Garrulous means _____.

2. Are you questioning my *veracity*? Have I ever lied to you?

   Veracity means _____.

3. A supervisor who is used to getting cooperation may not know how to deal wisely with a *refractory* employee.

   Refractory means _____.

4. Instead of reducing the severity of the illness, the new medication seems to have *exacerbated* it.

   Exacerbated means _____.

5. Why are you impatient? Your turn will come in a few minutes. Show some *forbearance*.

   Forbearance means _____.

6. I am glad to see that the members who were at odds with each other are now *reconciled*.

   Reconciled means _____.

7. Forgetfulness is a *venial* offense; it should not be confused with deliberate dishonesty, which in my view is unpardonable.

   Venial means _____.

8. The living room was tidy, but the kitchen had a *slatternly* appearance.

   Slatternly means _____.

9. We are not here to discuss unimportant matters. Why are you bringing up something of no *moment*?

   Moment means _____.

10. Gladys does not care for crossword puzzles, but Eunice has a *penchant* for such things.

    Penchant means _____.

Checking Up on Your Reasoning

Now that you have completed the foregoing exercise, compare the following answers and reasoning with your own.

NEW WORD	CONTRASTING CONTEXT CLUE	PROBABLE MEANING OF NEW WORD
1. *garrulous*	*says little*	talkative
2. *veracity*	*lied*	truthfulness
3. *refractory*	*cooperation*	uncooperative; obstinate
4. *exacerbated*	*reducing the severity of*	increased the severity of; intensified
5. *forbearance*	*impatient*	patience
6. *reconciled*	*at odds with each other*	restored to friendship
7. *venial*	*unpardonable*	pardonable; forgivable
8. *slatternly*	*tidy*	untidy
9. *moment*	*unimportant*	importance
10. *penchant*	*does not care*	liking

B. Details About the New Words

WORD	MEANING
bagatelle *n* ͵ba-gə-'tel	trifle; something of little value or importance

I did not know the pin's value when I gave it away, thinking it was just a bagatelle.

| **exacerbate** *v*
ig-'za-sər-͵bāt | make more severe or violent; aggravate |

If I had brought up our old disagreement, it would have exacerbated *our present quarrel, so I did not mention it.*

| **forbearance** *n*
fȯr-'bar-ən(t)s | self-control; patience |

Please, no more delays or postponements! Our forbearance *is nearly at an end.*

| **garrulous** *adj*
'gar-ə-ləs | talking too much about unimportant things; loquacious; talkative |

A long-distance telephone conversation with a garrulous *person is bound to be very expensive.*

WORD	MEANING

moment *n*
'mō-mənt
importance; consequence

Is the matter of such moment *that it needs instant attention, or can it be put off until tomorrow?*

---

penchant *n*
'pen-chənt
strong leaning; fondness; liking

Luis ordered a second dessert; he has a penchant *for sweets.*

---

reconcile *v*
're-kən-,sīl
1. make friendly again

The two are such bitter foes that it is unwise to try to recon-cile them.

2. settle; adjust

It is unlikely that their dispute will ever be reconciled.

---

refractory *adj*
ri-'frak-tə-rē
hard to control; resisting authority; unruly; obstinate

In interviewing the parents of the refractory *child, we learned that she defied them, too.*

---

slatternly *adj*
'sla-tərn-lē
dirty; untidy; slovenly

The tables had not been cleared, and the place looked so slatternly *that we decided to go to another restaurant.*

---

transitory *adj*
'tran(t)-sə-,tòr-ē
lasting a short time only; temporary; short-lived

Her stocks went up, but her delight was transitory *because they fell sharply the following week.*

---

venial *adj*
'vē-nē-əl
forgivable; pardonable; excusable

An occasional lateness is a venial *fault; it is not a crime.*

---

veracity *n*
ve-ra-se-tē
truthfulness; honesty

A person convicted of perjury in the past does not have a reputation for veracity.

C. Thinking with Your New Words

Read all of the following statements. Then answer each question below.

Statements

Joyce said Charley owed her a paper clip, and she insisted on getting it back.

Emma hated to go back to her regular job after serving as acting director for a week.

Myo used to collect seashells, but she has given up the hobby.

The money should have been returned to Gary on the first, but so far he has not pressed us for payment

There was dust on the furniture, the paint was peeling, and cobwebs hung from the walls. Steve asked the desk clerk for another room.

When Patricia revealed she was getting married, we congratulated her.

Shelly was unnecessarily rude to the officer who stopped him for going through a red light.

The president called for order, but Chester deliberately kept whistling until Ben gave him a stern look.

I still would not be talking to Pearl if Charlotte had not persuaded us to bury the hatchet.

Walt took my keys by accident. I am sure it was just a mistake.

If you are willing to listen, Henry can sit and chat for half the morning.

Some of the things Anne told us in the past we later found to be not exactly true.

Questions

1. Who showed forbearance?　　　　　　_____

2. Who made an issue over a
   bagatelle?   _____
3. Who brought about a
   reconciliation?   _____
4. Who enjoyed transitory prestige?   _____
5. Who made a momentous
   announcement?   _____
6. Who rebuked a refractory
   individual?   _____
7. Who made departures from
   veracity?   _____
8. Who was thought to have committed a venial error?   _____
9. Who seems to have outgrown a
   penchant?   _____
10. Who is inclined to be garrulous?   _____
11. Who rejected slatternly
    accommodations?   _____
12. Who exacerbated a difficult
    situation?   _____

D. Concise Writing

Express the thought of each sentence below in *no more than four words*, as in 1, below:

1. Stay away from those who are in the habit of talking
   at great length about things that are of little value or
   importance.
   Avoid garrulous people.

2. There are times when crowds of people are hard to control.

3. The blunders that Cy committed are of a kind that can be
   forgiven.

4. The feeling of despair that swept over me lasted only a
   short time.

5. No one questioned whether or not Sandy was telling the
   truth.

E. Analogies

Write the *letter* of the pair of words related to each other in the same way as the words in the capitalized pair.

1. ARSON : VENIAL
   a. fact : alterable
   b. phobia : abnormal
   c. self-defense : justifiable
   d. nourishment : essential
   e. carbon monoxide : lethal

   Answer_____

Hint: ARSON is something that is not VENIAL.

2. PERJURER : VERACITY
   a. dipsomaniac : alcohol
   b. enthusiast : zeal
   c. pyromaniac : self-control
   d. centenarian : longevity
   e. daredevil : audacity

   Answer_____

3. REFRACTORY : OBEY
   a reasonable : compromise
   b. garrulous : speak
   c. anxious : worry
   d. indecisive : hesitate
   e. subservient : rebel

   Answer_____

4. TRANSITORY : DURATION
   a. imperative : urgency
   b. inconsequential : moment
   c. insurmountable : difficulty
   d. invaluable : worth
   e. interminable : beginning

   Answer_____

Hint: Something TRANSITORY is of little DURATION.

5. FORBEARANCE : IMPATIENCE
   a. uniformity : monotony
   b. mania : craze
   c. discord : unanimity
   d. hypothermia : fatality
   e. exaggeration : hyperbole

   Answer_____

Review of Chapters 1–5

I. Fill the blanks below, choosing your answers from the following list:

deca	mono	phobia	sub
hyper	multi	poly	super
hypo	pent	quadr	uni
mania	phile		

1. Both _____ and _____ mean "one."
2. _____ at the end of a word means "lover."
3. _____ means "five."
4. _____ means "four."
5. Both _____ and _____ mean "over."
6. _____ at the end of a word means "abnormal fear."
7. Both _____ and _____ mean "under."
8. _____ at the end of a word means "exaggerated desire."
9. Both _____ and _____ mean "many."
10. _____ means "ten."

II. What single word can replace the italicized words? Find that word, partially spelled, in the list at the end of this exercise, and complete its spelling before using it.

1. It is a mistake to dely an important transaction over a(n) *trifling matter*.   _____

2. Presidential elections are held *every four years* in the United States. _____

3. The damage was *on the surface*. _____

4. The fact is that he runs a tiny business, but in his *delusions of grandeur* he fancies himself a captain of industry. _____

5. Luckily, the quantity of the toxic substance swallowed by the patient was *insufficient to cause death*. _____

6. She is a(n) *admirer of French culture*. _____

7. Elderly persons living in insufficiently heated housing may suffer from *subnormal body temperature*. _____

8. I have been a member of this organization for a *period of ten years*. _____

9. Mountain climbing is not for you if you have *an abnormal fear of heights*. _____

10. Bea's outfit was not *the only one of its kind* because I saw others wearing it, too. _____

11. Laboratory tests show that the quality of this product is *below minimum standards*. _____

12. A *person with a neurotic impulse to steal* needs psychiatric attention. _____

13. The Bible contains a very high percentage of *one-syllable* words. _____

14. Herb is *inclined to talk too much about trivial matters*. _____

15. The *two-hundredth anniversary* of the Alaska purchase will be observed in 2067. _____

16. The closing of this factory will
make the economic condition of
the area *worse*.   _____

17. Disease used to *destroy a large
portion* of the herds.   _____

18. The sisters refuse to talk to each
other, and it is futile to try to
make them *friendly again*.   _____

19. *Worship of more than one god*
was characteristic of several
early religions.   _____

20. There were occasions in Rome
when the government was con-
trolled by a *group of three rulers*.   _____

rec __ __ cile   __ __ ique   ex __ __ erbate
sub __ __ thal   ac __ __ phobia   __ __ perficial
__ __ gatelle   __ __ cade   mo __ __ syllabic
gar __ __ lous   fran __ __ phile klep __ __ maniac
__ __ centennial   tri __ __ virate __ __ lytheism
mega __ __ mania   submarg __ __ al hypo __ __ ermia
__ __ adrennially   __ __ climate

III. Eliminate the repetition in each passage below by
replacing the italicized word or expression with a synonym.
Choose your synonyms from the list of words at the end of this
exercise.

1. The committee is split right
down the middle on this issue,
but I do not know what has
caused the *split*.   _____

2. All the houses had the same
doors and windows, and the
garages were *all the same*, too.   _____

3. A sensible host will not serve
one alcoholic drink after another
to a known *alcoholic*.   _____

4. They keep a pair of cats and a(n)
pair of hounds.   _____

5. Oil tripled in price in a short time, and some said it would *triple* again. _____

6. Had we known you were going to deliver a(n) *long talk,* we would not have asked you to talk. _____

7. In music they lean toward the classics, and in politics they have a(n) *strong leaning* for the conservatives. _____

8. You have a reputation for telling the truth, so we do not doubt your *truthfulness.* _____

9. So far we have dealt with only one *facet* of a multifaceted problem. _____

10. Science has progressed so far in the last thousand years that one wonders what life will be like at the end of the next *thousand years*. _____

11. This matter is of little *importance*. There are several more important matters demanding our attention. _____

12. Why don't you tidy up your desk? It looks very *untidy*. _____

13. Haven't I been patient? Who has shown more *patience* than I? _____

14. It is a mistake to plant a(n) *light-loving* shrub in a spot that gets little light. _____

15. Conducting guests to their tables is not the busboy's duty, and for him to have done so was clearly *beyond the call of duty*. _____

aspect	forbearance	penchant	treble
brace	millennium	photophilic	uniform
dichotomy	moment	slatternly	veracity
dipsomaniac	monologue	supererogatory	

IV. Complete the spelling of the word hinted at. Each blank stands for one missing letter.

1. An adjective meaning "one-sided" ___ ___ ___ lateral
2. A noun meaning "book-lover" biblio ___ ___ ___ ___ ___
3. A noun meaning "craze" ___ ___ nia
4. An adjective meaning "many-sided" multi ___ ___ ___ ___ ___ ___ ___
5. A noun meaning "abnormal dislike" ___ ___ ___ bia
6. An adjective meaning "excusable" ven ___ ___ ___ ___
7. A verb meaning "make less sensitive" ___ ___ ___ ___ ___ sensitize
8. An adjective meaning "underwater" ___ ___ ___ aqueous
9. An adjective meaning "captious" ___ ___ ___ ___ ___ ___ critical
10. A noun meaning "abnormal fear of fire" pyro ___ ___ ___ ___ ___ ___
11. An adjective meaning "extra" ___ ___ ___ ___ ___ ___ numerary
12. A noun meaning "tenth" ___ ___ the
13. A noun meaning "person married to one mate at a time" mono ___ ___ ___ ___ ist
14. An adjective meaning "short-lived" ___ ___ ___ ___ ___ itory
15. An adjective meaning "useful in a subordinate capacity" ___ ___ ___ servient
16. An adjective meaning "tiresomely unvaried" ___ ___ ___ ___ tonous
17. A noun meaning "admirer of foreigners" xeno ___ ___ ___ ___ ___
18. An adjective meaning "designed for both sexes" ___ ___ ___ sex

19. An adjective meaning
    "too tiny to be
    observed with an
    optical microscope"   __ __ __ microscopic
20. An adjective meaning
    "beneath the skin"   __ __ __ cutaneous

V. Complete each of the following sentences by inserting the most appropriate word or number.

1. A Sinophile admires the _____.
2. Hypertensive patients have abnormally
   _____ blood pressure.
3. There are _____ decades in a century.
4. The Bible describes our life span as "threescore years and ten," or _____ years.
5. A Francophobe dislikes the _____.
6. Since you got twelve votes to Carmen's ten and my seven, you have been elected by a plurality of
   _____.
7. Anyone born in 1985 cannot become a sexagenarian until
   _____.
8. If you are hypotensive, you have abnormally
   _____ blood pressure.
9. Legend has it that Sir Patrick Spens and his crew lie 50 fathoms, or _____ feet, below the ocean's surface.
10. Nebraska, which gained statehood in 1867, will celebrate its sesquicentennial in _____.
11. A(n) _____ tends to bleed excessively from very slight injuries.
12. _____ is an abnormal fear of being in public places.
13. A _____ nation reflects many different cultures and beliefs.
14. To be a(n) _____, one must be in his or her seventies.
15. A unicorn is an imaginary beast with
    _____ horn.

Words of Concealment and Deception

There is a great deal of concealment in our complex world—some of it justifiable and some not. There is also a considerable amount of deception. A knowledge of the following words will help you to describe instances of concealment and deception. What one word, for example, precisely describes the following situation?

Certain employees in excellent health frequently absent themselves from work on Fridays, claiming illness.

The answer, of course, is *malingering*.

A. Preview

Here are some words for your vocabulary of concealment and deception.

abscond	collusion	duplicity	malinger
alias	con	facade	feign
anonymous	connive	impersonate	seclusion
cache	covert	insidious	suborn
canard	cryptic	latent	subterfuge

Complete each statement below by adding the most appropriate word from the above list.

1. By the _____ of the wooden horse, the Greeks gained entry into the fortified city of Troy.
2. The name the suspect gave at the time of his arrest proved to be a(n) _____.
3. She is crafty. Don't let her _____ you into signing anything.

4. This is a poor hiding place for our valuables. I know of a better _____.

5. After the tragedy, she retired from society and went into _____.

6. The teacher recognized Eva's _____ musical talent and encouraged her to develop it.

7. Be careful. He presents a(n) _____ of honesty, but he is very crooked.

8. I will not allow them to _____ me. Why should I commit perjury?

9. The fugitive is expert in disguises and may attempt to _____ a police officer.

10. All our dealings are in the open. We do not engage in _____ activities.

11. The cook must have been really ill when he asked to go home; he is not one to _____.

12. Eventually the magazine article was exposed as a(n) _____: the events it described had never occurred.

13. Fearing the indicted financier would _____, the prosecutor asked for very high bail.

14. The _____ message, written in code, had no meaning for the ordinary person.

15. It is useless for me to _____ interest in the subject. I am no good at pretending.

16. Do not rule out the possibilities of an ambush; the enemy is _____.

17. Each of the buyers made the same outrageously low offer; they seemed to be acting in _____ against me.

18. Though posing as a friend, she kept ridiculing me behind my back, until I discovered her _____.

19. You have the right to know the name of your accuser; you cannot be tried on _____ charges.

20. Jane suspects some of her lukewarm supporters may _____ with her opponents to defeat her.

B. Details About the New Words

WORD	MEANING
abscond *v* ab-'skänd	depart secretly and hide, especially to avoid prosecution

Fearing the indicted financier would abscond, *the prosecutor asked for very high bail.*

| **alias** *n*
 'ā-lē-əs | assumed name |

The name the suspect gave at the time of his arrest proved to be an alias.

| **anonymous** *adj*
 ə-'nä-nə-məs | supplied or written by one whose name is not known or is withheld |

You have the right to know the name of your accuser; you cannot be tried on anonymous *charges.*

| **cache** *n*
 'kash | safe place for hiding and storing treasure, supplies, etc. |

This is a poor hiding place for our valuables. I know of a better cache.

| **canard** *n*
 kə-'närd | false, deliberately made-up report or story |

Eventually the magazine article was exposed as a canard: *the events it described had never occurred.*

| **collusion** *n*
 kə-'lü-nə-zhən | secret agreement for a deceitful purpose; conspiracy |

Each of the buyers made the same outrageously low offer; they seemed to be acting in collusion *against me.*

| **con** *v*
 'kän | swindle, after first gaining the confidence of the victim; trick; coax |

She is crafty. Don't let her con *you into signing anything.*

WORD	MEANING
connive *v* kə-'nīv	cooperate secretly with someone for a deceitful purpose: conspire

Jane suspects some of her lukewarm supporters may connive *with her opponents to defeat her.*

covert *adj* 'kō-vərt	covered over; secret; surreptitious

All of our dealings are in the open; we do not engage in covert *activities.*

cryptic *adj* 'krip-tik	having or appearing to have a hidden meaning; baffling; mysterious

The cryptic *message, written in code, had no meaning for the ordinary person.*

duplicity *n* dü-'pli-sə-tē	double-dealing; hypocritical deception

Though posing as a friend, she kept ridiculing me behind my back, until I discovered her duplicity.

facade *n* fə-'säd	false front; artificial or superficial appearance

Be careful. He presents a facade *of honesty, but he is very crooked.*

feign *v* 'fān	make a false show of; pretend; simulate; counterfeit

It is useless for me to feign *interest in the subject. I am no good at pretending.*

impersonate *v* im-'pər-sᵊn-ˌāt	pretend to be some other person; assume the character of

The fugitive is expert at disguises and may attempt to impersonate *a police officer.*

insidious *adj* in-'si-dē-əs	lying in wait to entrap; crafty; treacherous

Do not rule out the possibility of an ambush; the enemy is insidious.

WORD	MEANING
latent *adj* 'lā-t°nt	present though invisible and inactive; potential

The teacher recognized Eva's latent *musical talent and encouraged her to develop it.*

malinger *v* mə-'liŋ-ger	pretend to be ill or incapacitated so as to avoid work or duty

The cook must have been really ill when he asked to go home; he is not one to malinger.

seclusion *n* si-'klü-zhən	condition of being withdrawn in a place hard to reach; solitude

After the tragedy she retired from society and went into seclusion.

suborn *v* sə-'bòrn	induce someone to testify falsely

I will not allow them to suborn *me. Why should I commit perjury?*

subterfuge *n* 'səb-tər-ˌfyüj	trick or plan to conceal one's true objective; stratagem; deception

By the subterfuge *of the wooden horse, the Greeks gained entry into the fortified city of Troy.*

C. Thinking with Your New Words

Read all of the following statements. Then answer each question below.

Statements

Though Regina had said it made no difference to her whether her sister or she got the position, it bothered her that she had not been chosen.

Simpson explained how cancer had taken him unawares, and how medical science had helped him strike back.

The painting sold to Peters as an original turned out to be a clever imitation.

When she went on vacation, Coretta stored her best jewelry in a compartment behind the medicine cabinet.

At the motel, Anderson registered as Anthony D. Russo, Jr.

Watkins left the country when he got word that a warrant was being issued for his arrest.

Stevens paid Mrs. Jackson $1,000 to testify that, at the time of the robbery, he was painting her house.

On Monday morning Jones called his supervisor to say he was in bed with a severe cold. Then he left to play golf.

Lucille proved that the reporter who had written about his experiences in Afghanistan had never visited that part of the world.

The caller, who would not give her name, said Simmons would be at the Bluestone Cafe, and that is where the police seized him.

Questions

1. Who exposed a canard?   _____
2. Who put on a facade of
   indifference?   _____
3. Who used an alias?   _____
4. Who absconded?   _____
5. Who was apprehended through
   an anonymous tip?   _____
6. Who was suborned?   _____
7. Who was conned?   _____
8. Who fought an insidious foe?   _____
9. Who used a cache?   _____
10. Who malingered?   _____

D. Concise Writing

Express the thought of each of the following sentences in *no more than four words*, as in 1, below:

1. We dislike those people who secretly cooperate with one another in order to achieve a deceitful purpose.
   We dislike connivers.

2. The charges were made by people who either did not bother or refused to give their names.

3. Who is the one who induced the witness to testify falsely?

4. No one discovered where we hide and store the things that we consider valuable.

5. A hermit enjoys being all alone, completely withdrawn from all other human beings, in a place that is hard to reach.

E. Analogies

Write the *letter* of the pair of words related to each other in the same way as the words in the capitalized pair.

1. ABSCOND : FUGITIVE
   a. agree : dissenter
   b. perpetrate : victim
   c. hesitate : procrastinator
   d. invite : guest
   e. exacerbate : helper
         Answer _____

Hint: A person who ABSCONDS is a FUGITIVE.

2. CRYPTIC : BAFFLE
   a. tiresome : refresh
   b. soothing : irritate
   c. lethal : kill
   d. unique : offend
   e. venial : pardon
         Answer _____

3. MALINGERER : ILL
   a. volunteer : willing
   b. casualty : injured
   c. tyro : inexperienced
   d. polymath : knowledgeable
   e. hypocrite : virtuous
         Answer _____

4. CONSPIRATOR : CONNIVE
   a. creditor : borrow
   b. aggressor : assault
   c. defector : support
   d. maverick : conform
   e. ingrate : appreciate
         Answer _____

5. LATENT : VISIBLE
a. alleged : proven
b. hyperbolic : exaggerated
c. slatternly : unappealing

d. supernatural : extraordinary
e. pretentious : showy
Answer _____

6. ANONYMITY : PRIVACY
a. drug abuse : health
b. accusation : reputation
c. insurance : property

d. tactlessness : wisdom
e. expertise : inexperience
Answer _____

Hint: ANONYMITY protects a person's PRIVACY.

7

Medical Vocabulary

The suffix -*itis*, from ancient Greek, means "inflammation of."
With this knowledge you should be able to unlock the meaning
of many -*itis* words. For example, *tonsillitis* means "an inflammation of the tonsils."

A. Preview

Match each of the following -*itis* words with its definition
below.

appendicitis	colitis	gingivitis	otitis
arthritis	cystitis	hepatitis	peritonitis
bronchitis	dermatitis	laryngitis	phlebitis
bursitis	encephalitis	nephritis	sinusitis
carditis	gastritis	neuritis	tonsillitis

Sample:

inflammation of the tonsils   __tonsillitis__

1. inflammation of the stomach   _____
2. inflammation of a joint or joints   _____
3. brain inflammation   _____
4. gum inflammation   _____
5. inflammation of a nerve   _____
6. inflammation of the appendix   _____
7. skin inflammation   _____
8. liver inflammation   _____
9. inflammation of the larynx   _____
10. inflammation of the colon   _____
11. inflammation of the peritoneum   _____
12. kidney inflammation   _____

13. inflammation of the bronchial tubes   _____
14. sinus inflammation   _____
15. heart inflammation   _____
16. inflammation of a vein   _____
17. bladder inflammation   _____
18. inflammation of a bursa (sac between a tendon and a bone)   _____
19. ear inflammation   _____

B. Details About the New Words

WORD	MEANING
appendicitis *n* ə-ˌpen-də-ˈsī-təs	inflammation of the *appendix*

The physician found that I had appendicitis *and arranged for the immediate removal of my inflamed appendix.*

| **arthritis** *n*
är-ˈthrī-təs | inflammation of the joints |

With advancing age, many people develop arthritis *in their knees, hips, or other joints.*

| **bronchitis** *n*
brän-ˈkī-təs | inflammation of the lining of the *bronchial* tubes, which convey air into the lungs |

A heavy smoker's fits of coughing and difficulty in breathing may be symptoms of bronchitis.

| **bursitis** *n*
bər-ˈsī-təs | inflammation of a sac, especially of the shoulder or elbow |

Improper grip on a tennis racket may cause tennis elbow, a form of bursitis.

| **carditis** *n*
kär-ˈdī-təs | inflammation of the heart |

In the least serious form of carditis, *only the outer layer of the heart is inflamed.*

WORD	**MEANING**

colitis *n*
kō-'lī-təs

inflammation of the colon

Raw vegetables are fine if you have a healthy colon, but not if you have colitis.

cystitis *n*
sis-'tī-təs

inflammation of the urinary bladder

The antibiotic prescribed for the patient with cystitis *provided quick relief.*

dermatitis *n*
‚dər-mə-'tī-təs

inflammation of the skin

The redness and swelling are gone, and the skin looks normal; dermatitis *has been cured.*

encephalitis *n*
in-‚se-fə-'lī-təs

inflammation of the brain

Encephalitis, *sometimes called "sleeping sickness," may cause serious brain damage.*

gastritis *n*
ga-'strī-təs

inflammation of the stomach

To fill the stomach with an excess of irritating foods and liquor is to invite an attack of gastritis.

gingivitis *n*
‚jin-jə-'vī-təs

inflammation of the gums

See your dentist if your gums bleed during toothbrushing. You may have gingivitis.

hepatitis *n*
‚he-pə-'tī-təs

inflammation of the liver

She had no trouble with her liver until she contracted hepatitis *from eating contaminated food.*

laryngitis *n*
‚lar-ən-'jī-təs

inflammation of the *larynx,* or voice box

Since you have laryngitis, *try not to talk; rest your local cords.*

WORD	MEANING

nephritis *n*
ni-'frī-təs
inflammation of the kidneys

Until last spring, when he had his first attack of nephritis, *there was no kidney problem in the patient's medical history.*

---

neuritis *n*
nú-'rī-təs
inflammation of a nerve

The pitcher had neuritis; *a nerve in his right arm was inflamed.*

---

otitis *n*
ō-'tī-təs
inflammation of the ear

Swimmer's ear, a form of otitis, *is usually caused by swimming in contaminated or overchlorinated water.*

---

peritonitis *n*
ˌper-ə-tᵊn-'i-təs
inflammation of the *peritoneum,* the membrane lining the abdominal cavity

If your diseased appendix had not been removed in time, it might have ruptured and poured its infectious contents into your abdominal cavity, causing peritonitis.

---

phlebitis *n*
fli-'bī-təs
inflammation of a vein

When Mom had phlebitis, *the inflamed vein developed a clot that luckily was dissolved by medication.*

---

sinusitis *n*
ˌsī-nə-'sī-təs
inflammation of the *sinuses,* hollow cavities connected by passageways to the nose

As soon as Betty's sinuses become blocked and infected, and she feels headachy, she knows her sinusitis *has returned.*

C. Building Additional Words

Your study in this chapter has already had at least two valuable outcomes:

1. You have learned that the suffix *-itis* means "inflamma-tion of."
2. You have met several roots that designate different parts of the body. For example, in learning that *hepatitis* means "inflammation of the liver," you became aware that the root *hepat* means "liver."

I. What does each of the following roots mean? Choose your answers from the body words at the foot of this exercise, and enter them as in 1, below.

1. Arthr(o)
   ___joint___

7. Gingiv(o)
   _____

2. Ot(o)
   _____

8. Hepat(o)
   _____

3. Phleb(o)
   _____

9. Nephr(o)
   _____

4. Dermat(o)
   _____

10. Neur(o)
   _____

5. Encephal(o)
   _____

11. Cyst(o)
   _____

6. Gastr(o)
   _____

12. Cardi(o)
   _____

bladder	brain	ear	gum	heart	joint
kidney	liver	nerve	skin	stomach	vein

II. Complete the spelling of the unfinished word by adding the correct root.

Sample:

Pain along the course of one or more nerves is known as
_____neur_algia.

1. A _____scope is an instrument for examining the interior of the urinary bladder.
2. The science of the ear and its diseases is known as
   _____logy.
3. A(n) _____surgeon performs surgery involving nerves, the spine, and other parts of the nervous system.
4. A(n) _____logist is a heart specialist.

5. _____logy is the scientific study of the nervous system.
6. A(n) _____ac is a person with a heart ailment.
7. A(n) _____oma is a tumor of the liver.
8. A(n) _____gram is a tracing showing the force and form of the movements of the heart.
9. A(n) _____gram is a tracing showing the changes in electric potential in the brain.
10. Loose, flabby gum tissues are a symptom of _____al disease.
11. A(n) _____logist is a kidney specialist.
12. A(n) _____intestinal ailment is one that involves both the stomach and the intestines.
13. A(n) _____ectomy is the surgical removal of all or part of the stomach.
14. The surgical removal of all or part of the liver is known as a(n) _____ectomy.
15. _____tomy is the opening of a vein to draw blood from a patient in the treatment of disease.
16. Pain in a joint is known as _____algia.
17. _____ic juice is secreted by glands in the lining of the stomach.
18. A(n) _____logist is a skin specialist.

D. Using Medical Terms

Replace the italicized words with a single word discussed in this chapter.

1. A noted *heart specialist* examined the President.   _____
2. It is unwise to ignore *an inflammation of the gums*.   _____
3. In the olden days, *bleeding a patient by opening a vein* was widely used as a general remedy.   _____
4. A *surgical operation to remove part of the stomach* is not needed if the patient responds to drug therapy.   _____
5. *The inflammation of the larynx* made it painful for her to speak.   _____

6. A special diet is prescribed for
   a(n) *heart patient*.   _____
7. The *pain along the course of a
   nerve* in her left arm is not bothering her so much today.   _____
8. *Inflammation of the sinuses*
   can make a person very
   uncomfortable.   _____
9. The appendix was removed
   before it could rupture; there is
   no danger of *an inflammation of
   the peritoneum*.   _____
10. Do you know that *inflammation
    of the liver* can be caused by
    receiving blood from an infected
    donor?   _____

E. Analogies

Insert the *letter* of the pair of words related to each other in the same way as the words in the capitalized pair.

1. CARDIOLOGIST : HEART
   a. neurologist : liver   *d.* dermatologist : skin
   b. meteorologist : weather   *e.* polyglot : languages
   c. pediatrician : child   **Answer** _____

Hint: The part of the body that a CARDIOLOGIST specializes in is the HEART.

2. ENCEPHALITIS : BRAIN
   a. colitis : stomach   *d.* sinusitis : nose
   b. nephritis : kidneys   *e.* peritonitis : appendix
   c. arthritis : muscle   **Answer** _____

3. BRONCHITIS : BREATHING
   a. static : reception   *d.* gingivitis : bleeding
   b. sleet : roadway   *e.* daylight : vision
   c. rest : recovery   **Answer** _____

Hint: BRONCHITIS interferes with BREATHING.

4. TONSILLECTOMY : TONSILS
a. gastrectomy : intestines   *d.* arthritis : knee
b. appendectomy : appendix   *e.* hepatectomy : kidney
c. phlebotomy : blood   **Answer** _____

5. ARTHRALGIA : JOINTS
a. neuralgia : discomfort   *d.* neuritis : pain
b. dichotomy : strife   *e.* cardialgia : heart
c. carditis : hypertension   **Answer** _____

8

Words of Beginning and Ending

How comfortable would you be as a passenger with a *tyro* at the wheel? What is a *swan song*? Could you properly be considered an expert in a subject once you have mastered its *rudiments*? *Tyro, swan song,* and *rudiments* are among the useful and interesting words of beginning and ending you will meet in this chapter.

A. Preview

Use each of the following no more than once in completing the sentences below.

antepenultimate	genesis	maiden	swan song
coup de grace	inchoate	penultimate	terminal
debut	infinite	preamble	tyro
demise	initiative	premiere	ultimate
finale	lapse	rudiment	ultimatum

1. The pianist has never performed publicly, but she will be making her _____ at Carnegie Hall April 12.
2. Bit by bit she has reduced her addiction; her _____ goal is to stop smoking.
3. Anyone who lacks aptitude for getting things started is poor in _____.
4. The director sent Antoine this _____: "If you miss another rehearsal, you will be dropped from the cast."
5. How did the fight start? What was the _____ of the quarrel?
6. The long road to the tennis finals begins with a thorough

mastery of the _____s of the game.

7. New York City has witnessed the birth and _____ of many newspapers.

8. Tonight's speech by the mayor will be her _____; the new administration takes over tomorrow.

9. The _____ is sold out, but a few tickets are available for the second performance.

10. After the _____, all the entertainers reappeared on stage for several curtain calls.

11. December 30 is the _____ day of the year.

12. The house is still in a(n) _____ state; only the frame has been erected.

13. The patient was afraid he had a(n) _____ illness, but his physician assured him he would recover.

14. Renew the policy before it expires. Do not allow it to _____.

15. The first of your last three chances is your _____ chance.

16. The vessel is nearing completion and will soon make its _____ voyage.

17. A(n) _____ stating underlying principles precedes the body of our Constitution.

18. Our patience is likely to end: it is not _____.

19. These critical times require an expert at the helm, not a(n) _____.

20. The challenger had the champion on the ropes again and again but could not administer the _____.

B. Details About the New Words

WORD	MEANING
antepenultimate _adj_ ˌan-ti-pi-'nəl-tə-mət	coming immediately before the next to the last

The first of your last three chances is your antepenultimate _chance._

WORD	**MEANING**

coup de grace *n*
ˌkü-də-ˈgräs
The challenger had the champion on the ropes again and again but could not administer the coup de grace.

decisive finishing blow

---

debut *n*
ˈdā-ˌbyü
The pianist has never performed publicly, but she will be making her debut *at Carnegie Hall April 12.*

first public appearance

---

demise *n*
di-ˈmīz
New York City has witnessed the birth and demise *of many newspapers.*

cessation of existence; death

---

finale *n*
fə-ˈna-lē
After the finale, *all the entertainers reappeared on stage.*

last scene or act; conclusion; end

---

genesis *n*
ˈje-nə-səs
How did the fight start? What was the genesis *of the quarrel?*

origin; coming into being

---

inchoate *adj*
in-ˈkō-ət
The house is still in an inchoate *state; only the frame has been erected.*

just begun; only partly in existence; incomplete

---

infinite *adj*
ˈin-fə-nət
Our patience is likely to end: it is not infinite.

endless; without boundaries or limits; exceedingly great

---

initiative *n*
i-ˈni-shə-tiv
If you lack aptitude for getting things started, you are poor in initiative.

ability to begin and follow through without being urged; enterprise

WORD	MEANING

lapse *v*
'laps
come to an end; become void

Renew the policy before it expires. Do not allow it to lapse.

maiden *adj*
'mā-dᵊn
first; earliest

The vessel is nearing completion and will soon be making its maiden *voyage.*

penultimate *adj*
pi-'nəl-tə-mət
next to the last

December 30 is the penultimate *day of the year.*

preamble *n*
'prē-,am-bəl
preliminary statement or event; introduction

A preamble *stating underlying principles precedes the body of our Constitution.*

premiere *n*
pri-'myer
first performance

The premiere *is sold out, but a few tickets are available for the second performance.*

rudiment *n*
'rü-də-mənt
first principle that must be learned; fundamental (usually plural)

How can you get to the finals if you have not yet learned the rudiments *of the game?*

swan song *n*
'swän 'sòŋ
farewell appearance; final creative work or performance

Tonight's speech by the mayor will be her swan song; *the new administration takes over tomorrow.*

terminal *adj*
'tər-mə-nᵊl
coming at the end; ending in death

The patient was afraid he had a terminal *illness, but his physician assured him he would recover.*

WORD	MEANING
tyro *n*	beginner in learning
'tī-rō	something; novice; neophyte

These critical times require an expert at the helm, not a tyro.

ultimate *adj*	last in a progression; final;
'əl-tə-mət	highest possible

Bit by bit she has reduced her addiction; her ultimate goal is to stop smoking.

ultimatum *n*	final, uncompromising demand
‚əl-tə-'mā-təm	or offer, leading to serious
	consequences if rejected

The director sent Antoine this ultimatum: "If you miss another rehearsal, you will be dropped from the cast."

C. Thinking with Your New Words

Read all of the following statements. Then answer each question below.

Statements

Reynolds notified Village Motors that he would institute legal proceedings if his deposit were not returned immediately.

Booker and Alan were old hands in the shipping department. Jack was new on the job.

Bernice has tickets for the new musical. Eva saw it when it opened.

In her final appearance on the courts, Helen won the singles championship. Then she retired.

Business had been poor, but only when Comstock canceled his annual order did Owens decide to close the plant.

Audrey never missed a meeting and never introduced a motion in her four years in the club.

On the day the trolley line was discontinued, Gina was a passenger on its last run.

In his political life Thomas E. Dewey served as District Attorney and Governor and narrowly missed election to the White House.

Dan's birthday is January 31, Rose's February 26, and Adele's May 30.

Gomez gave Burns a base on balls in the bottom of the ninth but struck out Lee, Simpson, and Rizzo to end the game.

Questions

1. Who seemed to lack initiative? _____
2. Who received an ultimatum? _____
3. Who was present at the demise of an institution? _____
4. Who was a tyro? _____
5. Who was born on the penultimate day of the month? _____
6. Who attended a premiere? _____
7. Who delivered a coup de grace? _____
8. Who never realized an ultimate career goal? _____
9. Who was the pitcher's antepenultimate victim? _____
10. Who did something we can call a swan song? _____

D. Concise Writing

Express the thought of each sentence in *no more than four words,* as in 1, below.

1. Alison has shown that she possesses the ability to get things started and follow them through.
   Alison has shown initiative.

2. Space in the universe is considered to have no limit whatsoever; it goes on and on, and never ends.

3. The first performance that he gave was one that people are not likely to forget.

4. That final uncompromising demand that you made was a disappointment to us.

---

5. It was the antepenultimate day of the month of May.

---

6. The preliminary statement with which she began could not have been dispensed with.

---

7. The insurance that Danny signed up for has come to an end and is now no longer in effect.

---

8. The plan that I have is only partly in existence and in a state of incompletion.

---

9. They were beginners who were learning something completely new to them, and in which they had had no prior experience of any kind.

---

10. We were present at the first public appearance that he made.

E. Analogies

Write the *letter* of the pair of words related to each other in the same way as the words of the capitalized pair.

1. ORIGIN : DEMISE
a. compass : course
b. remedy : pain
c. dawn : sunset
d. canard : untruth
e. court : impartiality
   Answer _____

2. NEOPHYTE : INEXPERIENCE
a. pioneer : enterprise
b. pauper : wealth
c. rebel : compliance
d. beginner : authority
e. partisan : openmindedness
   Answer _____

3. SCENE I : FINALE
a. curtain : stage
b. actor : script
c. January : December
d. threshold : door
e. preamble : constitution
   Answer _____

4. ULTIMATUM : NEGOTIATION
a. petition : dissatisfaction   d. crisis : leadership
b. typhoon : navigation   e. verdict : evidence
c. drought : scarcity   **Answer** _____

Hint: ULTIMATUM makes NEGOTIATION impossible.

5. INFINITY : END
a. unanimity : agreement   d. anarchy : confusion
b. feud : revenge   e. megalomania : derangement
c. immortality : death   **Answer** _____

9

Extra, Intra, and *Inter* Words

This chapter can help you become more proficient in understanding and using words beginning with three Latin prefixes:

Extra means "outside" or "beyond."

Extralegal matters are outside or beyond the jurisdiction of the law. For a long time the disposal of toxic wastes was an *extralegal* matter. Today it is closely regulated by law.

Intra means "within."

When the different factions within a political party cooperate, there is *intraparty* harmony.

Inter means "between" or "among."

An *intersession* is the period between two academic terms or sessions.

A. Preview

Complete the partially spelled word in each sentence below by adding *extra*, *intra*, or *inter*.

Sample:

You are far more alert than the ordinary person; you have _____extra__ordinary awareness.

1. The patient was given nourishment by _____venous feeding after her operation.
2. People of several races live there: it is an _____racial neighborhood.
3. Stick to the topic. Do not bring up _____neous matters.
4. The _____coastal Waterway provides sheltered passage for commercial and pleasure boats within the Atlantic coastline.

5. An _____ city bus offers no transportation beyond the city limits.

6. People generally marry within their own race and religion, but _____ marriage is not uncommon.

7. The competition between the regions is nothing new; there has always been _____ regional rivalry.

8. Does life exist only on earth? Is _____ terrestrial life impossible?

9. Though I do well in _____ mural sports, I do not consider myself good enough for interscholastic competition.

10. To be a good leader, one must excel in _____ personal relations, the art of getting along with others.

11. Some say there are ways beyond the five senses by which we become aware of things. Do you believe in _____ sensory perception?

12. The campaign has _____ denominational support: all the faiths in town are backing it.

13. Smoking in public places, formerly _____ legal, is coming increasingly within the jurisdiction of the law.

14. The fact that these nations have formed an international trading community shows that they are economically _____ dependent.

15. This is an _____ organizational problem: outside organizations have nothing to do with it.

16. The charge of adultery was dismissed because there was absolutely no proof of _____ marital relations.

17. The two cities are not connected by a bus line but there is an _____ urban railway.

18. The school does not send its athletes to compete with those of other schools; it is against _____ mural sports.

19. Make your revisions in the margin rather than between lines; _____ linear changes are hard to read.

20. It will be an _____ departmental gathering: members of other departments have not been invited.

B. Details About the New Words

WORD	MEANING
extralegal adj ˌek-strə-ˈlē-gəl	beyond the jurisdiction of the law; not regulated by law

Smoking in public places, formerly extralegal, *is coming within the jurisdiction of the law.*

extramarital adj ˌek-strə-ˈmar-ə-tᵊl	involving a sexual relationship outside one's marriage; adulterous

The charge of adultery was dismissed because there was no proof of extramarital *relations.*

extramural adj ˌek-strə-ˈmyùr-əl	outside the walls or boundaries of a school, university, etc.

The school does not send its athletes to compete with those of other schools; it is against extramural *sports.*

extraneous adj ek-ˈstrā-nē-əs	coming from the outside; not an essential part; irrelevant

Stick to the topic. Do not bring up extraneous *matters.*

extrasensory adj ˌek-strə-ˈsen-sə-rē	outside the ordinary senses; not limited to sight, hearing, touch, taste, and smell

Some say there are ways beyond the five senses by which we become aware of things. Do you believe in extrasensory *perception?*

extraterrestrial adj ˌek-strə-tə-ˈres-trē-əl	originating or existing outside the earth or its atmosphere

Does life exist only on earth? Is extraterrestrial *life impossible?*

interdenominational adj ˌin-tər-di-ˌnä-mə-ˈnā-shə-nᵊl	between, among, or shared by different *denominations* (religions)

The campaign has interdenominational *support: all the faiths in town are backing it.*

WORD	MEANING

interdependent *adj*
ˌin-tər-di-'pen-dənt

dependent on one another; mutually dependent

The fact that these nations have formed an international trading community shows they are economically interdependent.

---

interlinear *adj*
ˌin-tər-'li-nē-ər

inserted between lines already written or printed

Make your revisions in the margin; interlinear *changes are hard to read.*

---

intermarriage *n*
ˌin-tər-'mar-ij

marriage between persons of different religions, races, castes, etc.

People generally marry within their own race and religion, but intermarriage *is not uncommon.*

---

interpersonal *adj*
ˌin-tər-'pər-sᵊ-nəl

between persons

To be a good leader, one must excel in interpersonal *relations, the art of getting along with others.*

---

interracial *adj*
ˌin-tər-ˌrā-shəl

between, among, or involving people of different races

People of several races live there: it is an interracial *neighborhood.*

---

interregional *adj*
ˌin-tə-rē-jə-nəl

between regions

The competition between the regions is nothing new; there has always been interregional *rivalry.*

---

interurban *adj*
ˌin-tər-'ər-bən

between cities or towns

The two cities are not connected by a bus line, but there is an interurban *railway.*

---

intracity *adj*
ˌin-trə-'si-tē

within a city

An intracity *bus offers no transportation beyond the city limits.*

WORD	MEANING

intracoastal *adj*
ˌin-trə-ˈkōs-tᵊl
within and close to the coast

The Intracoastal *Waterway provides sheltered passage for commercial and pleasure boats within the Atlantic coastline.*

---

intradepartmental *adj*
ˌin-trə-di-ˌpärt-ˈmen-tᵊl
within a department

It will be an intradepartmental *gathering: members of other departments have not been invited.*

---

intramural *adj*
ˌin-trə-ˈmyür-əl
within the walls or boundaries of a school, university, etc.

Though I do well in intramural *sports, I do not consider myself good enough for interscholastic competition.*

---

intraorganizational *adj*
ˌin-trə-ˌòr-gə-nə-ˈzā-shə-nᵊl
within an organization

This is an intraorganizational *problem: outside organizations have nothing to do with it.*

---

intravenous *adj*
ˌin-trə-ˈvē-nəs
within or entering by way of the veins

The patient was given nourishment by intravenous *feeding after her operation.*

C. Building Additional Words

Complete the spelling of the unfinished word by adding *extra, intra,* or *inter.*

1. An _____ disciplinary humanities course may involve materials from literature, music, art, and other disciplines, or branches of learning.
2. There is considerable _____ service rivalry between the different branches of the Armed Forces.
3. A school's _____ curricular activities may include concerts, plays, debates, and interscholastic sports.
4. _____ city buses operate between two or more cities.

5. An _____ spinal injection beneath the membrane of the spinal cord is sometimes used to administer anesthesia.

6. Any comment that a judge privately makes outside of court, rather than from the bench, is _____ judicial.

7. An _____ hemispheric flight is a flight between hemispheres.

8. Diplomats may not be prosecuted for violating the laws of the territory in which they serve; they have _____ territorial privileges.

9. An _____ lining provides extra warmth.

10. _____ muscular fat is fat within a muscle.

11. An _____ coastal railway runs between Atlantic and Pacific ports.

12. _____ stellar space staggers the mind. The distance between stars is incredibly vast.

13. Astronauts have duties to perform within their space vehicle, and they are also given _____ vehicular assignments.

14. The Panama Canal is an _____ oceanic waterway linking the Atlantic and the Pacific.

15. Some cosmic rays reaching the earth originate outside the solar system; they are _____ solar.

D. Thinking with Your New Words

Read all the following statements. Then answer each question below.

Statements

While Armstrong and Aldrin were walking on the moon, Collins was in orbit around the moon in the command ship.

Auland received numerous summonses while a member of his nation's mission to the UN, but never had to pay a fine.

The jealous Othello murdered his wife Desdemona after he was misled into believing she had been unfaithful to him.

At 14, Nadia Comaneci became the first to earn a perfect score of 10 in an Olympic gymnastic event.

Dan was not talking to me and had quarreled with Edna, too. None of his neighbors would have anything to do with him.

After I dealt the cards, Cynthia stunned me by her uncanny knowledge of my hand, which she could not possibly have seen.

For several days after the surgery Cheryl was unable to take food by mouth.

The short Northwest Passage that Cartier and other explorers sought was never found.

We were more than halfway to the beach and looking forward to a cool dip in the ocean when Harriet said, "Let's go to the movies."

Dr. Arno of the State University taught an evening extension course in our local high school.

Questions

1. Who enjoyed extraterritorial rights?   _____
2. Who showed an extraordinary sense of balance?   _____
3. Who introduced an extraneous matter?   _____
4. Who was apparently fed intravenously?   _____
5. Who was innocent of extra-marital misconduct?   _____
6. Who participated in an extra-mural activity?   _____
7. Who missed an extravehicular experience?   _____
8. Who appeared to have extra-sensory perception?   _____
9. Who had poor interpersonal relations?   _____
10. Who envisioned an inter-oceanic link?   _____

E. Analogies

Write the *letter* of the pair of words related to each other in the same way as the words of the capitalized pair.

1. INTRAVENOUS : VEIN
a. intraspinal : skin
b. intrahepatic : liver
c. intradermal : brain
d. intranasal : nerve
e. intraneural : heart
Answer _____

2. INTERSESSION : FACULTY
a. armistice : war
b. interjection : punctuation
c. semester : instruction
d. intermission : cast
e. adjournment : trial
Answer _____

3. EXTRATERRITORIALITY : DIPLOMAT
a. seniority : employee
b. fine : offender
c. asylum : danger
d. expertise : tyro
e. immunization : vaccine
Answer _____

4. INTERLINING : GARMENT
a. curtain : window
b. insulation : house
c. parcel : contents
d. jacket : book
e. circumference : circle
Answer _____

5. INTERCONTINENTAL : CONTINENTS
a. interstellar : planets
b. intrastate : states
c. interlinear : pages
d. intramural : walls
e. interdenominational : religions
Answer _____

10

Loanwords

English is rich in *loanwords,* words "borrowed" from other languages. Actually, *loanwords* is a misnomer, for English has no intention of returning these useful words and expressions; they have been naturalized and incorporated into our language.

Take *alfresco,* for example. What advantage is there in dining *alfresco*?

Or *kudos.* Would you be pleased or offended if you were to receive *kudos*?

Or *persona non grata.* What kind of reception awaits you in a place where you are *persona non grata*?

English has made terms like *alfresco, kudos,* and *persona non grata* a permanent part of its vocabulary. In this chapter you will become familiar with these and other loanwords from several ancient and modern languages.

A. Preview

Each sentence below has one or more blanks. Fill these blanks with words or expressions from the following list, using each of them only once.

ad hominem	au revoir	faux pas	non sequitur
ad infinitum	brouhaha	hoi polloi	persona non
ad nauseam	chutzpah	honcho	grata
alfresco	de rigueur	in medias res	postmortem
arrivederci	entre nous	kudos	salaam
auf Wiedersehen	ersatz	non compos	sayonaras
		mentis	halom

1. Shall we dine _____, or do you prefer to eat indoors?
2. If you create another disturbance, you will be asked to

leave this library, and in the future you will be
_____ here.

3. It seemed unfair for the _____ to
get all the congratulations; surely, the subordinates who
did most of the work deserved some
_____, too.

4. Among the expressions English has borrowed for saying
"good-bye" are "_____," from
Italian; "_____," from German;
"_____," from French; and
"_____," from Japanese.

5. "_____," adopted from Hebrew,
may be used either for "hello" or "good-bye."

6. The _____ that erupted when a
popular player was called out at home ended when the TV
replay showed he had failed to touch the plate.

7. At the restaurant we are going to, jackets and ties are
_____, so dress formally.

8. You have already stated your position several times. What
is the sense of repeating it _____?

9. Some writers do not try to make themselves understood by
the masses. Apparently, they have little concern for
_____.

10. Since they were constructed of
_____ materials, the emergency
shelters were unfit for permanent occupancy.

11. I would not say she is _____; her
mind is as sound as yours or mine.

12. I am the director here, and you are just a beginner. Where
do you get the _____ to tell me
how to run this organization?

13. We must set aside funds for a new car. The present one
will not last _____.

14. He is neither a sultan nor a rajah. We do not have to
_____ when coming into his
presence.

15. In introducing the guest speaker, I mispronounced her
name. It was an embarrassing
_____.

16. I know you like Jim, and I do, too, but
_____, isn't he a bit conceited?

17. The novel begins _____, and bit
    by bit we learn about what happened earlier.
18. It was unfair of you to say that the driver whose car you
    damaged has a prison record. That was a(n)
    _____ remark.
19. After each game, we meet with the coach for a(n)
    _____ of the key plays.
20. It is a(n) _____ to assume I can
    get you a job with Acme Industries just because I said
    its president is my cousin. I have no influence with her
    whatsoever.

B. Details About the New Vocabulary

LOANWORD	MEANING
ad hominem *adj* ad-'hä-mə-ˌnem	appealing to a listener's or reader's prejudices, rather than to reason (from Latin)

It was unfair of you to say that the driver whose car you damaged has a prison record. That was an ad hominem *remark.*

ad infinitum *adv* ˌad-ˌin-fə-'nī-təm	endlessly; forever; without limit (from Latin)

We must set aside funds for a new car. The present one will not last ad infinitum.

ad nauseam *adv* ad-'nȯ-zē-əm	to a sickening degree; to the point of nausea or disgust (from Latin)

You have already stated your position several times. What is the sense of repeating it ad nauseam?

alfresco *adv* al-'fres-kō	in the open air; outdoors (from Italian)

Shall we dine alfresco, *or do you prefer to eat indoors?*

arrivederci *interj* ä-ˌrē-və-'der-chē	till we see each other again; good-bye (from Italian)

In parting, we may say arrivederci, *as the Italians do.*

LOANWORD	MEANING

auf Wiedersehen *interj*
aùf-'vē-dər-,zā-ən

till we see each other again;
good-bye (from German)

A further substitute for good-bye is to say auf Wiedersehen, *as the Germans do.*

au revoir *interj*
,ōr-ə-'vwär

till we see each other again;
good-bye (from French)

Still another alternative is to say au revoir, *as the French do.*

brouhaha *n*
'brü-,hä-,hä

noisy stir; hubbub; uproar;
hullabaloo; commotion (from
French)

There was quite a brouhaha *in the office when the proprietor announced she was retiring.*

chutzpah *n*
'hùt-spə

supreme self-confidence;
shameless audacity; nerve;
brazenness (from Hebrew)

I am the director here, and you are just a beginner. Where do you get the chutzpah *to tell me how to run this organization?*

de rigueur *adj*
də-rē-'gər

socially obligatory; required
by custom, etiquette, or
fashion; proper (from French)

At the restaurant we are going to, jackets and ties are de rigueur, *so dress formally.*

entre nous *adv*
,än-trə-'nü

between us; confidentially
(from French)

I know you like Jim, and I do, too, but entre nous, *isn't he a bit conceited?*

ersatz *adj*
'er-,säts

being an inferior substitute
or imitation; artificial;
synthetic (from German)

During the war, millions drank ersatz *coffee made from grain, instead of from coffee beans.*

LOANWORD	MEANING

faux pas *n*
'fō-,pä

error; social blunder;
tactless act (from French)

*In introducing the guest speaker, I mispronounced her name.
It was an embarrassing* faux pas.

hoi polloi *n pl*
hȯi-pə-'lȯi

(literally, "the many")
masses; common people
(from Greek)

*Some writers do not try to make themselves understood by
the masses. Apparently, they have little concern for* hoi
polloi.

honcho *n*
'hän-chō

person in charge; leader;
chief; boss (from Japanese)

*Mechanics in this shop do not start working on a car without
an OK from the* honcho.

in medias res *adv*
in-'me-dē-əs-'rās

in the middle of things,
rather than at the beginning
(from Latin)

The novel begins in medias res, *and bit by bit we learn about
what happened earlier.*

kudos *n*
'kyü-,dōs

praise for an achievement;
glory; fame (from Greek)

Don't congratulate me. The one who truly deserves the
kudos *is our pitcher, Manuel.*

non compos mentis *adj*
,nän-,käm-pəs-'men-təs

not of sound mind; not mentally
competent to handle one's
affairs (from Latin)

I would not say she is non compos mentis; *her mind is as
sound as yours or mine.*

non sequitur *n*
'nän-'se-kwə-tər

conclusion that does not
logically follow from what
has just been said (from
Latin)

It is a non sequitur *to assume I can get you a job with Acme
Industries just because I said its president is my cousin. I
have no influence with her whatsoever.*

LOANWORD	MEANING
persona non grata *n* pər-'sō-nə-,nän-'gra-tə	person who is unwelcome; un-acceptable person (from Latin)

If you create another disturbance, you will be asked to leave this library, and in the future you will be persona non grata *here.*

| **postmortem** *n*
,pōst-'mòr-təm | (literally, "following the death") detailed evaluation of some event just completed (from Latin) |

After each game, we meet with the coach for a postmortem *of the key plays.*

| **salaam** *v*
sə-'läm | bow very low, placing the right palm on the forehead (from Arabic) |

He is neither a sultan nor a rajah. We do not have to salaam *when coming into his presence.*

| **sayonara** *n*
'sī-ō-,nä-rä | farewell; good-bye (from Japanese) |

In taking leave of someone, we may say sayonara, *as the Japanese do.*

| **shalom** *interj*
shä-'lōm | (literally, "peace") term of greeting or farewell (from Hebrew) |

Shalom, adopted from Hebrew, may be used either for "hello" or "good-bye."

C. Thinking with Your New Vocabulary

Read all the following statements. Then answer each question below.

Statements

Andy wasn't even here when we got on line. How did he get ahead of us?

Charlotte visited a friend, Ruth went to a picnic, and Alex slept all afternoon.

Dr. Pell said José's paper was the finest she had read all semester.

Mona was caught in a traffic jam on the way to the airport to see Steven off, and by the time she got there the plane had left.

Carl was refused admission because of his earlier arguments with the manager and ushers over his smoking in the non-smoking section.

Did you see the severe look Lena gave Tony at the banquet when she saw him eating with his fingers?

After her stroke, Camille was confused; she could not recognize people or even sign her name.

Only Phil thought that Margaret was too bossy. When she gave him his assignment, he bowed low and said, "Thank you, Your Majesty."

Frank wanted to live in the city because he enjoyed its liveliness and its crowds. Ellen would have preferred a cottage in the woods.

In one of the last speeches of the campaign, Terry mentioned that her opponent had once been a drug addict.

Questions

1. Who liked hoi polloi?   _____
2. Who showed chutzpah?   _____
3. Who was persona non grata?   _____
4. Who dined alfresco?   _____
5. Who made an ad hominem
   appeal?   _____
6. Who lost a chance to say
   shalom?   _____
7. Who salaamed?   _____
8. Who was non compos mentis?   _____
9. Who committed a faux pas?   _____
10. Who bestowed kudos?   _____

D. Using Loanwords

Replace the italicized words with a single word or expression from Section B.

1. *Between you and me,* do you think Alvin should have been given the award? _____

2. Would you agree that printed invitations are *required by custom* for a wedding reception? _____

3. Every morning, breakfast was the same; we had waffles and syrup *to a sickening degree*. _____

4. Begin from the beginning and explain what happened. Do not start *in the middle of your story*.

5. Can the sun provide us with energy *till the end of time,* or will it burn itself up some day? _____

6. Sandra said Hawkins is unemployed, but she also said he is well-to-do. Your motion that we excuse him from paying dues is therefore a(n) *proposal of no relevance*. _____

7. When we adjourned in disagreement, the officers held a(n) *detailed evaluation of the meeting* to try to discover what had gone wrong. _____

8, 9, 10. Supply *three* answers to the following: "Very well, then," she said, shaking hands. *"Till we see each other again."* _____
_____
_____

E. Analogies

Write the *letter* of the pair of words related to each other in the same way as the words in the capitalized pair.

1. NON COMPOS MENTIS : SANE
   a. demented : dangerous   d. incompetent : healthy
   b. frail : robust   e. impulsive : restless
   c. inquisitive : rude   **Answer** _____

2. INDIVIDUAL : HOI POLLOI
   a. star : Milky Way   d. principal : faculty
   b. leader : followers   e. candidate : plurality
   c. employer : staff   **Answer** _____

3. HELLO : AU REVOIR
   a. farewell : welcome   d. greeting : rebuff
   b. demise : genesis   e. tyro : error
   c. debut : swan song   **Answer** _____

4. NON SEQUITUR : LOGIC
   a. hostility : silence   d. evidence : truth
   b. deluge : water   e. nonviolence : resistance
   c. indifference : concern   **Answer** _____

5. HYPOCRITE : CONTEMPT
   a. scapegoat : injustice   d. dipsomaniac : thirst
   b. contestant : victory   e. achiever : kudos
   c. bettor : jackpot   **Answer** _____

Review of Chapters 6–10

I. Fill the blanks, choosing your answers from the following list:

arthr	extra	inter	nephr
cardi	gastr	intra	neur
dermat	gingiv	itis	phleb
encephal	hepat		

1. "Brain" is the meaning conveyed by

_____.

2. A word containing _____ is a "vein" word.

3. _____, at the beginning of a word, means "outside."

4. _____, at the end of a word, means "inflammation."

5. Any word with _____ has something to do with the gums.

6. A word containing _____ is a "stomach" word.

7. A word containing _____ is a "heart" word.

8. _____, at the beginning of a word, means "within."

9. A word containing _____ has something to do with the joints.

10. _____, at the beginning of a word, means "skin."

11. Any word with _____ has something to do with the liver.

12. A word containing _____ is a "kidney" word.

13. _____ means "nerve."

14. _____, at the beginning of a word, means "between."

II. What word or expression can replace the italicized words? Find the answer, partially spelled, in the list at the end of this exercise, and complete its spelling before using it.

1. To most people, a Nobel Prize represents the *highest possible* achievement. _____

2. Besides lecturing a great deal, she is a heavy smoker, so it is no wonder that she has *inflammation of the larynx*. _____

3. He was then living under a(n) *assumed name*. _____

4. The day after the balloting, I read a(n) *detailed evaluation* of the election by a political analyst. _____

5. Few, if any, of us can "go it alone." We are *mutually dependent*. _____

6. By changing his position on the proposed legislation, the Governor has dealt it the *decisive finishing blow*. _____

7. Wouldn't you probably lose your deposit if the seller were to *depart secretly and go into hiding*? _____

8. Without thinking, I took a seat reserved for someone else; it was a(n) *tactless act*. _____

9. Despite its *superficial appearance* of luxury, the building is constructed of cheap materials. _____

10. *Inflammation of the liver* often accompanies mononucleosis. _____

11. The rebels stored weapons in a(n) *safe hiding place* in the woods. _____

12. Enough of your complaining! Why do you keep bringing up the same matter *to a sickening degree*?   _____

13. The court ruled that the patient was *no longer competent to manage her affairs*.   _____

14. I will not *cooperate secretly* with anyone to deprive you of what is rightfully yours.   _____

15. She is retiring next year; this is her *next-to-last* year on the job.   _____

16. We have no respect for those who *pretend to be ill* and over-burden their fellow employees.   _____

17. I did not know I had *invisible or inactive* talents until my teachers said I had great potential.   _____

18. If not renewed by next Friday, your policy will *become void*.   _____

19. The tip was *supplied by someone whose name is not known*.   _____

20. The medicine gave him tempo-rary relief from his *inflammation of the joints*.   _____

21. Next week, the new automobiles will make their *first appearance*.   _____

22. You were the victim of a(n) *deliberately made-up story*.   _____

23. That was the athlete's *final appearance;* he never competed professionally again.   _____

24. The conflict is *within the depart-ment;* no outsiders are involved.   _____

25. Their *hypocritical deception* has at last been uncovered.   _____

__ __ but	ad n __ __ seam
a __ __ nymous	__ __ che
__ __ nard	lat __ __ t
int __ __ dependent	__ __ timate
non compos m __ __ tis	int __ __ departmental

abs __ __ nd   __ __ ryngitis
__ __ an song   al __ __ s
f __ __ x pas   __ __ linger
__ __ nultimate   postm __ __ tem
arth __ __ tis   con __ __ ve
__ __ pse   hep __ __ itis
coup de gr __ __ e   dup __ __ city
__ __ cade

III. For the italicized word or words in each sentence below, find *two* synonyms. Choose all your synonyms from the list at the end of the exercise.

Sample: We are not going to *deceive* you. <u>con, defraud</u>

1. Anyone can see through your *deception*.
_____

2. Think of the *glory* that will be yours.
_____

3. I am not a(n) *novice*. _____

4. It was a(n) *secret* undertaking. _____

5. This cannot go on *forever*. _____

6. An actor can *simulate* grief. _____

7. She was not present at the *conclusion*.
_____

9. What *nerve*! _____

10. There are *endless* possibilities for error.
_____

10. Some luxuries are beyond the means of *the masses*.
_____

11. Unlike cotton or silk, rayon is a(n) *artificial* fiber.
_____

12. I'm not in charge; there's the *boss*. _____

13. How quiet it became once that *hubbub* ended!
_____

14. We're leaving now. *Good-bye*. _____

ad infinitum	commoners	end	hoi polloi	sayonara
au revoir	commotion	endlessly	honcho	stratagem
brazenness	con	ersatz	infinite	subterfuge
brouhaha	counterfeit	fame	kudos	surreptitious
chief	covert	feign	limitless	synthetic
chutzpah	defraud	finale	neophyte	tyro

IV. Eliminate the repetition in each passage below by replacing the italicized word with a synonym from the following list:

alfresco	demise	extraneous	initiative	preamble
collusion	de rigueur	genesis	insidious	seclusion

1. A term paper with a lengthy *introduction* may discourage the reader. Therefore, make your introduction as brief as the circumstances allow. _____

2. I did not know the owner had passed away. When did you learn of her *passing*? _____

3. Do you know the *origin* of this feud? It originated in a bet. _____

4. The guests were not obliged to bring anything, but some felt that a small gift for the hostess was *obligatory*. _____

5. The dictator has not hesitated to torture imagined conspirators into confessing their supposed *conspiracy* with his enemies. _____

6. You are leading a solitary life. Do you enjoy *solitude*? _____

7. It was an outdoor wedding; the ceremony was conducted *outdoors*, in the garden. _____

8. Be relevant. Do not introduce *irrelevant* matters. _____

9. The individual you are dealing with has been *treacherous* in the past, so beware of treachery. _____

10. Is Bruce really an enterprising executive? What *enterprise* has he shown? _____

V. Complete each sentence below by inserting the most appropriate word or expression from the following list:

cryptic	in medias res	rudiments	sinus
extraterrestrial	interurban	shalom	suborn
inchoate	persona non grata		

1. As a neophyte, I am just beginning to learn the _____ of the trade.
2. The _____ references made by the conspirators in their conversations with one another were, of course, meaningless to outsiders.
3. "_____" and "Peace be with you" are similar in meaning.
4. Some think we should settle our pressing problems here on earth before getting too involved in _____ matters.
5. A(n) _____ is a cavity in the skull.
6. The concept is still _____, so let me develop it further in my own mind before I announce it.
7. She once told me to leave, so I know I am _____ in her house.
8. We took a taxi to the next town, as there was no _____ bus.
9. The attempts made to _____ the witness failed because she ignored threats and offers of bribes.
10. As our table waited to be served, we saw diners at some of the other tables already _____, and this made us even hungrier.

Anti Words

Anti, from Greek, meaning "against" or "opposite," is easily one of the most active prefixes in our language, as we can see by the frequency with which new *anti* words are being coined.

The meanings of many *anti* words are self-evident. An *antiperspirant,* for example, is a substance intended to reduce perspiration. But some meanings are less obvious. What, for instance, is an *antimacassar*? or an *antipyretic*? These are among the *anti* words we will be discussing in this chapter.

A. Preview

Use each of the following words no more than once in answering the questions below.

antibiotic	antidote	antioxidant	antiscorbutic
antibody	antiestablishment	antipathy	antiseptic
anticlimax	antihistamine	antipersonnel	antithesis
anticoagulant	antihypertensive	antipodes	antitrust
anticorrosive	antimacassar	antipyretic	antiviral

1. A person who accidentally swallows a poison can usually be saved if the correct _____ is given in time.
2. The outdoor railing was given two coats of a good _____ paint to inhibit rust.
3. The body, when invaded by antigens (foreign substances), produces _____s to resist the invaders.
4. We have drugs that are effective against bacteria, but not against viruses. Nobody knows when a practical _____ substance will be discovered.
5. Penicillin is an _____: it destroys bacteria that causes infections.

6. Edna is the _____ of her brother. He is aloof, but she is friendly.

7. Aspirin is an _____: it reduces fever.

8. You seem to have an _____ to Louise. Why don't you like her?

9. The mouthwash recommended by the dentist contains an _____ to arrest the growth of harmful bacteria.

10. _____ drugs are often prescribed for persons with high blood pressure.

11. A heart patient may be given an _____ to reduce the danger of internal clotting.

12. Now she supports the government's policies, but for a long time she was _____.

13. Vitamin C is _____: it fights scurvy.

14. When it is noon in England, it is midnight in New Zealand and Australia because these places are England's _____.

15. _____s help protect the arms and backs of sofas against soiling.

16. Three corporations have been charged with conspiring to fix prices in violation of the _____ laws.

17. An _____ may give relief from the sneezing, runny nose, inflamed eyelids, and other unpleasant effects of histamine.

18. Note how the italicized words produce _____ in the following: He has an insatiable appetite for wealth, fame, and *pickled herring*.

19. The nation that suffered extremely high casualties protested that its foe had used _____ bombs.

20. _____s inhibit oxidation in the foods to which they are added and extend their shelf life.

B. Details About the New Words

WORD	MEANING
antibiotic *n* ˌan-ti-bī-'ä-tik	drug, usually derived from living organisms, that combats bacterial infection

Antibiotics, *like penicillin and streptomycin, hasten recovery from infectious diseases.*

| **antibody** *n*
'an-ti-ˌbä-dē | immunizing substance formed in the body to counteract an invading *antigen* (foreign body) |

When threatened with tetanus (lockjaw), our bodies produce an antibody *to kill the invading tetanus germs.*

| **anticlimax** *n*
an-ti-'klī-ˌmaks | sudden drop in importance or dignity, either in writing or speaking, creating a humorous effect |

She uses anticlimax. *For example, she said that for her birthday she wants jeweled earrings, a camcorder, and a new flyswatter.*

| **anticoagulant** *n*
ˌan-ti-kō-'a-gyə-lənt | substance that delays or prevents *coagulation* (clotting of the blood) |

Anticoagulants *have saved the lives of many patients who have clot-related diseases.*

| **anticorrosive** *adj*
ˌan-tē-kə-'rō-siv | counteracting or preventing *corrosion* (gradual wearing away, especially of metals) |

The outdoor railing was given two coats of a good anticorrosive *paint to inhibit rust.*

| **antidote** *n*
'an-ti-ˌdōt | remedy that counteracts a poison |

A substance labeled as poison must carry a description of its antidote.

WORD	MEANING

antiestablishment *adj*
ˌan-tī-ə-'sta-blish-mənt

opposed to the principles of a ruling class or inner circle

Millions of citizens opposed the government's policies, and their antiestablishment *views eventually won out.*

antihistamine *n*
ˌan-ti-'his-tə-mən

drug that helps prevent histamine from causing allergic reactions or cold symptoms

Cold-sufferers who feel drowsy after taking an antihistamine *should avoid driving.*

antihypertensive *adj*
ˌan-ti-ˌhī-pər-'ten-səv

effective in reducing high blood pressure

With the help of antihypertensive *pills, plus weight reduction and restriction of salt use, Sam's blood pressure was brought under control.*

antimacassar *n*
ˌan-ti-mə-'ka-sər

small cover for arms or backs of sofas or chairs, either as a decoration or a protection from soiling (originally, against hair oil imported from Macassar)

Which would you prefer for protecting your furniture— slipcovers or antimacassars?

antioxidant *n*
ˌan-tē-'äk-sə-dənt

chemical compound that slows down *oxidation* (changes produced by oxygen) and checks deterioration

The addition of antioxidants *prevents soaps, oils, gasoline, rubber, and food products from spoiling.*

antipathy *n*
an-'ti-pə-thē

strong feeling against someone or something; dislike; aversion

A student with an antipathy *to books and teachers is likely to become a dropout.*

WORD	MEANING
antipersonnel adj ˌan-ti-ˌpər-sᵊ-'nel	designed for use against an enemy nation's military personnel or civilians, rather than its equipment

The nation that suffered extremely high casualties protested that its foe had used antipersonnel *bombs.*

antipodes n pl an-'ti-pə-ˌdēz	(literally, with feet opposite) parts of the earth, or their inhabitants, directly opposite one another on the globe

A pair of small Indian Ocean islands, New Amsterdam and St. Paul, are the antipodes *of Washington, D.C.*

antipyretic n ˌan-ti-pī-'re-tik	substance that reduces fever

Her temperature is now normal; the antipyretic *has brought down her fever.*

antiscorbutic adj ˌan-ti-skȯr-'byü-tik	preventing or relieving scurvy

Sailors on long sea voyages used to suffer from scurvy in the days before the antiscorbutic *properties of limes and other citrus fruits became known.*

antiseptic n ˌan-tə-'sep-tik	substance that combats the germs that cause *sepsis* (disease or decay); germicide

Alcohol, boric acid, and hydrogen peroxide are common antiseptics.

antithesis n an-'ti-thə-səs	exact opposite; contrast

I have found you disloyal and untrustworthy. You are the antithesis *of what a true friend should be.*

WORD	MEANING
antitrust *adj* ˌan-ti-ˈtrəst	opposing, or intended to oppose, trusts (combinations of firms for the illegal purpose of destroying competition and controlling prices)

Three corporations have been charged with conspiring to fix prices in violation of the antitrust *laws.*

antiviral *adj* ˌan-ti-ˈvī-rəl	acting to make a virus ineffective

In 1796, Edward Jenner made an antiviral *vaccine from cowpox; it provided immunity against the smallpox virus.*

C. Building Additional Words

Construct and enter the correct *anti* word. The last letter of that word has been written in as a clue.

Sample:

The installation of _____ antipollutio n devices in automobiles has greatly reduced air pollution.

1. Patriotic organizations are denouncing the magazine article as "_____ c propaganda."
2. The noise level in this city is too high because we are not enforcing the _____ e laws.
3. Now Frank sees people; he has become social. Before, he was decidedly _____ l.
4. The Senator is a friend of labor; he is not _____ r.
5. If you are opposed to vivisection (medical experimentation on living animals), you are an _____ t.
6. Many use an _____ t to check underarm perspiration.
7. Protect the coolant in your engine against freezing by adding _____ e.
8. We now have superior _____ l drugs to help the millions suffering from malaria.

9. _____t gunners brought down three of the attacking planes.

10. Can our present _____e defenses adequately protect us against hostile missiles?

11. You say you are not opposed to the feminist movement. Why, then, do some of your statements have an _____t slant?

12. If sensibly enforced, our _____r regulations should appreciably reduce the amount of litter on our streets and highways.

13. One goal of the _____y program is to train individuals in the job skills they need to escape poverty.

14. The dozens of wrecked tanks on the battlefield testify to the success of the defenders' _____k weapons.

15. When a toxin endangers your health, your body responds by producing the specific _____n as a countermeasure.

D. Thinking with Your New Words

Read all the following statements. Then answer each question below.

Statements

Vasco da Gama's 1497–99 voyage from Portugal to India was a feat of navigation, but more than half the crew died of scurvy.

Paula frequently wrote to her representatives in Congress to protest the administration's policies on domestic and foreign issues.

If the medication Dr. Tausig prescribed for Juana had failed to dissolve the clot in her leg, he would have had her hospitalized.

Alice preferred to stay home to watch TV or read, instead of being with people.

Dr. Evans told Judy that an antibiotic would not help her cold, and he advised her to take aspirin to bring down her fever.

Sidney reported that the new pills had some unpleasant side effects, but he was glad they had lowered his blood pressure.

Yoko used to be friendly with Rita and Alan until she realized how selfish they were; now she will have nothing to do with them.

Ernie said the commander should have concentrated on destroying the enemy's equipment, instead of inflicting as many casualties as possible.

Basil told his guests that he could offer them Kentucky bourbon, French brandy, Scotch whiskey, or tap water.

The poison Joyce took by accident could have been fatal if she had not quickly been given liberal doses of milk of magnesia.

Questions

1. Who was antiestablishment? _____
2. Who took an antihyper-
   tensive drug? _____
3. Who used an anticlimax? _____
4. Who deplored antipersonnel
   tactics? _____
5. Who received an antidote? _____
6. Who recommended an
   antipyretic? _____
7. Who appeared to be antisocial? _____
8. Who took an anticoagulant? _____
9. Who developed an antipathy? _____
10. Who sorely needed antiscor-
    butic food? _____

E. Discussion with Your New Words

Answer each of the following in one or two sentences or a brief paragraph:

1. Would a guest with antiestablishment views be persona non grata in your home? Why, or why not?

_____

_____

_____

2. You announced the winner would get a new car, a year's
   supply of facial tissues, and a trip to Hawaii. If you had
   wanted to achieve anticlimax, where in your sentence
   should you have mentioned the prize you originally put in
   the penultimate slot?

   _____

   _____

   _____

3. Does someone who always travels first class necessarily
   have an antipathy to hoi polloi? Explain.

   _____

   _____

   _____

4. Would you be offended if a new boss questions your judgment in a field in which you are the antithesis of a tyro?
   Why, or why not?

   _____

   _____

   _____

5. Why are scientists like Sir Alexander Fleming, discoverer
   of the antibiotic penicillin, and Jonas Salk, developer of
   the first effective polio vaccine, entitled to the highest
   kudos?

   _____

   _____

   _____

12

"Cutting" Words

The root *tom* (from Greek) and the roots *cid, cis,* and *sect* (from Latin) all have the same meaning: "cut." Here are some sample words with these "cut" roots:

TOM: An appende*ctom*y is the "cutting" out or surgical removal of the appendix.

CID: Homi*cid*e is the "cutting" down or killing of one person by another.

CIS: Con*cis*e writing is writing from which all unnecessary words have been "cut."

SECT: To bi*sect* a line is to "cut" it into two equal sections, or "cuts."

A. Preview

Use each of the following no more than once in answering the questions below.

anatomy	fratricidal	incisive	sectionalism
conciseness	gingivectomy	intersect	suicidal
dissect	herbicide	laparotomy	tome
entomology	homicidal	lobotomy	trisect
excise	incision	rescission	vivisection

1. Do human needs justify _____, or is animal welfare more important?
2. It is fortunate when a surgeon can _____ a malignant tumor in the early stages of growth.
3. Broadway and Forty-second Street _____ at Times Square.
4. The nurse removed the splinter without having to make a(n) _____ in my finger.

5. A single-volume encyclopedia occupies much less space than one of many _____s.
6. Having studied _____, the physician knows the exact location of the body's organs and the nerves and blood vessels to which they are connected.
7. Hundreds of thousands perished in the _____ War Between the States.
8. A selective _____ destroys weeds without injuring desirable plants.
9. An operation in the abdominal area may begin with a(n) _____.
11. Some of the legislators who supported the tax increase are now clamoring for its _____.
12. The periodontist performed a(n) _____ to dislodge pockets of bacteria.
12. For the sake of _____, remove "to accept" from the following sentence: "They refused to accept our offer."
13. There was intense competition between the newer and older industrial regions for federal contracts; _____ was rife.
14. A specialist in _____ can easily distinguish a termite from an ant.
15. The series of killings was attributed to a(n) _____ maniac.
16. You have a(n) _____ mind that quickly gets to the root of a problem.
17. A(n) _____ is considered for a seriously ill mental patient only when other approaches, such as tranquilizers, fail to alleviate the extreme pain.
18. Only two cuts are needed to _____ a piece of lumber.
19. Sometimes we have to _____ a passage sentence by sentence and word by word to get its precise meaning.
20. It would have been _____ for Tom, in his poor state of health, to work twelve hours a day.

B. Details About the New Words

WORD	MEANING
anatomy *n* ə-'na-tə-mē	"cutting apart" or dissection of a body or organism to determine the location, structure, and interrelationships of its parts; science of structure, morphology

Having studied anatomy, *the physician knows the exact location of the body's organs and the nerves and blood vessels to which they are connected.*

| **conciseness** *n*
kən-'sīs-nəs | brevity and compactness in expression resulting from the avoidance ("cutting out") of needless words and elaborate detail |

For the sake of consciseness, *remove "to accept" from the following sentence: "They refused to accept our offer."*

| **dissect** *v*
di-'sekt | cut apart piece by piece for study; analyze closely |

Sometimes we have to dissect *a passage sentence by sentence and word by word to get its precise meaning.*

| **entomology** *n*
ˌen-tə-'mä-lə-jē | branch of zoology dealing with insects, so named for their "cut in," notched, segmented bodies (Both the Latin *insect* and the Greek *entomo* mean "cut in.") |

A specialist in entomology *can easily distinguish a termite from an ordinary ant.*

| **excise** *v*
ek-'sīz | remove by cutting out |

It is fortunate when a surgeon can excise *a malignant tumor in the early stages of growth.*

WORD	MEANING

fratricidal *adj*
ˌfra-trə-'sī-dəl

of or relating to fratricide (act of killing one's brother, sister, or fellow citizen)

Hundreds of thousands perished in the fratricidal *War Between the States.*

gingivectomy *n*
ˌjin-jə-'vek-tə-mē

surgical excision of gum tissue

The periodontist performed a gingivectomy *to dislodge pockets of bacteria.*

herbicide *n*
'(h)ər-bə-ˌsīd

chemical for destroying or inhibiting plant growth; weed killer

A selective herbicide *destroys weeds without injuring desirable plants.*

homicidal *adj*
ˌhä-mə-'sī-dəl

having a tendency toward homocide; murderous

The series of killings was attributed to a homicidal *maniac.*

incision *n*
in-'si-zhən

cut, especially for surgical purposes; gash

The nurse removed the splinter without having to make an incision *in my finger.*

incisive *adj*
in-'sī-siv

sharp; keen; penetrating

You have an incisive *mind that quickly gets to the root of a problem.*

intersect *v*
ˌin-tər-'sekt

cut across each other; cross

Broadway and Forty-second Street intersect *at Times Square.*

laparotomy *n*
ˌla-pə-'rä-tə-mē

surgical incision into the abdominal cavity

An operation on an abdominal organ may begin with a laparotomy.

WORD	MEANING

lobotomy *n*
lō-'bä-tə-mē

surgical operation on a lobe of the brain

A lobotomy *is considered for a seriously ill mental patient only when other approaches, such as tranquilizers, fail to alleviate the extreme pain.*

---

rescission *n*
ri-'si-zhən

act of *rescinding* ("cutting back"); cancelation; annulment

Some of the legislators who supported the tax increase are now clamoring for its rescission.

---

sectionalism *n*
'sek-shnə-ˌli-zəm

exaggerated devotion to the interests of one section; regional prejudice

The newer and older industrial regions competed intensely for federal contracts; sectionalism *was rife.*

---

suicidal *adj*
ˌsü-ə-'sī-dᵊl

tending toward *suicide* (act of voluntarily taking one's life); self-destructive; destructive of one's own interests

It would have been suicidal *for Tom, in his poor state of health, to work twelve hours a day.*

---

tome *n*
'tōm

one volume, or "cut," of a work of two or more volumes; any heavy, large, or scholarly book

Would you rather own a single-volume encyclopedia, or one of several tomes?

---

trisect *v*
'trī,sekt

cut into three equal parts

Only two cuts are needed to trisect *a piece of lumber.*

---

vivisection *n*
'vi-və-ˌsek-shən

practice of subjecting living animals to surgical experimentation to advance medical knowledge

Do human needs justify vivisection, *or is animal welfare more important?*

C. Building Additional Words

A word ends in *-ectomy* if it describes the partial or complete "cutting out" of a part of the body. (*-ec* in Greek means "out.")

A gast*rectomy* is the surgical removal, or "cutting out," of all or part of the stomach.

A word ends in *-tomy* if it describes a "cutting," rather than a "cutting out."

A gast*rotomy* is a "cutting," or surgical incision, into the stomach.

Each surgical operation below (1 to 18) can be expressed in one word. Build that word by adding *-ectomy* or *-tomy* to one of the following roots:

arterio (artery)	neuro (nerve)
cholecyst (gallbladder)	osteo (bone)
cranio (skull)	parathyroid (parathyroid)
hepato (liver)	pneumon (lung)
hystero (uterus; womb)	prostato (prostate)
laryngo (larynx)	spleno (spleen)
masto (breast)	thyroid (thyroid)
mastoid (mastoid)	tonsillo (tonsils)
nephro (kidney)	tracheo (windpipe)

Spelling hint. If a root ends in *o*, drop the *o* before *-ectomy*, but keep it before *-tomy*.

gastro + ectomy = gastrectomy (*o* dropped)
gastro + tomy = gastrotomy (*o* kept)

Samples:

Removal of the tonsils	tonsillectomy
Opening of the skull, as in brain surgery	craniotomy

1. Removal of the spleen
2. Removal of the larynx
3. Excision of a nerve, or part of a nerve
4. Cutting into the windpipe
5. Excision of a breast
6. Opening of an artery
7. Removal of the thyroid

8. Incision of the uterus, as in a
   Caesarian birth   _____
9. Excision of the liver   _____
10. Removal of the gallbladder   _____
11. Incision of a kidney, as to
    remove a kidney stone   _____
12. Cutting of a nerve, as to relieve
    pain   _____
13. Excision of the parathyroid   _____
14. Removal of the uterus   _____
15. Removal of the mastoid   _____
16. Excision of a lung   _____
17. Dividing of a bone, as to correct
    a deformity   _____
18. Excision of the prostate   _____

D. Thinking with Your New Words

Read all the following statements. Then answer each question below.

Statements

Aunt Susan's cancerous liver was excised and replaced by a healthy one from an anonymous donor.

First Marva made a small cut into the box; then she cut along the dotted lines, and the cover came off.

When a motion was made to annul the previous motion, Israel voted for it.

After removing the wormy part, Jackie sliced the rest of the apple for me; it was delicious.

By the time he was six, Brian had had his tonsils and adenoids taken out.

Andy's abdominal scar has healed very well and is now hardly visible.

Thorndike's first house was at the corner of Blake and Wilson Avenues.

Macduff came into the world by Caesarian section.

In his newsletter, Senator Berg reported he had brought more than $300,000,000 in government contracts to the state, and that he would work to surpass that figure in his second term.

Donna took many courses on insects and their habits, and now she works for the Department of Agriculture.

Questions

1. Who had an adenoidectomy? _____
2. Who had a hepatectomy? _____
3. Who made an incision? _____
4. Who had a laparotomy? _____
5. Who supported a rescission? _____
6. Who specialized in entomology? _____
7. Who was imbued with
   sectionalism? _____
8. Who was delivered by a
   hysterotomy? _____
9. Who lived at an intersection? _____
10. Who made an excision? _____

E. Analogies

Write the *letter* of the pair of words related to each other in the same way as the words in the capitalized pair.

1. INCISION : SCALPEL
   a. injection : hypodermic   *d.* needle : stitch
   b. wound : scar   *e.* beard : razor
   c. antiseptic : infection   **Answer** _____

2. ENTOMOLOGY : INSECTS
   a. criminology : detectives *d.* astronomy : stars
   b. philately : coins   *e.* eulogy : achievements
   c. anthology : authors   **Answer** _____

3. ANTIMACASSAR : SLIPCOVER
   a. wrapper : contents   *d.* book : jacket
   b. place mat : tablecloth   *e.* antioxidant : food
   c. awning : shade   **Answer** _____

4. HERBICIDE : PLANTS
a. anticoagulant : clots   d. fratricide : casualties
b. homicide : weapons   e. antibiotic : microorganisms
c. antihistamine : colds   **Answer** _____

5. ANTIPATHY : COOPERATION
a. hostility : friction   d. dichotomy : enmity
b. bias : justice   e. anatomy : morphology
c. rescission : veto   **Answer** _____

13

"Before" and "After" Words

Three prefixes meaning "before" are the Latin *ante-* and *pre-* and the Greek *pro-*.

Anterevolutionary America is America in the time of the thirteen colonies, i.e., *before* the Revolutionary War.

Pre-Columbian art is art that flourished in America *before* the coming of Columbus.

A *proscenium* is the part of a stage *before*, or *in front of*, the curtain.

Two prefixes meaning "after" are the Latin *post-* and the Greek *meta-*.

Postoperative care is care that a patient needs *after* an operation.

The *metatarsal* bones are the five bones of the human foot that come *after* the *tarsus* (ankle) and before the toes.

A. Preview

Use each of the following no more than once in completing the sentences below.

antecedent	metacarpal	posterity	prescient
antediluvian	metaphysics	posthumous	presentiment
antemeridian	metastasis	postprandial	prognosis
antepenult	metempsychosis	predecease	prophesy
anterior	posterior	prerecord	prophylaxis

1. Radio and TV programmers often _____ material for broadcast at a later time.
2. The people coming to dinner are not philosophers so please do not discuss _____.

3. Some say the soul migrates to a new body when the body dies. Do you believe in _____?

4. Julius Caesar heard a soothsayer _____ that there would be trouble on the Ides of March.

5. David Copperfield was a(n) _____ child, his father having died six months before David was born.

6. Compared to the new models now in dealer showrooms, our twelve-year-old jalopy looks _____.

7. Before the game, I had a(n) _____ of defeat, and the final score showed I was right.

8. Let us solve the problem of pollution now, instead of leaving it to our _____.

9. The chances of recovery from cancer are enhanced if the malignant tumor can be excised early, before _____ begins.

10. In "the runner who fell," "who" is a pronoun and "runner" is its _____.

11. Mr. Somers has plenty of life insurance, so his wife and children will be well provided for if he should _____ them.

12. Our incisors are _____ teeth: they are at the front of the mouth.

13. I have no foreknowledge of future events. I am not _____.

14. The _____ is favorable. The patient should recover.

15. I get hungry before noon, so I really appreciate my _____ coffee break.

16. The dinner was delicious, and the _____ conversation equally enjoyable.

17. Proper dental _____ includes brushing and flossing after meals, plus periodic visits to the dentist for checkups and removal of tartar and plaque.

18. In *com-mu-ni-ca-tion*, *ca* is the penult, and *ni* is the _____.

19. The _____ bones connect the wrist with the fingers.

20. Our molars are _____ teeth: they are toward the back of the mouth.

B. Details About the New Words

WORD	MEANING
antecedent *n* ˌan-tə-'sē-dᵊnt	word that a pronoun refers to (an antecedent usually comes before its pronoun)

In "the runner who fell," "who" is a pronoun and "runner" is its antecedent.

antediluvian *adj* ˌan-ti-də-'lü-vē-ən	(literally, of the time before the Flood described in the Bible) very old; primitive

Compared to the new models now in dealer showrooms, our twelve-year-old jalopy looks antediluvian.

antemeridian *adj* ˌan-ti-mə-'ri-dē-ən	occurring before noon

I get hungry before noon, so I really appreciate my antemeridian *coffee break.*

antepenult *n* ˌan-ti-'pē͵nəlt	syllable before the *penult* (next-to-last syllable); third syllable from the end of a word

In com-mu-ni-ca-tion, ca *is the penult, and* ni *is the* antepenult.

anterior *adj* an-'tir-ē-ər	situated before or toward the front

Our incisors are anterior *teeth; they are at the front of the mouth.*

metacarpal *adj* ˌme-tə-'kär-pəl	having to do with any of the five long bones after the *carpus* (wrist) and before the fingers

The metacarpal *bones connect the wrist and the fingers.*

WORD	MEANING
metaphysics *n pl* ,me-tə-'fi-ziks	branch of philosophy dealing with the nature of existence (In Aristotle's collected works, his treatise on this subject was placed after his *Physics*; hence the name *metaphysics*.)

The people coming to dinner are not philosophers, so please do not discuss metaphysics.

metastasis *n* mə-'tas-tə-səs	(literally, an after condition) spread of a malignancy from its original site to other parts of the body

The chances of recovery from cancer are enhanced if the malignant tumor can be excised early, before metastasis *begins.*

metempsychosis *n* mə-,tem(p)-si-'kō-səs	supposed after existence, or passing of the *psyche* (soul) at death into another body, either human or animal; transmigration of souls

Some say the soul migrates to a new body when the body dies. Do you believe in metempsychosis?

posterior *adj* pō-'stir-ē-ər	coming after; situated behind or toward the back

Our molars are posterior *teeth; they are toward the back of the mouth.*

posterity *n* pä-'ster-ə-tē	those born after a person; descendants; future generations

Let us solve the problem of pollution now, instead of leaving it to our posterity.

posthumous *adj* 'päs-chə-məs	born after the death of one's father; published or occurring after one's death

David Copperfield was a posthumous *child, his father having died six months before David was born.*

WORD	MEANING

postprandial *adj*   occurring after a meal; after
ˌpost-ˈpran-dē-əl   dinner
The dinner was delicious, and the postprandial *conversation was equally enjoyable.*

predecease *v*   die before another person
ˌprē-di-ˈsēs
Mr. Somers has plenty of life insurance, so his wife and children will be well provided for if he should predecease *them.*

prerecord *v*   record in advance, before use
ˌprē-ri-ˈkòrd   or broadcasting
Radio and TV programmers often prerecord *material for broadcast at a later time.*

prescient *adj*   seeming to have knowledge of
ˈprē-shənt   events before they occur; gifted
     with foresight
I have no foreknowledge of future events. I am not prescient.

presentiment *n*   feeling that something
pri-ˈzen-tə-mənt   unfortunate is about to happen
     before that event occurs;
     foreboding
Before the game, I had a presentiment *of defeat, and the final score showed I was right.*

prognosis *n*   forecast; prediction of the
präg-ˈnō-səs   probable course of an illness;
     prognostication
The prognosis *is favorable; the patient should recover.*

prophesy *v*   foretell; indicate beforehand;
ˈprä-fə-ˌsī   predict
Julius Caesar heard a soothsayer prophesy *that there would be trouble on the Ides of March.*

WORD	MEANING
prophylaxis n ,prō-fə-'lak-səs	(literally, "guarding beforehand") preventive treatment against disease

Proper dental prophylaxis *includes brushing and flossing after meals, plus periodic visits to the dentist for checkups and removal of tartar and plaque.*

C. Building Additional Words

Construct the necessary word by adding one of the following prefixes:

ante	meta
pre	post
pro	

1. The bride and groom had not freely chosen each other; their spouses had been _____ selected for them by their parents.
2. Everyone who came into the world after the explosion of the first atomic bomb is considered to have been born into the _____ atomic age.
3. In their _____ election statements, both candidates expressed confidence that they and their parties would be swept into office.
4. The _____ position to raise the sales tax will be put before the voters at the next general election.
5. Selma graduated from Yale in 1991 and returned for _____ graduate study in 1993.
6. A(n) _____ dated check bears an earlier date than the one on which it was written.
7. Should I make some introductory remarks before telling my story, or do you think a(n) _____ logue is unnecessary?
8. A(n) _____ morphosis is an *after* form, transformation, or changeover.
9. A(n) _____ dated check bears a later date than the one on which it was written.
10. A child between the ages of nine and twelve is a(n) _____ adolescent.

11. Being neither an expert nor a prophet, I refuse to
_____ gnosticate the outcome.

12. A _____ paid shipment is one that is paid for in
advance.

13. I took a seat in the _____ room that leads into the
director's office.

14. Only a _____ designated alternate is authorized
to cast a vote for an absent delegate.

15. The defendant insisted that the killing of the victim was
un_____ meditated.

D. Thinking with Your New Words

Read all the following statements. Then answer each question below.

Statements

Scott said *deSPICable*, Martha said *DESpicable*. The instructor indicated both were correct.

Four years ago Dr. Logan told Adrienne's parents he did not expect her to recover, but she did.

Roberto told Harriet the stock would go to 98 by May 15, and, believe it or not, it did!

You would not have recognized Patricia. She has lost considerable weight, and she has become a blonde.

Rip Van Winkle fell asleep when our country was a British colony, and when he awoke it was an independent nation.

Valdine injured the bone between her wrist and ring finger.

Terry was at the piano, Alan was backstage, Tony and Bill were in the wings, and Leila emerged from the curtain to address the audience.

Delwyn said he would never forget the people who helped him so much during his recovery from surgery.

The Salk vaccine is mainly responsible for the practical disappearance of crippling paralytic polio.

Herman slipped and broke a bone between the ankle and little toe on his left foot.

Questions

1. Who sustained a metatarsal injury?
_____
2. Who underwent a metamorphosis?
_____
3. Who retired in an anterevolutionary era?
_____
4. Who has left a priceless legacy to posterity?
_____
5. Who stressed the antepenult?
_____
6. Who defied a prognosis?
_____
7. Who suffered a metacarpal injury?
_____
8. Who was prescient?
_____
9. Who required postoperative care?
_____
10. Who was on the proscenium?
_____

E. Discussion with Your New Words

Answer each of the following in a brief paragraph.

1. Why may we call the Tories who lived in the thirteen colonies both "anterevolutionary" and "antirevolutionary"?

_____

_____

_____

_____

2. Which would be more serious for a writer—a metacarpal fracture, or a metatarsal one? Explain.

_____

_____

_____

_____

3. Is the *proboscis* (trunk) a posterior or an anterior part of the elephant's anatomy? Explain.

_____

_____

_____

_____

4. As a matter of health, should those who have three full meals a day generally avoid antemeridian and postprandial snacks? Why, or why not?

_____

_____

_____

_____

5. Many have prophesied that it would be suicidal for any nation to start a nuclear war. Do you agree? Why, or why not?

_____

_____

_____

_____

"People" Words

Question: What is a *Pollyanna*?

Answer: *Pollyanna,* the heroine of stories by Eleanor H. Porter, was always looking on the bright side of things, despite her difficult life as an orphan.

A *Pollyanna* is "anyone who is excessively and persistently optimistic."

Question: What does *Draconian* mean?

Answer: *Draco,* an Athenian of the seventh century before Christ, wrote a code of law in which the death penalty was prescribed for numerous minor offenses.

Draconian today means "extremely harsh or severe."

This chapter deals with "people" words—words derived from the names of real people (like *Draco*) or fictional people (like *Pollyanna*).

A. Preview

Use each of the following no more than once in completing the sentences below.

Adonis	chauvinist	Machiavellian	philippic
atlas	cicerone	malapropism	quisling
Baedeker	Damoclean	mentor	quixotic
bowdlerize	gargantuan	mesmerize	sadistic
boycott	John Hancock	odyssey	stentorian

1. The show is spellbinding: it will _____ you.
2. If your cousin gets to the food first, there will be very little for the rest of us; he has a(n) _____ appetite.
3. Without a microphone I would have needed a(n)

_____ voice to be heard at the
outdoor rally.

4. He did not hesitate to use lies, fraud, bribery, character
   assassination, spies, and even thugs to stay in office; he
   was _____.

5. Read the document carefully. Then affix your
   _____ on the dotted line.

6. I would like to check on the boundaries of Hungary. Do
   you have a recent _____?

7. The father began teaching his daughter the piano when she
   was only three, and her progress showed he was an excellent _____.

8. The enraged captain whipped the rebellious seaman with
   _____ glee.

9. Nowadays most tourists do not have the time for an
   eighty-four-day _____ through
   the Middle East and the Orient.

10. Emily's blind date was ordinary-looking, and mine was no
    _____ either.

11. Some of the residents near the nuclear power plant regard
    it as a(n) _____ threat; others
    feel no imminent danger.

12. The _____ who gave military
    secrets to our potential enemies has been living abroad.

13. If I had not misplaced my _____,
    I would have visited more of the truly important places in
    Paris.

14. Pat said she has a "ravaging" appetite for pizza. Of course,
    she meant "ravenous," but I did not want to embarrass her
    by pointing out the _____.

15. If the fare goes up any more, many riders will walk or
    form car pools. They will _____
    the transit system.

16. Any plan for the instant rehabilitation of career criminals
    is _____: it will not work.

17. We must guard against being dragged into conflicts by
    _____s; their patriotism is blind.

18. In an impassioned _____, the
    former cabinet official rebuked the prime minister and
    demanded his resignation.

19. Thanks to the loquacious _____,
    we learned a great deal about art and history on our tour of
    Florence.

20. Some of the classics studied in high school have been
_____d, as you may discover
when you later read the unexpurgated editions.

B. Details About the New Words

Word	Meaning
Adonis n ə-'dä-nəs	very handsome man (Adonis was a handsome youth loved by Aphrodite, goddess of love and beauty.)

Emily's blind date was just ordinary-looking, and mine was no Adonis *either.*

atlas n 'at-ləs	book of maps (Atlas, an earth giant, was forced to support the heavens on his shoulders. A representative of Atlas in this task used to appear on the front page of map collections.)

I would like to check on the boundaries of Hungary. Do you have a recent atlas?

Baedeker n 'bā-də-kər	guidebook; handbook (Karl Baedeker (1801–1859) published in Germany a series of guidebooks to foreign countries.)

If I had not misplaced my Baedeker, *I would have visited more of the truly important places in Paris.*

bowdlerize v 'bōd-lə-,rīz	expurgate; clear of words or passages thought to be objectionable (Thomas Bowdler (1754–1825) published an expurgated edition of Shakespeare's works.)

Some of the classics studied in high school have been bowdlerized, *as you may discover when you later read the unexpurgated editions.*

WORD	MEANING
boycott *v* 'boi-ˌkät	join with others to refuse to use, buy, or deal with (Charles C. Boycott (1832–1897), agent in Ireland for an English landlord, treated the tenants so unfairly that they refused to pay their rents to him.)

If the fare goes up any more, many riders will walk or form car pools. They will boycott *the transit system.*

| **chauvinist** *n*
 'shō-və-nist | fanatical patriot; jingoist (Nicolas Chauvin, a legendary French soldier, was excessively devoted to Napoleon I.) |

We must guard against being dragged into conflicts by chauvinists; *their patriotism is blind.*

| **cicerone** *n*
 ˌsi-sə-'rō-nē | guide who explains to tourists the history and special features of a place (Cicero (106–43 B.C.) was a Roman orator. Cicerones are usually talkative.) |

Thanks to the loquacious cicerone, *we learned a great deal about art and history on our tour of Florence.*

| **Damoclean** *adj*
 ˌda-mə-'klē-ən | involving imminent disaster (In ancient Syracuse, Damocles, who had overpraised the king's happiness, was allegedly forced to sit under a sword suspended by a single hair to teach him the insecurity of the king's position.) |

Some of the residents near the nuclear power plant regard it as a Damoclean *threat; others feel no imminent danger.*

WORD	MEANING

gargantuan *adj*
gär-'gan(t)-shə-wən

enormous; gigantic; prodigious (Gargantua, the amiable giant king in *Gargantua* by Rabelais, has an enormous capacity for food and drink.)

If your cousin gets to the food first, there will be very little for the rest of us; he has a gargantuan *appetite.*

John Hancock *n*
'jän-'han-ˌkäk

person's signature (On the Declaration of Independence, the signature of the American statesman John Hancock (1737–1793) is the first, the largest, and the most legible.)

Read the document carefully. Then affix your John Hancock *on the dotted line.*

Machiavellian *adj*
ˌma-kē-ə-'ve-lē-ən

crafty; deceitful; cunning (Niccolo Machiavelli (1469–1527) wrote about the use of deceit and cunning to gain and hold power, with morality subordinated to political expediency.)

He did not hesitate to use lies, fraud, bribery, character assassination, spies, and even thugs to stay in office; he was Machiavellian.

---

malapropism *n*
'ma-lə-ˌprä-ˌpi-zəm

humorous misuse of words by a person unaware of the error (Mrs. Malaprop, a character in Sheridan's play *The Rivals,* makes many such errors.)

Mrs. Malaprop thinks Captain Absolute is "the very pineapple of politeness." Her confusion of "pineapple" with "pinnacle" is, of course, a ridiculous malapropism.

WORD	MEANING
mentor *n* 'men-,tòr	wise, trusted adviser or teacher (In the *Odyssey,* Mentor is the trusted friend of Odysseus and tutor of Odysseus's son Telemachus.)

The father began teaching his daughter the piano when she was only three; he was an excellent mentor.

| **mesmerize** *v*
 'mez-mə-,rīz | hypnotize; spellbind; enthrall (Franz Anton Mesmer (1734–1815) was a German physician who used hypnotism.) |

The show is spellbinding: it will mesmerize *you.*

| **odyssey** *n*
 'ä-də-sē | long, wandering journey (Homer's *Odyssey* describes the wanderings of Odysseus on his way home from the Trojan War, a journey that took ten years.) |

Nowadays most tourists do not have the time for an eighty-four-day odyssey *through the Middle East and the Orient.*

| **philippic** *n*
 fə-'li-pik | bitter denunciatory speech; tirade; jeremiad (In his *Philippics,* the orator Demosthenes (384–322 B.C.) denounced Philip II of Macedon.) |

In an impassioned philippic, *the former cabinet official rebuked the prime minister and demanded his resignation.*

| **quisling** *n*
 'kwiz-liŋ | traitor; collaborator (Vidkun Quisling (1887–1945), a Norwegian, betrayed his country to the Nazis and was installed by them as its puppet ruler.) |

The quisling *who gave military secrets to our potential enemies has been living abroad.*

WORD	MEANING
quixotic adj kwik-'sä-tik	impractically idealistic; visionary (Don Quixote, hero of a novel by Cervantes, is a naïve idealist who tries to combat evil in an unrealistic and absurd manner.)

Any plan for the instant rehabilitation of career criminals is
quixotic: *it will not work.*

sadistic adj sə-'dis-tik	deriving pleasure by inflicting pain on others; deliberately cruel (The Marquis de Sade (1740–1814) described such abnormal behavior in his writings.)

The enraged captain whipped the rebellious sailor with
sadistic *glee.*

stentorian adj sten-'tōr-ē-ən	very loud (In Homer's *Iliad*, Stentor, a Greek herald, speaks with the loudness of fifty voices.)

Without a microphone I would have needed a stentorian
voice to be heard at the outdoor rally.

C. Using "People" Words

Replace the italicized words with a single word that you
have learned in this chapter.

1. The assailant pounded his help-
   less victim with *deliberately
   cruel* blows.   _____

2. The Eighth Amendment to
   the Constitution specifically
   prohibits *extremely severe*
   punishments.   _____

3. You are *impractically idealistic* if you believe all people are honest and unselfish. _____

4. The employees on the picket line are urging the public to *refuse to buy* their employer's products. _____

5. Would you rather go through the exhibit by yourself, or with a *guide who can explain the special qualities of each painting*? _____

6. You would be a *blind, fanatical patriot* if you were to claim that your country could never be wrong. _____

7. Is it ever justifiable for an editor to *remove words or passages thought to be objectionable from* a book? _____

8. With her talent as an actress, she can easily *cast a spell on* any audience. _____

9. If you expect to win against great odds all the time, you are a *foolish optimist*. _____

10. The cast is headed by a(n) *very handsome male* with no previous stage experience. _____

D. Thinking with Your New Words

Read all of the following statements. Then answer each question below.

Statements

The utility company mailed Bruce's check back to him because he had forgotten to sign it.

Pierre Laval, who had collaborated with the Nazis during their occupation of his native land, was tried in a French court and executed in 1945.

Luckily, Caroline came along when we visited the restored

Colonial village. She had been there several times, so she was able to explain everything to us.

Toshi was on the plane that was hijacked over the Mediterranean and flown to seven airports on three continents before he regained his freedom.

Audrey lived in an upper-floor apartment across the courtyard, and whenever she spoke, all the other tenants could hear what she was saying.

There is a series of tall tales about Paul Bunyan, a legendary American hero of phenomenal size and strength.

In the hills above Hobart's home, there was an old earthen dam that the townspeople feared might burst some day, but no one did anything about it.

Whenever Joan had to drive to an unfamiliar area, she always checked the route in advance in her book of road maps.

Cozan blasted Kegel for committing the organization to expenditures without membership approval. After recalling similar charges against Kegel in the past, Cozan called for a vote of censure.

Walter was so enraged by Carmen that he vowed to "illiterate" her from his memory.

Questions

1. Who had a stentorian voice? _____
2. Who was a quisling? _____
3. Whose John Hancock was missing? _____
4. Who was the target of a philippic? _____
5. Who committed a malapropism? _____
6. Who was involved in an odyssey? _____
7. Who consulted an atlas? _____
8. Who was gargantuan? _____
9. Who lived in a Damoclean setting? _____
10. Who acted as a cicerone? _____

E. Analogies

Write the *letter* of the pair of words related to each other in the same way as the words in the capitalized pair.

1. DRACONIAN : SEVERE
a. costly : exorbitant
b. permissive : lenient
c. Damoclean : safe
d. sadistic : rude
e. old : antediluvian

Answer _____

2. CICERONE : SIGHTSEER
a. Baedeker : tourist
b. mentor : guidance
c. understudy : actor
d. investor : broker
e. audio : video

Answer _____

3. QUISLING : TREASON
a. renegade : loyalty
b. perjurer : arson
c. accomplice : guilt
d. murderer : homicide
e. smuggler : contraband

Answer _____

4. POLLYANNA : OPTIMISM
a. diehard : resistance
b. malingerer : illness
c. reactionary : change
d. insurgent : establishment
e. environmentalist : pollution

Answer _____

5. LARGE : GARGANTUAN
a. obese : stout
b. youthful : mature
c. wise : Machiavellian
d. emaciated : thin
e. small : tiny

Answer _____

New Words from Similar Words in the Context

If you meet a strange word, do not become flustered. Look for a context clue. In Chapter 5 we learned how to define a strange word when an opposite is present in the context. In this chapter we shall practice defining such a word when there is a synonymous or similar expression in the context, as is often the case.

Words like *bellicose* and *imprimatur,* possibly unfamiliar to you, can readily be understood if met in such contexts as the following:

> Scratchy Wilson, in "The Bride Comes to Yellow Sky," was not ordinarily quarrelsome. Only when he got drunk did he become *bellicose.*

Here, we get the meaning of *bellicose* from the synonym *quarrelsome.*

> The change cannot be made unless the director approves. We are waiting for her *imprimatur.*

Here, the clue is *approves.* Obviously, *imprimatur* means *approval.*

Note that a slight adjustment, such as from *approves* to *approval,* sometimes has to be made.

A. Preview

Write the meaning of the italicized words below. In each case, a clue in the form of a similar word or expression appears in the context.

1. She has the *alchemy* to turn hostile listeners into friends. I do not possess that magic.

   Alchemy means _____.

2. I tried to strike up a conversation with your neighbor, but he was uncommunicative. Is he always so *taciturn*?

   Taciturn means _____.

3. Her friends found her explanation *diverting*, though she really had not meant to amuse them.

   Diverting means _____.

4. Dad had no objection to your ordering a new dishwasher, but when you considered the deluxe model he *demurred* at the added cost.

   Demurred means _____.

5. The string beans had been thoroughly picked over by earlier shoppers, but I was able to *cull* about a half pound for tonight's dinner.

   Cull means _____.

6. Stop giving us ambiguous answers. Say yes or no. Don't *equivocate*.

   Equivocate means _____.

7. Have you read the lavish tributes in the campaign literature of the various candidates? Do their accomplishments really merit such *panegyrics*?

   Panegyrics means _____.

8. They filed a *mendacious* accident report: it was full of lies.

   Mendacious means _____.

9. His creditors kept sending bills and telephoning to demand payment. Their *dunning* made his life unbearable.

   Dunning means _____.

10. After the meeting, I stayed for the *collation*, reasoning that a light meal would not spoil my appetite for dinner.

    Collation means _____.

11. The washboard has fallen into *desuetude;* the horse-drawn buggy, too, is seldom used these days.

    Desuetude means _____.

12. Sam shouldn't criticize Nora for *preening*. He likes to neaten up his appearance too, doesn't he?

    Preening means _____.

13. There you go *carping* again! You are always finding fault with the way I do things.

    Carping means _____.

14. The idea that life exists on planets beyond the earth is purely *hypothetical:* it is based on supposition.

    Hypothetical means _____.

15. He may give the impression of being *ingenuous,* but let me assure you he is not naïve.

    Ingenuous means _____.

16. We were told that a little *baksheesh* would work miracles, so we gave the concierge a twenty-five-franc tip.

    Baksheesh means _____.

17. I was not shocked by his *pusillanimous* behavior. I knew he was a coward.

    Pusillanimous means _____.

18. What a difficult situation you have gotten us into! How will we ever be able to extricate ourselves from this *quagmire*?

    Quagmire means _____.

19. When little was known about a disease, the treatment was *empirical;* it was based on observation and trial-and-error experience, rather than on scientific knowledge.

    Empirical means _____.

20. She said I would *rue* my decision to turn down the managership. The truth is I have never regretted it.

    Rue means _____.

B. Details About the New Words

WORD	MEANING
alchemy *n* 'al-kə-mē	medieval chemistry concerned with finding a way to change base metals into gold and a single cure for all diseases; hence, magic, or magic power

She has the alchemy *to turn hostile listeners into friends. I do not possess that magic.*

| **baksheesh** *n*
'bak-,shēsh | gift of money; tip; gratuity |

We were told that a little baksheesh *would work miracles, so we gave the concierge a twenty-five-franc tip.*

| **bellicose** *adj*
'be-li-,kōs | inclined to fight or quarrel; pugnacious; warlike |

Scratchy Wilson, in "The Bride Comes to Yellow Sky," was not ordinarily quarrelsome. Only when he got drunk did he become bellicose.

| **carp** *v*
'kärp | find fault unreasonably; complain in a petty, nagging way |

There you go carping *again! You are always finding fault with the way I do things.*

| **collation** *n*
kə-'lā-shən | light meal |

After the meeting I stayed for the collation, *reasoning that a light meal would not spoil my appetite for dinner.*

| **cull** *v*
'kəl | select; pick out; choose |

The string beans had been thoroughly picked over by earlier shoppers, but I was able to cull *about a half pound for tonight's dinner.*

WORD	MEANING

demur *v*
di-'mər

object; take exception

Dad had no objection to your ordering a new dishwasher, but when you considered the deluxe model he demurred *at the added cost.*

---

desuetude *n*
'de-swi-,tüd

condition of no longer being used; disuse

The washboard has fallen into desuetude; *the horse-drawn buggy, too, is seldom used these days.*

---

divert *v*
də-'vərt

amuse; entertain; give pleasure to

Her friends found her explanation diverting, *though she really had not meant to amuse them.*

---

dun *v*
'dən

make repeated, insistent demands for payment

His creditors kept sending bills and telephoning to demand payment. Their dunning *made his life unbearable.*

---

empirical *adj*
im-'pir-i-kəl

relying solely on observation or experience

When little was known about a disease, the treatment was empirical; *it was based on observation and trial-and-error experience, rather than pure scientific knowledge.*

---

equivocate *v*
i-'kwi-və-,kāt

be deliberately ambiguous; use misleading terms so as not to commit oneself

Stop giving us ambiguous answers. Say yes or no. Don't equivocate.

---

hypothetical *adj*
,hī-pə-'the-ti-kəl

based on or involving a *hypothesis* (supposition); conjectural

The idea that life exists on planets beyond the earth is purely hypothetical: *it is based on supposition.*

WORD	MEANING

imprimatur *n*
'im-prə-'mä-,túr
(literally, let it be printed) authorization; sanction; approval

The change cannot be made unless the director approves. We are waiting for her imprimatur.

ingenuous *adj*
in-'jen-yə-wəs
innocent and simple; artless; naïve

He may give the impression of being ingenuous, *but let me assure you he is not naïve.*

mendacious *adj*
men-'dā-shəs
lying; untrue; deceitful

They filed a mendacious *accident report: it was full of lies.*

panegyric *n*
,pa-nə-'jir-ik
formal speech or piece of writing in high praise of a person or thing; eulogy; tribute

Have you read the lavish tributes in the campaign literature of the various candidates? Do their accomplishments really merit such panegyrics?

preen *v*
'prēn
dress oneself carefully or smartly; fuss in dressing; primp

Sam shouldn't criticize Nora for preening. *He likes to neaten up his appearance too, doesn't he?*

pusillanimous *adj*
,pyü-sə-'la-nə-məs
lacking in courage; cowardly; timid

I was not shocked by his pusillanimous *behavior. I knew he was a coward.*

quagmire *n*
'kwag-,mīr
wet, boggy ground that gives way under the foot; difficult situation

What a difficult situation you have gotten us into! How will we ever be able to extricate ourselves from this quagmire?

WORD	MEANING
rue *v* 'rü	feel remorse for; wish undone; regret

She said I would rue *my decision to turn down the managership. The truth is I have never regretted it.*

taciturn *adj* 'ta-sə-,tərn	habitually disinclined to talk; silent; uncommunicative

I tried to strike up a conversation with your neighbor, but he was uncommunicative. Is he always so taciturn?

C. Thinking with Your New Words

Read all of the following statements. Then answer each question below.

Statements

Of William Shakespeare, Ben Jonson wrote:

> *Thou art a monument without a tomb,*
> *And art still alive while thy book doth live,*
> *And we have wits to read and praise to give.*

Jonathan Kaplan attempted to remove the stain with cold water. When that did not work, he applied some detergent. When that, too, failed, he tried a liquid stain remover.

Subsequently, Amos Parker—the principal witness for the prosecution—was convicted of perjury.

Jenny Smith got a junk-mail notice that she was being considered for a $10,000,000 prize; she scorned it as an advertising gimmick. Mildred Jones got the same notice and was overjoyed at her good fortune.

Standing before the mirror, Lou Marquez smoothed his hair, adjusted his tie, and removed a tiny food stain from his chin with a damp washcloth.

Midway through the dance, Sandra McCloud rolled out a table with bagels, cream cheese, pastries, and beverages; they were quickly consumed.

We enjoyed the Asian food and the service. Faye Ibrahim insisted on paying the bill but allowed Olga Evans to leave the tip.

Jean Stanowski did a sword-swallowing act, performed card tricks, and pulled a rabbit from her sleeve. All enjoyed the show.

To her coworkers, Evelyn Tarrant vowed she would rebel if given any more jobs; but each time her supervisor gave her additional duties, she did not protest.

Dean Panaroni inquired about my hobbies, Professor Gorman asked what courses I had found most difficult in college, and Dr. Josephs wanted to know what area I would specialize in if I were admitted to the bar.

In one speech, Jennifer Gale implied she supported the budget; in another, she gave the impression she was against it.

My check had to be initialed by Carmelita West in the Credit Department before the cashier would accept it.

Questions

1. Who was the subject of a panegyric? _____
2. Whose imprimatur was essential? _____
3. Who made mendacious statements? _____
4. Who preened? _____
5. Who equivocated? _____
6. Who was ingenuous? _____
7. Who asked a hypothetical question? _____
8. Who dispensed the baksheesh? _____
9. Who was pusillanimous? _____
10. Who provided a collation? _____
11. Who diverted the audience? _____
12. Who used an empirical approach? _____

D. Concise Writing

Express the thought of each sentence in *no more than four words,* as in 1, below.

1. No one in the world wants to have neighbors who are inclined to quarrel or fight.
   Nobody wants bellicose neighbors.

2. He likes to use misleading terms so as not to commit himself.

3. The claims that she has been making are full of untruths.

4. We're in a difficult situation from which it may not be possible for us to extricate ourselves.

5. Who is the one who has been sending you one insistent notice after another to pay up what you owe?

6. The conclusion that Jim has reached is based on supposition.

7. His unreasonable faultfinding has the effect of getting on people's nerves.

8. They wish the mistakes that they have made could be undone.

9. Roberta says little; she is as a matter of habit not inclined to do much talking.

10. Many formal speeches of high praise are not interesting to read or to listen to.

E. Discussion with Your New Words

Answer each of the following in a brief paragraph.

1. How would you react if you were to hear or read a panegyric about a quisling? Explain.

_____

_____

_____

2. In the middle of the hottest day of the year, the air conditioning in the busy restaurant you are managing malfunctions. Your attempts to contact the owner fail. Would it be a faux pas to order the expensive emergency repairs necessary without his imprimatur? Why, or why not?

_____

_____

_____

3. Would you demur at signing the nominating petition of someone with a Machiavellian bent? Explain.

_____

_____

_____

4. Who incurs the greater risk, a politician who makes a mendacious statement, or one who equivocates? Why?

_____

_____

_____

5. Would it be ingenuous to advocate that our country unilaterally renounce the use of nuclear weapons? Why, or why not?

_____

_____

_____

How Words from Outdoor Fields... [?]   141

How many times have I you, wife to waltz and I [?]
very over this way. Expl...

Review of Chapters 11–15

I. Complete the sentences below, choosing your answers from the following list:

ante	crani	pneumon	splen
anti	hepat	post	tom
cholecyst	hyster	pre	trache
cid	mast	pro	
cis	meta	sect	

1. A word containing _____ has something to do with the skull.
2. Both _____ and _____ mean "after."
3. "Breast" is the meaning conveyed by _____.
4. The presence of _____, _____, _____, or _____ in a word is usually a clue that it is a "cutting" word.
5. "Womb" is the meaning conveyed by _____.
6. A word containing _____ has something to do with the windpipe.
7. _____, in a medical word, is a reference to the spleen; _____ is a reference to the gall-bladder; and _____ is a reference to the liver.
8. A(n) _____ word is an "against" word.
9. The presence of _____, _____, or _____ in a word is usually a clue that it is a "before" word.
10. A word containing _____ has something to do with a lung.

II. Complete the spelling of the word hinted at. Each space stands for one missing letter.

1. A noun meaning "dislike" or "aversion": an __ __ pathy
2. An adjective meaning "silent": ta __ __ turn
3. An adjective meaning "primitive": an __ __ diluvian
4. A noun meaning "traitor": qu __ __ ling
5. A noun meaning "fanatical patriot": __ __ auvinist
6. A verb meaning "hypnotize": __ __ smerize
7. A verb meaning "amuse" or "entertain": __ __ vert
8. A noun meaning "descendants": posteri __ __
9. An adjective meaning "impractically idealistic": __ __ ixotic
10. An adjective meaning "gifted with foresight": __ __ escient

III. For the italicized word in each sentence below, find two synonyms in the following list:

Baedeker	eulogy	Machiavellian	rescission
bellicose	forecast	panegyric	sanction
cancelation	gargantuan	prodigious	select
cull	handbook	prognosis	timid
cunning	imprimatur	pusillanimous	warlike

1. What an *enormous* feast!

2. Her *prognostication* proved to be quite accurate.

3. Consult your *guidebook* for suggestions about where to dine.

4. Prepare for a fight; we are dealing with a *pugnacious* opponent.

5. Without the majority leader's *approval*, the bill is unlikely to get through the Senate.

6. Rarely have we encountered anyone so *crafty*.

7. Soon after the measure was passed, a clamor was raised for its *annulment*.

8. You are generous with praise; your *tribute* was more than he deserved.

_____

9. Aren't you embarrassed by your *cowardly* reaction to the challenge?

_____

10. It took days to *choose* the best applications from the batch we received.

_____

IV. Reduce the number of words in each passage below by replacing the italicized expression with a single word. Find that word, partially spelled, in the following list, and complete the spelling before using it.

vi __ __ section   anti __ __ tablishment   anti __ __ retic
p __ __ decease   her __ __ cide   __ uivocate
__ __ tithesis   s __ __ tionalism   ca __ __ __
r __ __ __   __ __ onis   ment __ __
__ __ yssey   an __ __ diluvian   antico __ __ ulant
boy __ __ tt   __ __ tersect   __ __ tastasis
__ __ sterity   col __ __ tion

1. The cancer is confined to one area; there has been no *spread of the malignancy.*

_____

2. Her views are definitely *opposed to the principles of the ruling inner circle.*

_____

3. Do you favor *surgical experimentation on living animals in the name of medical research*?

_____

4. No sooner were the words out of my mouth than I began to *feel remorse for* what I had said.

_____

5. Aspirin is a widely used *fever-reducing substance.*

_____

6. It is possible, but unlikely, that all of the heirs named in a person's will may *die before* him.

_____

7. I dislike people who *complain in a nagging way.*

_____

8. No *handsome youth* of the 1920s was more idolized than Rudolph Valentino. _____

9. Usually there are traffic signals where busy roads *cut across each other*. _____

10. How can we tell where they stand if they continue to *be deliberately ambiguous*? _____

11. The fast-acting *clot-preventing substance* probably saved the patient's life. _____

12. An unexpected rail strike converted my short trip to the office into a nightmarish *long, wandering journey*. _____

13. Let the members of Congress set aside petty *regional prejudice* and do what is best for the whole nation. _____

14. The meeting will be followed by a(n) *light meal*. _____

15. Had you listened to your *wise, trusted advisor*, you would not have gotten into trouble. _____

16. *Future generations* may criticize us if we fail to act decisively against pollution. _____

17. The result was the *exact opposite* of what we had intended. _____

18. Consumers may *refuse to deal with* an organization that pays no attention to their complaints. _____

19. When no one laughed at his first stale joke, he proceeded to tell another *very old* story. _____

20. A(n) *weed killer* is highly toxic. _____

V. Eliminate repetition by replacing the italicized word or expression with one of the following words:

alchemy	coagulation	incision	postprandial
antigen	demur	morphology	tirade
aversion	hypothetical		

1. The magic moon has turned everything to silver with its *magic power.* _____

2. We plan to take a(n) *after-dinner* stroll when dinner is over. _____

3. Your conclusion is *conjectural* rather than certain, for it is based on conjecture. _____

4. An antibody counteracts a(n) *foreign body.* _____

5. This is where you should make the first *cut* if you want to cut open the carton. _____

6. We listened to one *bitter denunciation* after another as the candidates took turns denouncing each other. _____

7. We dislike them, and they have a(n) *dislike* for us. _____

8. I have no objection to the proposed change, and I will put it into effect unless you *object.* _____

9. *Clotting* had to be avoided at all costs, as a clot in a blood vessel could have been fatal. _____

10. Have you studied anatomy? Are you familiar with the *anatomy* of the frog? _____

16

"Going" Words

"Going" words, as treated in this chapter, are words having something to do with the action of "going."

The showman P. T. Barnum once made effective use of a "going" word to solve a problem. His exhibits were so interesting that he had trouble getting the crowds to leave, until he hit upon this idea. He erected a sign, "To the Egress," with an arrow pointing the way. Those who followed the arrow, expecting to see another jungle beast, soon found themselves on the outside. An *egress* is an exit.

A. Preview

Use each of the following "going" words no more than once in completing the sentences below.

amble	founder	obituary	safari
concomitant	incursion	obsolescent	somnambulist
congregate	itinerary	peregrination	transition
exodus	labyrinth	peripatetic	wanderlust
flounder	meander	retrogress	yaw

1. One of the main reasons for the
   _____ of businesses from this
   locality is the lack of parking facilities.
2. Why do you call this style
   _____? It certainly is not on the
   way out.
3. Let us quicken our gait. We will not get to the post office
   in time if we continue to _____.
4. Do you prefer a(n) _____
   instructor, or one who does not move about during the
   lesson?

5. Many improve. Some make no progress. A few even
_____.

6. Lady Macbeth was a(n) _____:
she walked in her sleep.

7. Business after business has gone into bankruptcy, and this
one may _____, too.

8. Problems are sure to arise during the
_____ from the old administration to the new.

9. A higher salary is not the only benefit; there are
_____ advantages that go with
the promotion.

10. It is easy to lose your way in the
_____ of subterranean passageways connecting the buildings.

11. The towns are only seventeen miles apart by air but thirty-
three by water because the river
_____s.

12. Just back from Egypt, they are already planning a trip to
Japan. Their _____ urges them
on.

13. One of my favorite actresses has just passed away. I read
her _____ in today's paper.

14. A(n) _____ moved through the
tall grass, hoping to catch glimpses of lions, elephants, and
other wildlife.

15. Whoever does the steering must hold the ship to a straight
course without letting it _____.

16. Must you always _____ on our
lawn? Why don't you meet somewhere else?

17. Sometimes a math problem stumps me, and I
_____ for a while before finding
the solution.

18. When will you show the color slides of the famous places
you visited in your _____s
through Scandinavia?

19. Denver was the first stop on our
_____. Then we flew to Seattle.

20. The _____ was repelled, and the
raiders fled without achieving their objective.

B. Details About the New Words

WORD	MEANING
amble *v* 'am-bəl	walk unhurriedly; go leisurely; saunter

Let us quicken our gait. We will not get to the post office in time if we continue to amble.

| **concomitant** *adj*
kən-'kä-mə-tənt | accompanying; concurrent |

A higher salary is not the only benefit; there are concomitant *advantages that go with the promotion.*

| **congregate** *v*
'käŋ-gri-,gāt | gather into a crowd; assemble |

Must you always congregate *on our lawn? Why don't you meet somewhere else?*

| **exodus** *n*
'ek-sə-dəs | going out; mass departure (like that of the Israelites from Egypt) |

One of the main reasons for the exodus *of businesses from this locality is the lack of parking facilities.*

| **flounder** *v*
'flaun-dər | struggle awkwardly to move or obtain a footing; proceed clumsily with frequent mistakes |

Sometimes a math problem stumps me, and I flounder *for a while before finding the solution.*

| **founder** *v*
'faun-dər | come to grief; go to the bottom; sink; collapse |

Business after business has gone into bankruptcy, and this one may founder, *too.*

| **incursion** *n*
in-'kər-zhən | sudden, brief invasion; inroad; raid |

The incursion *was repelled, and the raiders fled without achieving their objective.*

WORD	MEANING

itinerary *n*
ī-'ti-nə-,rer-ē
route of a journey

Denver was the first stop on our itinerary. *Then we flew to Seattle.*

---

labyrinth *n*
'la-bə-,rinth
place full of confusing interconnecting passageways and blind alleys; maze; anything extremely intricate and perplexing

It is easy to lose your way in the labyrinth *of subterranean passageways connecting the buildings.*

---

meander *v*
mē-'an-dər
follow a winding intricate course (like the Meander River in Asia Minor, now called the Menderes); wander aimlessly; ramble

The towns are only seventeen miles apart by air but thirty-three by water because the river meanders.

---

obituary *n*
ə-'bi-chə-,wer-ē
published notice of death ("going"), including a short biographical account

One of my favorite actresses has just passed away. I read her obituary *in today's paper.*

---

obsolescent *adj*
,äb-sə-'le-sᵊnt
going out of use; becoming *obsolete* (outmoded)

Why do you call this style obsolescent? *It certainly is not on the way out.*

---

peregrination *n*
,per-ə-grə-'nā-shən
travel; journey

When will you show the color slides of the famous places you visited in your peregrinations *through Scandinavia?*

---

peripatetic *adj*
,per-ə-pə-'te-tik
walking about from place to place; itinerant

Do you prefer a peripatetic *instructor, or one who does not move about during the lesson?*

WORD	MEANING

retrogress *v*
,re-tre-'gres

move backward to an earlier or worse condition; degenerate

Many improve. Some make no progress. A few even retrogress.

---

safari *n*
sə-'fär-ē

journey or hunting expedition, especially in eastern Africa; any lengthy, adventurous expedition

A safari moved through the tall grass, hoping to catch glimpses of lions, elephants, and other wildlife.

---

somnambulist *n*
säm-'nam-byə-list

person who walks in his or her sleep; sleepwalker

Lady Macbeth was a somnanbulist: she walked in her sleep.

---

transition *n*
tran-'si-shən

process or period of passing from one condition, place, or action to another; change

Problems are sure to arise during the transition *from the old administration to the new.*

---

wanderlust *n*
'wän-dər-,ləst

strong, restless longing to travel

Just back from Egypt, they are already planning a trip to Japan. Their wanderlust *urges them on.*

---

yaw *v*
'yȯ

deviate abruptly from a straight course; swerve; veer

Whoever does the steering must hold the ship to a straight course without letting it yaw.

C. Building Additional "Going" Words

Complete each unfinished word below by adding one of the following Latin roots:

ambulat or *amble*, meaning "walk" or "go"
cur, curr, or *curs,* meaning "run"
grad or *gress,* meaning "step" or "go"
it, meaning "go"

Sample:

How do we get out of here? Where is the
ex *it*_____?

1. The road to the summit is circu_____ous: it goes round and round.

2. A school's _____iculum is the sequence of courses the students take as they move along toward graduation.

3. The part that "goes" before the body of a constitution or a similar document is the pre_____.

4. Turn down the TV. If you awaken the neighbors, you will in_____ their displeasure.

5. The room was windowless. Except for the door, there was no means of in_____ or egress.

6. Are the negotiations making pro_____, or are you retrogressing?

7. A few patients were bedridden and unable to walk, but all the rest were _____ory.

8. We went on an ex_____ion to Bear Mountain.

9. Anyone becomes a trans_____or who goes beyond the bounds of law or morality.

10. The crude airplane invented by the Wrights was the pre_____or (or forerunner) of the modern jetliner.

11. Fame is usually trans_____ory; it goes away quickly.

12. Please stick to the topic. Do not di_____.

13. If you like walking, why not join me and my dog in our early morning per_____ion?

14. Learning is a step-by-step process. Growth, too, is _____ual.

15. The in_____iation ("going-in" ceremony) for new members was brief and dignified.

16. The 6-0 decision shows that all the judges con_____ed in the verdict.

17. Plastics are not biode_____able (easily decomposable by bacteria into harmless substances).

18. Gasoline was cheaper last month. The _____ent ("going" or present) price is about ten cents more per gallon.
19. Soon after the operation, the patient was encouraged to walk. Surgeons nowadays favor early _____ion.
20. Dennison is being up_____ed (stepped up in rank) to a full partner.

D. Thinking with Your New Words

Read all of the following statements. Then answer each question below.

Statements

Harold II, last of the Saxon kings of England, was defeated by William the Conqueror in 1066 at the Battle of Hastings.

Rebecca could have gotten twice as much work done with half the staff if she had had up-to-date computer software.

On his cruise, Rupert saw plastic half-gallon beverage containers floating in the middle of the Atlantic.

When Felicia resigned from the committee, more than half of its members left with her.

The incoming president is retaining the entire cabinet except Nathaniel Canterbury, who will be replaced.

My cousin Dorothy was supposed to visit us in Baltimore for a week before going to Boston and Cape Cod. Instead, she stayed with us for two weeks and then accompanied us to New Orleans.

Gretta sold cosmetics in a department store, Martin worked at a checkout counter in a supermarket, and Ralph solicited magazine subscriptions door to door.

Bernard was sure he would remember the way, but he became confused by the circuitous streets, lost his sense of direction, and eventually had to knock on a door for help. He was directed back to Alma's house, and she guided him out of the development.

The afternoon edition reported Ambassador Brown's speech at the United Nations, Moses Dempsey's retirement from professional basketball, and Agnes Latham's demise at 86.

Alan covered the distance from the stadium to the Main Building in four minutes without rushing, but Dan—who had left the same time as Alan—took a quarter of an hour.

Questions

1. Who was a peripatetic salesperson? _____
2. Who foundered? _____
3. Who encountered nonbiodegradable wastes? _____
4. Who used obsolescent equipment? _____
5. Who floundered? _____
6. Who changed an itinerary? _____
7. Who was the subject of an obituary? _____
8. Who was the victim of a transition? _____
9. Who must have ambled? _____
10. Who led an exodus? _____

E. Analogies

Write the *letter* of the pair of words related to each other in the same way as the words in the capitalized pair.

1. OBSOLESCENT : OBSOLETE
   a. youthful : aging
   b. expiring : deceased
   c. convalescing : ill
   d. trainee : veteran
   e. reminiscent : forgetful
   Answer _____

2. CARP : CRITICIZE
   a. request : demand
   b. dun : bill
   c. like : admire
   d. ail : malinger
   e. acquiesce : demur
   Answer _____

3. WANDERLUST : TRAVEL
a. nostalgia : past
b. pusillanimity : achievement
c. rue : guilt

d. ingenuousness : experience
e. bellicosity : moderation

Answer _____

4. PERAMBULATION : FEET
a. manipulation : hands
b. eavesdropping : toes
c. inhalation : air

d. arthritis : joints
e. mastication : food

Answer _____

5. DIGRESSOR : MEANDER
a. interrogator : reply
b. payee : pay
c. mentor : teach

d. procrastinator : expedite
e. heir : estate

Answer _____

Words of Crime and Punishment

Is a person who maliciously sets fire to a building committing a *felony* or a *misdemeanor*? What is a *penal* offense? a *capital* offense? What is involved in *embezzlement*? Who is a *poacher*? a *vandal*? a *recidivist*?

A. Preview

Use each of the following words no more than once in completing the sentences below.

accessory	embezzlement	inculpate	poacher
capital	exculpate	larceny	recidivist
charlatan	extradition	misdemeanor	subpoena
contraband	felony	penal	vandal
culpability	incarceration	plagiarism	venue

1. A verdict of guilty seems likely; most of the evidence tends to _____ the defendant.
2. Claiming her client cannot get a fair trial in this district, the attorney is asking for a change of _____ .
3. Many who oppose the building of more prisons sincerely believe that _____ fails to rehabilitate the criminal.
4. A farmer reported that someone has been hunting on his property. The authorities are looking for the _____ .
5. The injured passenger is suing the bus company for criminal negligence, but it has denied _____ .
6. Armed robbery is not a(n) _____ ; it is a grave crime.

7. Now that the fugitive has been arrested in New Mexico, North Dakota is asking for her return to face trial, but she has decided to fight _____.

8. The person accused of the stabbing will be charged with a(n) _____.

9. The shoplifter was arrested and is being prosecuted for _____.

10. Should a(n) _____, who time and again has lapsed into crime after supposedly being rehabilitated, be again given parole?

11. The _____s who broke into the museum overnight defaced the walls with graffiti and damaged priceless works of art.

12. For plotting against the throne, a(n) _____ offense, the convicted traitors paid with their heads.

13. The alleged burglars have been apprehended, and the woman whose van they had borrowed to transport their loot is being held as a(n) _____.

14. Pamela Noonan is filing charges of _____ against the writer who took several pages from her book and reprinted them as his own work.

15. The defense attorney has called a witness whose testimony he hopes will _____ his client.

16. Though several of his patients have come to his defense, the record shows he never attended medical school and left high school without earning a diploma. He is evidently a(n) _____.

17. If the treasurer has diverted pension funds to his own use, he has committed _____.

18. Some of the industrial pollution tolerated in the past would be regarded as a(n) _____ offense today.

19. The tenant in whose apartment the smuggled goods were found faces charges of possession of _____.

20. The person who witnessed the crime has been served with a(n) _____ directing her to appear in court to give testimony.

B. Details About the New Words

WORD	MEANING
accessory *n* ak-'se-sə-rē	person who, though not present at the time of a crime, aids in its commission or helps the perpetrator to escape; accomplice

The alleged burglars have been apprehended, and the woman whose van they had borrowed to transport their loot is being held as an accessory.

capital *adj* 'ka-pə-t³l	(literally, "having to do with the head") involving or punishable by the death penalty

For plotting against the throne, a capital *offense, the convicted traitors paid with their heads.*

charlatan *n* 'shär-lə-tən	person who fraudulently claims to have expert skill or knowledge; fake; quack; impostor

Anyone who practices medicine without ever having attended medical school is obviously a charlatan.

contraband *n* 'kän-trə-,band	goods illegally imported or exported; smuggled merchandise

The tenant in whose apartment the smuggled goods were found faces charges of possession of contraband.

culpability *n* ,kəl-pə-'bi-lə-tē	quality or state of being *culpable* (deserving blame or censure); blameworthiness

The injured passenger is suing the bus company for criminal negligence, but it has denied culpability.

WORD	MEANING

embezzlement *n*
im-'be-zəl-mənt

stealing of money, securities, etc., entrusted to one's care

If the treasurer has diverted pension funds to his own use, he has committed embezzlement.

---

exculpate *v*
'ek-skəl-ˌpāt

free from blame or fault; prove guiltless; exonerate

The defense attorney has called a witness whose testimony he hopes will exculpate *his client.*

---

extradition *n*
'ek-strə-'di-shən

surrender of an alleged criminal by one state or country to the jurisdiction of another for trial

Now that the fugitive has been arrested in New Mexico, North Dakota is asking for her return to face trial, but she has decided to fight extradition.

---

felony *n*
'fe-lə-nē

major crime, such as murder, rape, arson, or burglary, for which the penalty ranges from execution to imprisonment of more than a year

The person accused of the stabbing will be charged with a felony.

---

incarceration *n*
in-ˌkär-sə-'rā-shən

imprisonment; jailing; confinement

Many who oppose the building of more prisons sincerely believe that incarceration *fails to rehabilitate the criminal.*

---

inculpate *v*
in-'kəl-ˌpāt

incriminate; make appear guilty

A verdict of guilty seems likely; most of the evidence tends to inculpate *the defendant.*

WORD	MEANING
larceny *n* 'lär-sᵊn-ē	unlawful taking away of another's property, with intent to defraud the owner; theft

The shoplifter was arrested and is being prosecuted for larceny.

misdemeanor *n* ,mis-di-'mē-nər	minor offense punishable by fine or imprisonment of usually less than a year; misdeed

Armed robbery is not a misdemeanor; *it is a grave crime.*

penal *adj* 'pē-nᵊl	involving punishment; having to do with penalties or correctional institutions

Some of the industrial pollution tolerated in the past is now a penal *offense.*

plagiarism *n* 'plā-jə-,ri-zəm	act of *plagiarizing* (stealing the writing of another and passing it off as one's own)

Pamela Noonan is filing charges of plagiarism *against the writer who took several pages from her book and reprinted them as his own work.*

poacher *n* 'pō-chər	one who *poaches* (hunts or fishes illegally)

A farmer reported that someone has been hunting on his property. The authorities are looking for the poacher.

recidivist *n* rə-'si-də-vist	(literally, "one who falls back") person with a tendency to relapse; chronic offender; habitual criminal

Should a recidivist, *who time and again has lapsed into crime after supposedly being rehabilitated, be again given parole?*

WORD	MEANING
subpoena *n* sə-'pē-nə	(literally, "under penalty") order summoning a person to testify in court under a penalty for failure to appear

The person who witnessed the crime has been served with a subpoena directing her to appear in court to give testimony.

vandal *n* 'van-dəl	person who maliciously defaces, spoils, or destroys public or private property

The vandals who broke into the museum overnight defaced the walls with graffiti and damaged priceless works of art.

venue *n* 'ven-yü	locality from which a jury is drawn and in which the trial is held

Claiming her client cannot get a fair trial in this district, the attorney is asking for a change of venue.

C. Thinking with Your New Words

Read all of the following statements. Then answer each question below.

PART ONE

Statements

Attorney General Di Lorenzo met with Senator Alvarez, Assemblyman Goldsmith, and Warden Alderman.

Andrea O. failed in her endeavor to have her case tried in some locality other than Big Horn.

The company headed by Elizabeth S. was mentioned as a polluter of the river, but she vehemently denounced the allegation.

Marisa W. posted signs around the perimeter of her acreage reading "Private Property: No Hunting."

After the jailbreak, Emil P. hid out in a mountain cabin put at his disposal by Phil E., a friend.

Despite fourteen arrests and four indictments, William T. has not spent a day in jail, though he has paid some fines.

Joe G., who stole the Greens' car for a joyride, was permitted to plead guilty to malicious mischief and was put on a year's probation instead of being sent to jail.

Hobart G. was afraid to testify and would have stayed away from the court if not for the penalty for nonappearance.

Joshua B., arrested for reckless driving, was later charged with homicide when one of the victims died of injuries sustained in the fiery collision.

Only when it was announced that Pamela E. had won the writing contest did she begin to worry; she had taken her essay word for word from a magazine.

Questions

1. Who was sentenced for a misdemeanor rather than a felony? _____
2. Who was prosecuted for a felony rather than a misdemeanor? _____
3. Who headed a penal institution? _____
4. Who was served with a subpoena? _____
5. Who was an accessory? _____
6. Who repeatedly avoided incarceration? _____
7. Who committed plagiarism? _____
8. Who was denied a change of venue? _____
9. Who was concerned about poachers? _____
10. Who denied culpability? _____

PART TWO

Statements

Until Hattie N.'s confession, Marcia B. was the prime suspect.

At the last minute, Governor Carlson commuted Sanford M.'s sentence to life imprisonment.

Bill L. discovered that turnstile-jumping is not a joke when he was charged with theft of services.

The investigation showed Ruth V. had used funds of which she was the custodian to build a cabana and swimming pool on her property.

It turned out that the diplomas in Doc B.'s office were forgeries, and that he had been practicing without a license.

Between jobs as gas station attendant, roofer's helper, and security guard, Fred G. has been in and out of correctional institutions.

During questioning by the authorities, Sally O. was careful not to incriminate anyone else.

Friday night, Henry T. went on a spree of overturning garbage cans and smashing street lights.

In Helene Q.'s luggage, customs officers found cocaine with a street value of more than three million dollars.

When Iowa petitioned California for the return to Dudley M. to stand trial in Des Moines, he instructed his attorney to contest the move.

Questions

11. Who committed petty larceny? _____
12. Who was a charlatan? _____
13. Who avoided inculpating others? _____
14. Who was a vandal? _____
15. Who escaped capital punishment? _____
16. Who was caught with contraband? _____

17. Who was an embezzler? _____
18. Who resisted extradition? _____
19. Who was exculpated? _____
20. Who was a recidivist? _____

D. Concise Writing

Express the thought of each sentence in *no more than four words,* as in 1, below.

1. The stealing of money, securities, or other property entrusted by others to one's care is something that cannot be forgiven.
   Embezzlement is unforgivable.

2. Do those who maliciously deface, spoil, or destroy public or private property deserve to be sent to prison?

   _____

3. The testimony that she gave under oath in court made others appear guilty.

   _____

4. The practice of strewing litter on the streets is a minor crime that is punishable by a fine or by imprisonment of usually less than a year.

   _____

5. There are many people who put their trust in individuals who fraudulently claim to have expert skill or knowledge.

   _____

6. The confession that he made proved that we were not guilty.

   _____

7. Were any major crimes, such as murder, rape, arson, or burglary, reported?

   _____

8. Goods that have been illegally imported into, or exported from, a country are subject to confiscation.

   _____

9. An individual who was seen to be hunting out of season was taken into custody.

   _____

10. Former convicts who keep committing additional crimes after having supposedly been rehabilitated do not deserve leniency.

   _____

E. Discussion with Your New Words

Answer each of the following in a brief paragraph.

1. Which penalty in your opinion is more fitting for a convicted murderer—incarceration for life with no possibility of parole, or capital punishment? Explain your position with reasons.

_____

_____

_____

_____

_____

_____

_____

2. Should a prosecutor agree to allow an alleged felon to plead guilty to a misdemeanor to save the state the expense of a long and costly trial whose outcome is by no means certain? Why, or why not?

_____

_____

_____

_____

_____

_____

3. We are told that 10 percent of the criminals commit 50 percent of the crimes. Should we then hold only recidivists in our penal institutions and grant early parole to all the other convicts? Why, or why not?

_____

_____

_____

_____

_____

_____

4. After a trial in which evidence you believe could have
   exculpated you was suppressed, you are fined $200.
   Would you appeal the verdict through the labyrinth of the
   lower courts—even to the Supreme Court, if necessary—
   or would you try to forget about the whole thing? Explain.

_____

_____

_____

_____

_____

_____

5. Deborah never locks her car and habitually leaves her keys
   in the ignition. One day her car is stolen. Has she, or has
   she not, been an accessory to the crime of larceny?
   Explain.

_____

_____

_____

_____

_____

_____

18

Character and Personality Words

Both of the following sentences have the same meaning:

Alice always feels deep sympathy and sorrow for the sufferings and misfortunes of others, and she would like to alleviate their pain or remove its cause. [26 words]

Alice is *compassionate*. [3 words]

Obviously, *compassionate* is rich in meaning. By learning such words, you can become a better listener, reader, speaker, and writer.

Like *compassionate,* each lesson word in this chapter deals with character and/or personality, and each of them is rich in meaning.

A. Preview

Use each of the following "character and personality" words no more than once in completing the sentences below.

altruistic	gregarious	intrepid	parsimonious
biased	gullible	irrational	sanguine
captious	impassive	obsequious	skeptical
contrite	impetuous	obstreperous	supercilious
diffident	indolent	opinionated	vindictive

1. In this dog-eat-dog world, where almost everyone is out for personal gain, it is heartening to meet a(n) _____ person.
2. My father was _____ when I said I had gotten a $100 raise, until I showed him my paycheck.

3. Don't be _____. Why must you believe everything you hear?

4. Before the test, you looked _____. Evidently, you were sure you would do well.

5. I am not _____. I do not seek revenge.

6. I was too hasty in resigning. I acted on impulse. It is no good to be _____.

7. Your ability should give you confidence in yourself. You have no reason to feel _____.

8. They yell, they shout, they make so much noise! Walter and I find them _____.

9. Fear of the unknown did not deter our _____ astronauts from undertaking their daring mission.

10. Anyone who makes a decision that defies reason is _____.

11. Since Wong is your best friend, I would expect him to be _____ in your favor when you are involved in controversy with others.

12. Donald at first had no regret for what he had done, but later he became _____.

13. Harriet has finished her report, but I haven't even begun to work on mine. You know how _____ I am.

14. If one has to be _____ to get ahead in this firm, I will quit now. It revolts me to be overly subservient.

15. It is futile to discuss anything with a(n) _____ person who clings stubbornly to fixed views.

16. Throughout the trial, the defendant was _____; he showed no emotion.

17. At lunch, Joyce usually sits with friends, but Ann keeps to herself; she is not _____.

18. You are always looking for something to criticize. Must you be so _____?

19. Your well-to-do friend is a(n) _____ giver; he contributed a dime.

20. Clementine considers herself superior and will have nothing to do with ordinary people like you and me, but her sister is not _____.

B. Details About the New Words

WORD	MEANING
altruistic *adj* ˌal-tru-ˈis-tik	concerned for the welfare of others; unselfish

In this dog-eat-dog world, where almost everyone is out for personal gain, it is heartening to meet an altruistic *person.*

biased *adj* ˈbī-əst	prejudiced; unduly or unfairly influenced

Since Wong is your best friend, I would expect him to be biased *in your favor when you are involved in controversy with others.*

captious *adj* ˈkap-shəs	quick to find fault, especially over petty matters; carping

You are always looking for something to criticize. Must you be so captious?

contrite *adj* kən-ˈtrīt	sorrowful for a misdeed that one has committed; deeply repentant

Donald at first had no regret for what he had done, but later he became contrite.

diffident *adj* ˈdi-fə-dənt	lacking confidence; timid; shy

Your ability should give you confidence in yourself. You have no reason to feel diffident.

gregarious *adj* gri-ˈgar-ē-əs	seeking or enjoying the company of others; sociable

At lunch, Joyce usually sits with friends, but Ann keeps to herself; she is not gregarious.

WORD	**MEANING**

---

gullible adj
'gə-lə-bəl

easily deceived or tricked; credulous

Don't be gullible. *Why must you believe everything you hear?*

---

impassive adj
im-'pa-siv

feeling or revealing no emotion; calm; unmoved

Throughout the trial, the defendant showed no emotion: he was impassive.

---

impetuous adj
im-'pech-wəs

acting suddenly without forethought; rash, impulsive

I was too hasty in resigning. I acted on impulse. It is no good to be impetuous.

---

indolent adj
in-də-lənt

inclined to avoid work; lazy; idle

Harriet has finished her report, but I haven't even begun to work on mine. You know how indolent *I am.*

---

intrepid adj
in-'tre-pəd

not afraid; bold; dauntless

Fear of the unknown did not deter our intrepid *astronauts from undertaking their daring mission.*

---

irrational adj
ir-'ash-nəl

not *rational* (capable of reasoning); illogical; absurd; senseless

Anyone who makes a decision that defies reason is irrational.

---

obsequious adj
əb-'sē-kwē-əs

much too attentive (to a superior); excessively submissive; servile; fawning

If one has to be obsequious *to get ahead in this firm, I will quit now. It revolts me to have to be overly subservient.*

---

obstreperous adj
əb-'stre-pə-rəs

excessively noisy; boisterous; unruly

They yell, they shout, they make so much noise! Walter and I find them obstreperous.

WORD	MEANING

opinionated *adj*
ə-'pin-yə-,nā-təd

holding obstinately to one's own opinion

It is futile to discuss anything with an opinionated *person who clings stubbornly to fixed views.*

parsimonious *adj*
,pär-sə-'mō-nē-əs

extremely frugal; miserly; stingy

Your well-to-do friend is a parsimonious *giver; he contributed a dime.*

sanguine *adj*
'saŋ-gwən

confidently optimistic; hopeful

Before the test, you looked sanguine. *Evidently, you were sure you would do well.*

skeptical *adj*
'skep-ti-kəl

disbelieving; doubting; not easily convinced

My father was skeptical *when I said I had gotten a $100 raise, until I showed him my paycheck.*

supercilious *adj*
,sü-per-'si-lē-əs

showing haughty contempt; disdainful; full of pride and scorn

Clementine considers herself superior and will have nothing to do with ordinary people like you and me, but her sister is not *supercilious.*

vindictive *adj*
vin-'dik-tiv

inclined to seek vengeance; unforgiving; spiteful

I am not *vindictive. I do not seek revenge.*

C. Thinking with Your New Words

Read all of the following statements. Then answer each question below.

Statements

We could hear everything Jane was saying though she sat

three tables away. She laughed more than anyone else at her own jokes. The library was really peaceful when she left.

When he returned from vacation, Stanley was extremely carefree and relaxed, taking his time with everything and doing very little. The boss thought of firing him.

The instructor assured Gloria she did not need further instruction, but Gloria enrolled for ten more lessons to prepare for the road test.

Frost showed there was absolutely no need for a fence, but neighbor Jones would not budge from a favorite saying of his ancestors, "Good fences make good neighbors," so it was no use arguing with him.

Rose was depressed when her car was towed away, but heartened by her neighbor Sonia's offer to drive her to the hairdresser, the dentist, the supermarket, and anywhere else.

We invited Burton to parties and picnics but he never came. His usual excuse was that he had to finish a book or was going fishing. After a while, we stopped inviting him.

Because he was never a college man, Campbell was unimpressed by college learning, and when he had an opening, he would give preference to applicants who had not gone beyond high school.

Lisa never questioned the advertising claim that the vehicle could go up to fifty miles on a gallon of fuel, but Audrey doubted it.

Gladys was humiliated when Phyllis did not invite her, so Gladys made a big party and did not invite Phyllis.

You could always sense from Nora's expression whether she was holding a good or bad hand, but Jennifer had a poker face.

Despite his ample income, Otis prepared his own meals, rarely bought clothes, and never took a vacation.

Baxter kept himself at the beck and call of the director, whom he addressed as "Sir." He continually praised the director for superior judgment and never disagreed with him.

After hastily cashing her salary check, Brenda gambled it away recklessly on lottery tickets. Then she went to Nancy for a $20 loan.

Asked for his opinion of Theresa's paper, Philip faulted her for misspelling the name of a minor character and not dotting all her *i*'s.

When Santia heard of her father's death, she rued the harsh words she had spoken to him at their last meeting.

Questions

1. Who was not gregarious? _____
2. Who was vindictive? _____
3. Who seemed altruistic? _____
4. Who was obsequious? _____
5. Who was obstreperous? _____
6. Who was impetuous? _____
7. Who seemed indolent? _____
8. Who seemed impassive? _____
9. Who became contrite? _____
10. Who was diffident? _____
11. Who was parsimonious? _____
12. Who seemed opinionated? _____
13. Who was biased? _____
14. Who was skeptical? _____
15. Who seemed captious? _____

D. Concise Writing

Express the thought of each sentence in *no more than four words,* as in 1, below.

1. Don't be so quick to find fault, especially over a petty matter.
   Don't be so captious.

2. Are those who govern us unselfishly concerned for the welfare of others?

3. There are times when we are in a frame of mind in which we are not easily convinced.

4. Michael is overly attentive to the superiors who supervise his work.

5. Most boys and girls in their teens enjoy being in the company of others.

6. The individuals who had been maliciously defacing public and private property seem to be sorry for what they have done.

7. Many of those who are victimized are out to get revenge.

8. Those who oppose us continue to hold obstinately to their opinions.

9. Once in a while, every one of us doesn't feel like doing any work.

10. The fans who have been supporting us remain confidently optimistic.

E. Analogies

Write the *letter* of the pair of words related to each other in the same way as the words in the capitalized pair.

1. INDOLENCE : INDUSTRY
a. contrition : guilt
b. bias : objectivity
c. embezzlement : trust
d. impetuosity : haste
e. carping : pettiness
Answer_____

2. THIEF : LARCENY
a. poacher : game
b. equivocator : veracity
c. assailant : battery
d. witness : subpoena
e. perpetrator : culpability
Answer_____

3. ALTRUISM : SELFISHNESS
a. generosity : parsimony
b. gullibility : deception
c. indolence : advancement
d. skepticism : inaction
e. incarceration : punishment
Answer_____

4. TRAGEDY : COMPASSION
a. antipathy : cooperation *d.* applause : recognition
b. comedy : drama   *e.* contempt : cowardliness
c. intrepidity : admiration   **Answer_____**

5. ARSON : FELONY
a. treason : misdemeanor   *d.* spy : espionage
b. white lie : perjury   *e.* hydrogen : element
c. contraband : arrest   **Answer_____**

Body Vocabulary

We know that *visual* has to do with the eyes, and *auditory* with the ears. But what part of the body is involved when you *genuflect*? What is the location of a *plantar* wart? Where does a *visceral* feeling come from?

This chapter will deal with "body" vocabulary—words having to do with different parts or functions of the body.

A. Preview

Use each of the following "body" words no more than once in filling the blanks below.

carpal	genuflect	manual	spleen
cerebral	gustatory	olfactory	subcutaneous
cervical	guttural	plantar	supine
corporal	labial	prone	tactile
digital	lachrymose	pulmonary	vascular
eviscerate	lingual	sanguinary	visceral

1. Use light _____ pressure on the keyboard.
2. Do you have _____ dexterity? I am clumsy with my hands.
3. The child's _____ plea moved his parents to permit him to watch TV for an additional thirty minutes.
4. My gut feeling was that Parker would lose the election. Several others had the same _____ reaction.
5. We are in a(n) _____ position when we lie on our backs, and in a(n)

_____ position when we lie on our stomachs.

6. If he had seen some of the other worshipers _____, he might have bent his knee, too.

7. Luckily, my _____ sense alerted me to the scent of smoke, and my _____ sense enabled me to grope my way in the dark to the fire exit.

8. It is too bad she hurt her neck again because she has not fully recovered from a previous _____ injury.

9. Strenuous or repeated use of the wrist, as in racquetball or typing, may cause _____ tunnel syndrome, a painful condition.

10. *B*, *p*, and *m* are _____ sounds because they are made with the lips; *l* and *r* are _____ sounds because they are made with the tongue.

11. The skin was discolored but not broken; there had been _____ bleeding.

12. _____ punishment can cause serious bodily injury.

13. The _____ contains many blood vessels; it is a highly _____ organ.

14. It is not necessary to _____ the turkey since the butcher has already removed the entrails.

15. The _____ artery carries blood into the lungs.

16. Sealing envelopes is not a brainy job; it requires little _____ effort.

17. He made a(n) _____ sound, as if he were clearing his throat.

18. A great deal of blood was spilled. It was a(n) _____ conflict.

19. Bernice can recognize a brand of coffee by its taste, but my _____ sense is not so keen.

20. A(n) _____ wart occurs on the sole of the foot.

B. Details About the New Words

WORD	MEANING

carpal *adj*
'kär-pəl

having to do with the *carpus* (wrist) or bones of the wrist

Strenuous or repeated use of the wrist, as in racquetball or typing, may cause carpal *tunnel syndrome, a painful condition.*

cerebral *adj*
sə-'rē-brəl

having to do with the *cerebrum* (brain); intellectual

Sealing envelopes is not a brainy job; it requires little cerebral *effort.*

cervical *adj*
'ser-vi-kəl

pertaining to a *cervix* (neck)

It is too bad she hurt her neck again because she has not fully recovered from a previous cervical *injury.*

corporal *adj*
'kòr-pə-rəl

having to do with or inflicted on the body; bodily

Corporal *punishment can cause serious bodily injury.*

digital *adj*
'di-jə-tᵊl

1. involving a finger or fingers

Use light digital *pressure on the keyboard.*

2. involving *digits* (the numbers one through nine and the zero)

A digital *watch is a timepiece with no clockface or hands—just numbers.*

eviscerate *v*
i-'vi-sə-,rāt

remove the *viscera* (entrails, intestines, guts) from; disembowel; gut

It is not necessary to eviscerate *the turkey since the butcher has already removed the entrails.*

WORD	MEANING

genuflect *v*
'jen-yə-ˌflekt

bend the knee, as in reverence or worship; kneel

If he had seen some of the other worshipers genuflect, *he might have bent his knee, too.*

gustatory *adj*
'gəs-tə-ˌtòr-ē

having to do with the sense of taste or tasting

Bernice can recognize a brand of coffee by its taste, but my gustatory *sense is not so keen.*

guttural *adj*
'gə-tə-rəl

produced in the throat; harsh; rasping; throaty

He made a guttural *sound, as if he were clearing his throat.*

labial *adj*
'lā-bē-əl

involving the lips; pronounced with the help of one or both lips

B and p are labial *sounds; m, too, is made with the lips.*

lachrymose adj
'la-krə-ˌmōs

given to shedding or causing tears; tearful; mournful

The child's lachrymose *plea moved his parents to permit him to watch TV for an additional thirty minutes.*

lingual *adj*
'liŋ-gwəl

having to do with the tongue, language, or languages; pronounced with the aid of the tongue

L and r are lingual *sounds; they are made with the tongue.*

manual *adj*
'man-yə-wəl

having to do with a hand or the hands; worked by hand

Do you have manual *dexterity? I am clumsy with my hands.*

olfactory *adj*
äl-'fak-tə-rē

concerned with the sense of smell

Dogs have a superior sense of smell. Our own olfactory *powers are relatively limited.*

plantar *adj*
'plan-tər

having to do with the sole of the foot

A plantar *wart occurs on the sole of the foot.*

WORD	MEANING

prone *adj*
'prōn

1. lying face downward

When I tire of sleeping on my back, I roll over to a prone *position*

2. having a bent or inclination; predisposed

Mobs are prone *to violence.*

---

pulmonary *adj*
'pəl-mə-,ner-ē

having to do with the lungs

The pulmonary *artery carries blood into the lungs.*

---

sanguinary *adj*
'saŋ-gwə-,ner-ē

bloody; having to do with bloodshed; bloodthirsty

A great deal of blood was spilled. It was a sanguinary *conflict.*

---

spleen *n*
'splēn

1. ductless organ, near the stomach, containing many blood vessels

The spleen *destroys and replaces worn-out red blood cells.*

2. malice; anger; bad temper (The *spleen* was once regarded as the seat of many emotions.)

After being called out on strikes, the enraged batter vented his spleen *on the umpire.*

---

subcutaneous *adj*
,səb-kyú-tā-nē-əs

situated, occurring, or applied beneath the skin

The skin was discolored but not broken; there had been sub-cutaneous *bleeding.*

WORD	MEANING
supine *adj* sù-'pīn	1. lying on the back, face upward

I left the infant on his back, face upward, but when I returned he was not in a supine *position.*

	2. mentally or morally inactive; lethargic; listless

Isn't the legislature doing anything about crime? We cannot understand its supine *disregard of the problem.*

| **tactile** *adj*
 'tak-t^əl | having to do with the sense of touch |

Walking cautiously in the fog, I relied on my tactile *sense to tell me whether I was on grass or pavement.*

| **vascular** *adj*
 'vas-kyə-lər | having to do with, composed of, or provided with vessels that convey blood or lymph |

Some vascular *surgeons specialize in removing varicose veins.*

| **visceral** *adj*
 'vi-sə-rəl | having to do with or occurring in the *viscera* (internal organs, intestines, guts, etc.) |

My gut feeling was that Parker would lose the election. Several others had the same visceral *reaction.*

C. Building Additional Body Words

Complete each unfinished word below by adding one of the following Latin roots:

carp, meaning "wrist"
corp or *corpor*, meaning "body"
lingua or *lingu*, meaning "tongue" or "language"
man or *manu*, meaning "hand"
splen, meaning "spleen"
tact or *tang*, meaning "touch"

1. Again I must ask you to keep your hands off the controls. Please do not _____ipulate them.
2. A meta_____al bone is one of the five long bones after the wrist and before the fingers.
3. A _____ectomy is the surgical removal of the spleen.
4. Not a cent of the missing money had been touched, and the rest of the loot, too, was recovered in _____.
5. If you speak only one language, you are mono_____l; if you speak two, you are bi_____l.
6. I rarely see my cousin. There has been almost no con_____ between us.
7. _____istics is the science of language.
8. A _____ual is a small helpful book that can be carried in the hand.
9. Soon after, the victim's _____se was washed up by the tide.
10. The company's stock, fixtures, computers, vehicles—in short, all things that can be touched—are its _____ible assets.
11. A firm's reputation is one of its most valuable in_____ible assets.
12. A _____ful salesperson never keeps a customer waiting needlessly; to do so would not only be rude but _____less.
13. Where are the sub_____l salivary glands? Under the tongue, of course.
14. The thirteen colonies were in_____ated into a new, independent nation.
15. Our staff is an example of teamwork. We have a fine esprit de_____s.
16. Most people cut their own fingernails, but some seek the services of a _____icurist.
17. A person who knows many languages is a polyglot, or _____ist.
18. A very small drop of blood contains about 5,000,000 red blood cells and up to 10,000 white blood cells, so you can see why such cells are called _____uscles, meaning "tiny bodies."
19. The care of the estate has been given into my hands

as trustee, and I will be faithful to that
_____ date.
20. The _____script is authentic; it is in the
author's own hand.
21. In some multi_____l communities,
voting instructions have to be printed in several languages.
22. For freeing his people from the hand (or power) of their
colonial overlord, Gandhi was hailed as an
e_____cipator.
23. A _____ation is a body legally authorized to function with the rights and duties of a single
individual.
24. The suspect claims that excessive violence was used when
_____acles were clamped on her wrists.
25. Supervisors should be able to control their tempers. A
_____etic outburst over an employee's
minor infraction of the rules is unforgivable.

D. Thinking with Your New Words

Read all of the following statements. Then answer each
question below.

PART ONE

Statements

John grew up in a home where Italian was spoken, yet the
only language he knew was English.

Olga's hands and lips had become chapped from her
working outdoors in subfreezing weather.

To relieve the soreness, Philip gargled with a warm salt solution.

Angelina's coughing was attributed to her heavy smoking. Her
physician warned she might get emphysema if she did not quit.

In assembling the new mower, Hanlon found the directions
in the instruction booklet unforgivably vague.

Carol had expected Bruce to stick to his principles, so his
surrender to the opposition turned her stomach.

Alphonse was awakened by the scent of freshly brewed
coffee emanating from the kitchen.

In "The Great Lover," Rupert Brooke praised "the cool kindliness of sheets that soon /Smooth away trouble, and the rough male kiss of blankets."

Erica, the nurse on duty, removed a nasty splinter from Roderigo's right thumb.

Nettie considered the matter for a few minutes and came up with a solution, but Marcia refused to bother her head about the problem.

Questions

1. Who was monolingual? _____
2. Who courted a pulmonary disaster? _____
3. Who avoided cerebral exertion? _____
4. Who experienced a visceral reaction? _____
5. Who responded to an olfactory stimulus? _____
6. Who had a labial irritation? _____
7. Who recorded tactile impressions? _____
8. Who did subcutaneous probing? _____
9. Who experienced frustration with a manual? _____
10. Who made guttural sounds? _____

PART TWO

Statements

At lunch, Chester bit his tongue. It bled and hurt so badly that he had to stop eating.

Dotty found it difficult to get along with Amy, her carping roommate.

Magdalena, the guide with Harvey's group, was fluent in several languages.

When Kit was down with a cold, he complained that the food he was served had no taste, though I found it delicious.

As Fowler emerged, handcuffed to a detective, he bent down his head to frustrate the TV photographers.

Jason repeatedly telephoned Harriet but could not reach her. All his letters, too, were returned unopened.

The dealer allowed Agnes to handle the vase at her own risk; when she dropped it she had to pay for it.

Billings, the security guard, saw one of the customers take a necklace from the counter and drop it into her bag, but at that moment he did absolutely nothing about it.

Hastily covering the puddle in the Queen's path with his velvet cloak, Sir Walter sank to one knee and with a sweep of his arm invited her to pass.

The citizens wept when Antony showed them Caesar's corpse and the many wounds the assassins had inflicted.

Questions

11. Who genuflected?
12. Who had been manacled? _____
13. Who sustained a lingual injury? _____
14. Who was a linguist? _____
15. Who suffered a gustatory
    impairment? _____
16. Who could not establish contact? _____
17. Who was prone to petty
    fault-finding? _____
18. Who was a clumsy manipulator? _____
19. Who seemed supinely
    indifferent? _____
20. Who was a lachrymose
    spectacle? _____

E. Discussion with Your New Words

Answer each of the following in a brief paragraph.

1. Will digital timepieces eventually make traditional clocks
   obsolete? Why, or why not?

_____

_____

_____

2. What effect would a plantar wart probably have on the
   behavior of a peripatetic teacher? Explain.

_____

_____

_____

_____

3. Is a habitually impetuous person likely to be an accident-
   prone driver? Explain.

_____

_____

_____

_____

4. Would you personally intervene between vindictive foes
   to prevent a sanguinary clash? Why, or why not?

_____

_____

_____

_____

5. Some favor corporal punishment. Others are skeptical of
   its efficacy. Which side are you on? Support your answer
   with at least two reasons.

_____

_____

_____

_____

Figurative Expressions

Words can be used in a literal or a figurative sense. For example, in "my injured *foot*," *foot* is used in its *literal* (plain) sense of a part of the body. But in "the *foot* of the mountain," *foot* is used in a *figurative* (nonliteral) sense. When used figuratively, *foot* means not a part of the body, but the base or lowest part, as the *foot* of a page, the *foot* of a staircase, etc.

When asked whether you have an *ax to grind,* you are certainly not being asked whether you have an ax. And if you ever have to *eat crow,* you will not do any eating—at least not in a literal sense. *Ax to grind* and *eat crow* are figurative expressions, and that is what we shall be discussing in this chapter.

A. Preview

Use each of the following figurative expressions no more than once in completing the statements below. (Minor changes, such as "have" to "has," are permissible.)

busman's holiday	hold a candle to	poker face
come home to roost	hold water	red herring
Dutch treat	lame duck	roll out the red carpet
eat crow	pay the piper	stick in one's craw
fish or cut bait	play possum	stick to one's last
French leave	play the devil's	whistle in the dark
have an ax to grind	advocate	white elephant

1. When the head of a friendly nation comes to confer with our President, we usually _____.
2. When the wells of those who are wasting water run dry, they will see that their extravagance has

_____.

3. Don't ask Harvey whether you should switch from oil to gas heat. He sells heating oil; he

   _____.

4. Russ should have called in a plumber instead of trying to install the dishwasher himself. The experience has taught him that it pays to _____.

5. You were warned that failure to change the engine oil regularly might cause irreparable damage, but you did not listen. Now, you must _____.

6. For Eli, a carpet-installer, the weekend was a(n) _____. He installed new carpeting in his own home.

7. The only survivor was a private who had the presence of mind to _____ and was mistaken by the raiders for a corpse.

8. The plan seems like a good one, but let us examine it further to see if it will _____.

9. We are fortunate to be living in a democracy, but let me _____ and point out some shortcomings of democracy.

10. The gas-guzzling car we bought last year has already cost us a fortune in repairs. Let's get rid of that

    _____.

11. I am more than a match for Rose in tennis, but I cannot _____ her in golf.

12. Our procrastinating allies give us only half-hearted support. Let us tell them now to

    _____.

13. Sally would not go to lunch with me until I agreed that it would be a(n)

    _____.

14. Howard earns less than others doing the same work. The injustice of this disparity has been explained to him as a matter of seniority, but it continues to

    _____.

15. When the father saw the price tag on the dollhouse his daughter wanted, he tried to interest her in a much less expensive doll carriage, but she was not diverted by that

    _____.

16. The motel operator incurred a substantial loss when a guest who had stayed more than a week took

    _____.

17. From her _____, it was

impossible to tell whether the letter she had just opened
contained good or bad news.
18. The pollster has predicted that the Democrats will win by
a landslide. If they should lose, he will
_____.
19. Though beset with injuries, the Wildcats say they are confident of victory, but we believe they are
_____.
20. If Senator Sims is defeated in November, he will be
a(n) _____ until the winner is
sworn in next January.

B. Details About the New Expressions

EXPRESSION	MEANING
busman's holiday	holiday spent in an activity the same as, or similar to, one's occupation, as a bus driver who takes his family for a Sunday drive

For Eli, a carpet-installer, the weekend was a busman's
holiday. *He installed new carpeting in his own home.*

come home to roost	have disagreeable repercussions; boomerang

*When the wells of those who are wasting water run dry, they
will see that their extravagance has* come home to roost.

Dutch treat	meal or entertainment for which each participant pays his or her own share

*Sally would not go to lunch with me until I agreed that it
would be a* Dutch treat.

eat crow	be forced into a humiliating or extremely disagreeable situation

*The pollster has predicted that the Democrats will win by a
landslide. If they should lose, he will* eat crow.

EXPRESSION	MEANING
fish or cut bait	proceed wholeheartedly or drop out altogether; stop procrastinating or temporizing

Our procrastinating allies give us only half-hearted support. Let us tell them now to fish or cut bait.

French leave	unauthorized, hasty, or secret departure

The motel operator incurred a substantial loss when a guest who had stayed more than a week took French leave.

have an ax to grind	have a selfish motive or ulterior purpose to promote

Don't ask Harvey for advice on whether to switch from oil to gas heat. He sells heating oil; he has an ax to grind.

hold a candle to	compare favorably with

I am more than a match for Rose in tennis, but I cannot hold a candle to *her in golf.*

hold water	remain sound, logical, or consistent; stand up

The plan seems good, but let us examine it further to see if it will hold water.

lame duck	elected official who remains in office for a brief period after a successor has been elected

If Senator Sims is defeated in November, he will be a lame duck *until the winner is sworn in next January.*

pay the piper	suffer the unfavorable consequences of one's actions

You were warned that failure to change the engine oil regularly might cause irreparable damage, but you did not listen. Now, you must pay the piper.

EXPRESSION	MEANING
play possum	pretend to be dead or alseep; dissemble (Opossums feign death when threatened.)

The only survivor was a private who had the presence of mind to play possum *and was mistaken by the raiders for a corpse.*

play the devil's advocate	uphold the wrong side of a cause for the sake of argument

We are fortunate to be living in a democracy, but let me play the devil's advocate *and point out some shortcomings of democracy.*

poker face	expressionless face, as that of an experienced poker player

From her poker face, *it was impossible to tell whether the letter she had just opened contained good or bad news.*

red herring	something used to distract attention from the real issue (from the practice of drawing a red herring across a trail to confuse hunting dogs)

When the father saw the price tag on the dollhouse his daughter wanted, he tried to interest her in a much less expensive doll carriage, but she was not diverted by that red herring.

roll out the red carpet	show impressive courtesy (from the practice of rolling out a red carpet for arriving dignitaries to step on)

When the head of a friendly nation arrives to confer with our President, we usually roll out the red carpet.

EXPRESSION	MEANING
stick in one's craw	be intolerable and unacceptable to one

Howard earns less than others doing the same work. The injustice of this sticks in his craw.

stick to one's last	keep to one's own trade or field (from the proverb "Let the cobbler stick to his last," a last being a shaped form on which a shoe is made or repaired)

Russ should have called in a plumber instead of trying to install the dishwasher himself. The experience has taught him that it pays to stick to one's last.

whistle in the dark	put on a show of confidence in the face of impending danger or defeat; try to keep up one's courage

Though beset with injuries, the Wildcats say they are confident of victory, but we believe they are whistling in the dark.

white elephant	possession entailing expense and trouble far greater than its usefulness to the owner

The gas-guzzling car we bought last year has already cost us a fortune in repairs. Let's get rid of that white elephant.

C. Thinking with Your New Vocabulary

Read all of the following statements. Then answer each question below.

Statements

Lorber built a $50,000 in-ground swimming pool on his property with two cabanas, but his family seldom used it, preferring the beach.

When Belle suggested we ask the waitress for separate checks, Charley overruled her, insisting that all of us were his guests.

Though she lost at the polls, Compton was still our mayor for an additional nine weeks.

Agnes scoffed at the idea of annual dental checkups, until she had to have two teeth extracted.

Judge Smith was humiliated when his private car was towed away for illegal parking.

During summer vacations, Chuck worked as a volunteer in the local hospital because he thought the service would look good on his applications to medical schools.

The Queen received a twenty-one gun salute, and her national anthem, as well as that of the host country, was played.

Schultz had repeatedly told Mrs. Worth he wanted to buy her property, but he delayed signing the papers until she told him of another prospective buyer. Only then did he put down his deposit.

Herman was not alarmed when his campaign manager, Lydia, began listing the reasons he should not be elected; he realized she was doing it to help him prepare replies to possible detractors.

Freida, a dressmaker, bought some material from which she made a pair of beautiful curtains for her kitchen on her day off.

Questions

1. Who ate crow? _____
2. Who had a white elephant? _____
3. Who spent a busman's holiday? _____
4. Who was a lame duck? _____
5. Who was accorded red-carpet treatment? _____
6. Who paid the piper? _____

7. Who was in effect told to fish or cut bait? _____

8. Who played the devil's advocate? _____

9. Who had an ax to grind? _____

10. Who proposed a Dutch treat? _____

D. Using Figurative Language

Replace the italicized words with a figurative expression from Section B of this chapter.

1. She introduced a *matter whose only purpose was to take the attention of the group from the basic issue under discussion.* _____

2. The inmate used to *pretend to be asleep* when the guards made their rounds. _____

3. This unwise decision may *cause a great deal of trouble for us in the future.* _____

4. Two employees were charged with taking *the rest of the day off without permission,* after clocking in at 8:58 A.M. Friday. _____

5. Some people panic when things look bad; others *put on a show of confidence* to keep up their morale. _____

6. My features are an open book. I do not have a *talent for concealing my feelings.* _____

7. Our attorney has predicted that none of the

charges against us will
*stand up under exami-
nation and scrutiny* in a
court of law.   _____

8. It is all right to do
minor repairs, like
changing a furnace
filter or a faucet
washer, but otherwise
you should *keep to the
trade or profession you
were trained for.*   _____

9. Your failure to appoint
Ned as head of the
committee, as you had
promised, is sure to *be
unbearable and unac-
ceptable to him.*   _____

E. Using Some Additional Figurative Expressions

Complete the sentences below by inserting the most appropriate of the following additional figurative expressions.

burn the midnight oil—work or study far into the night
bury the hatchet—settle a disagreement; make peace
go begging—be in little demand
have a bone to pick—have something to argue or complain
about
have a chip on one's shoulder—have a disposition to
quarrel

1. We try not to offend anyone, but if you should ever
_____ with us,
please let us know so that we may quickly resolve the
matter.

2. The team's T-shirts and caps are sure to
_____ if it con-
tinues to be a consistent loser.

3. The former foes are now friends; they decided to
_____.

4. It is hard to get along with someone who
_____.

5. If Sally's report is due tomorrow, and she hasn't written a word of it yet, she will probably
_____.

F. Discussion with Figurative Language

Answer each of the following in a brief paragraph.

1. Is it xenophobic to object to the expense of rolling out the red carpet for visiting foreign dignitaries? Why, or why not?

_____

_____

_____

_____

2. Why might you be skeptical about proposals for new legislation sponsored by lame ducks?

_____

_____

_____

3. Why would it stick in your craw to see a fellow employee who could not possibly hold a candle to you promoted over you to a supervisory position?

_____

_____

_____

4. Should we feel compassion for the perpetrator of a canard who has to eat crow? Explain.

_____

_____

_____

_____

5. Describe a situation in which reasonable people might
   agree that taking French leave is a venial offense.

_____

_____

_____

_____

Review of Chapters 16–20

I. Complete the sentences below, choosing your answers from the following list:

cerebr	gust	manu	tact
corpor	labi	sangu	viscer
digit	lingu		

1. "Hand" is the meaning conveyed by _____.
2. A _____ word is a "gut" word.
3. A word containing _____ has something to do with the tongue.
4. "Finger" is the meaning conveyed by _____.
5. A word containing _____ has something to do with the brain.
6. _____ appears in several words dealing with the sense of touch.
7. "Blood" is the meaning conveyed by _____.
8. "Body" is the meaning conveyed by _____.
9. A _____ word is a "lip" word.
10. _____ may be a sign that the word in which it appears has to do with the sense of taste.

II. Replace the italicized words in each passage below with a single word. Find that word, partially spelled, in the following list, and complete the spelling before using it.

fl __ __ under	cont __ __ band	cong __ __ gate
__ __ inerary	ob __ __ lescent	__ __ cessory
me __ __ der	__ __ ptious	la __ __ rinth
__ __ ndal	re __ ___ divist	tran __ __ tion
con __ __ ite	al __ __ uistic	__ __ odus

1. A first offender is usually given a more lenient sentence than a(n) *habitual criminal*.   _____

2. They laughed when they saw me *struggle to obtain a footing*.   _____

3. In our swiftly changing technology, equipment purchased today may be *on the way out of use* by tomorrow.   _____

4. I was *deeply repentant* because my carelessness was responsible for the accident.   _____

5. Shoppers waiting for the store to open *gather into a crowd* at the main entrance.   _____

6. Is there anything we can do to stop the *mass departure* from our cities?   _____

7. The tourists have been notified of the change in the *route of the journey*.   _____

8. It takes time for newcomers to learn their way through the *confusion of intersecting streets* of a busy city.   _____

9. Rarely have we met anyone so *unselfishly concerned for the welfare of others*.   _____

10. Where did they hide the *smuggled goods*?   _____

11. A few pursue their objective in a straight course; the rest *wander aimlessly*.   _____

12. It is hard to forgive a(n) *person who maliciously destroys public property*.   _____

13. The *process of going* from adolescence to adulthood is gradual.   _____

14. The person who provided the murderer with a weapon was considered a(n) *helper in the commission of the crime*.   _____

15. How can we get along with
    someone who is so *prone to find*
    fault over petty details?   _____

III. For the italicized word in each sentence below, find *two* synonyms. Choose all your synonyms from the list at the end of the exercise.

1. Bail enables a suspect to avoid *imprisonment*.

   _____
2. This is *senseless*. _____
3. She remained *unmoved*. _____
4. You *bloodthirsty* villain! _____
5. Don't be so *stingy*. _____
6. His voice was *throaty*. _____
7. What is the use of being *spiteful*? _____
8. Be *bold*. _____
9. Without help, they will *founder*. _____
10. Tigers swiftly *gut* their prey. _____
11. She explained her theory to a *doubting* audience.

   _____
12. We were in the thick of a *boisterous* crowd.

   _____
13. Speak up. Don't be *shy*. _____
14. Don't listen to that *quack*. _____
15. The *raid* was repelled. _____

bloody	eviscerate	intrepid	sanguinary
calm	guttural	irrational	sink
charlatan	illogical	jailing	skeptical
collapse	impassive	miserly	timid
dauntless	impostor	obstreperous	unforgiving
diffident	incarceration	parsimonious	unruly
disbelieving	incursion	rasping	vindictive
disembowel	inroad		

IV. Replace the italicized words with one of the following figurative expressions:

ax to grind	pay the piper
come home to roost	poker face

have a bone to pick   red herring
hold a candle to   roll out the red carpet
hold water   white elephant

1. The experts are analyzing our proposal to see if it will *stand up*.
   _____

2. Hunters caught poaching must *suffer the consequences*.
   _____

3. Do you *have something to argue or complain about* with me?
   _____

4. His *expressionless features* offered no clue as to what he was thinking.
   _____

5. Some claim that the dictator's exaggeration of a minor spying incident was a(n) *distraction to divert attention from other issues*.
   _____

6. Why should we invest in a(n) *project that is far more costly than it can ever be worth*?
   _____

7. You were not so altruistic in supporting the director's bid for a higher post because, as her likely successor, you had a(n) *selfish motive*.
   _____

8. A novice in chess cannot *compare favorably with* a veteran player like you.
   _____

9. What will you do if your schemes *boomerang*?
   _____

10. For a distinguished guest we *make an impressive show of hospitality*.
    _____

V. Complete the spelling of the word hinted at. Each blank stands for one missing letter.

1. A wart on the sole of a foot is known as a plant __ __ wart.
2. Punishment is cor __ __ ral when it is inflicted on the body.
3. Freshly brewed coffee is __ __ factory because it excites our sense of smell.
4. It is also gus __ __ tory because it stimulates our taste buds.

5. We receive __ __ ctile impressions from things that stimulate our sense of touch, like sandpaper or silk.
6. A cer __ __ cal pain is a pain in the neck.
7. Pul __ __ nary diseases are diseases of the lungs.
8. When you lie on your back, you are in a(n) __ __ pine position.
9. When you lie on your stomach, you are in a(n) __ __ one position.
10. A bruise shows there has been damage to small sub __ __ taneous blood vessels.
11. With the words "Off with his head," Richard III condemned Lord Hastings to __ __ pital punishment.
12. We should not have to ge __ __ flect to obtain what is justly ours.
13. Many noses have been bloodied in s __ __ guinary scuffles over trifling differences.
14. We make a gut __ __ ral sound when we clear our throats.
15. With a(n) __ __ nual transmission, you must shift gears by hand.

VI. *Concise Writing*. Express the thought of each sentence below in *no more than four words*.

1. People who are given to shedding tears are abnormally sensitive.

   _____

2. There was little demand for expensive goods imported from abroad.

   _____

3. They settled the issue over which they had been quarreling and made peace with each other.

   _____

4. The remarks that she made were full of spite and malicious anger.

   _____

5. Elected officials who remain in office for a brief period after their defeat at the polls have a feeling that they are not important.

   _____

21

"Living" Words

All of the words in this chapter have something to do with living. Many have interesting origins. For example, consider *troglodyte*.

A *troglodyte*, of Greek origin, is literally "one who enters or lives in holes"; hence, a cavedweller. *Troglodyte* can mean either (1) a prehistoric person who lived in caves; or (2) one who resembles a cavedweller because of living in seclusion, or having outmoded or reactionary attitudes; or (3) an animal like an ant that lives underground.

A. Preview

Use each of the following "living" words no more than once in completing the sentences below.

aerobic	biopsy	exurbanite	resuscitate
amphibian	coeval	macrobiotic	troglodyte
animated	ecology	microorganism	viable
biocidal	expatriate	reclusive	vita
biodegradable	extant	reincarnation	viviparous

1. No fish can live in rivers or lakes contaminated by heavy discharges of _____ wastes.
2. Some believe that a(n) _____ diet can help them achieve superior health and longevity.
3. Conservationists oppose the draining of the swamps because it would disturb the _____ of the area.
4. As a(n) _____, Jackson commutes from his semirural home to his city office about twice a week.
5. A meeting between George Eliot (1819–1880) and

Katharine Mansfield (1888–1923) could not have occurred; they were not _____s.

6. To _____ a victim of cardiac arrest, emergency measures should begin without a second's delay.

7. If you think my reorganization plan will not work, can you suggest a(n) _____ alternative?

8. We need oxygen to live: we are _____.

9. Some _____s, like viruses, were invisible until the invention of the electron microscope.

10. Only a few hundred lines of the writings of Ennius are _____; the rest are lost.

11. Patricia calls Sam a _____ because he rejects technological progress.

12. The meeting was dull until a motion was made to hold a dance; then the discussion became _____.

13. Humans are _____: they produce living young.

14. When war threatens to break out in a foreign country, most of the _____s who live there return to their homelands.

15. Applicants for the position were asked to submit a(n) _____ and three letters of recommendation.

16. The disposal of plastics is a serious problem because some of them are not _____.

17. Some believers in _____ think the soul passes into another human body after death; others say it is embodied in a nonhuman species.

18. A(n) _____ will be performed to determine whether the lump is malignant or benign.

19. Why do you live by yourself, without a telephone, away from family and friends? Do you enjoy being _____?

20. The frog is a tailless _____ with strong hind legs especially adapted for leaping.

B. Details About the New Words

WORD	MEANING

aerobic *adj*
ə-'rō-bik

1. able to live or grow only in the presence of oxygen

We need oxygen to live: we are aerobic.

2. having to do with exercise that increases oxygen intake and conditions the heart and lungs

Walking, running, and swimming are forms of aerobic *exercise.*

---

amphibian *n*
am-'fi-bē-ən

Any animal or plant that can live both on land and in water

The frog is a tailless amphibian *with strong hind legs especially adapted for leaping.*

---

animated *adj*
'a-nə-,mā-təd

alive; lively; spirited

The meeting was dull until a motion was made to hold a dance; then the discussion became animated.

---

biocidal *adj*
,bī-ə-'sī-dəl

destructive to living organisms

No fish can live in rivers or lakes contaminated by heavy discharges of biocidal *wastes.*

---

biodegradable *adj*
,bī-ō-də-'grā-də-bəl

capable of being readily decomposed by living microorganisms

The disposal of plastics is a serious problem because some of them are not biodegradable.

---

biopsy *n*
'bī-,äp-sē

removal and diagnostic examination of bits of tissues, cells, or fluids from the living body

A biopsy *will be performed to determine whether the lump is malignant or benign.*

WORD	MEANING
coeval n kō-'ē-vəl	contemporary; person of the same period or age

A meeting between George Eliot (1819–1880) and Katharine Mansfield (1888–1923) could not have occurred; they were not coevals.

| **ecology** n
i-'kä-lə-jē | interrelationship between living organisms and their environment |

Conservationists oppose the draining of the swamps because it would disturb the ecology of the area.

| **expatriate** n
ek-'spā-trē-,ət | one who lives in a foreign country |

When war threatens to break out in a foreign country, most of the expatriates who live there return to their homelands.

| **extant** adj
'ek-stənt | still in existence; not lost or destroyed |

Only a few hundred lines of the writings of Ennius are extant; the rest are lost.

| **exurbanite** n
ek-'sər-bə-,nīt | former citydweller who lives in an *exurb* (region beyond the suburbs) but continues to earn a living in the city |

An an exurbanite, Jackson commutes from his semirural home to his city office about twice a week.

| **macrobiotic** adj
,ma-krō-bī-'ä-tik | having to do with or consisting mainly of whole grains and vegetables, whose consumption is thought to promote health and long life |

Some believe that a macrobiotic diet can help them achieve superior health and longevity.

WORD	MEANING
microorganism *n* ˌmī̩krō-'or-gə-'ni-zəm	any microscopic or ultramicroscopic living animal or plant

Some microrganisms, *like viruses, were invisible until the invention of the electron microscope.*

reclusive *adj* ri-'klü-siv	solitary; living in seclusion, apart from others; like a recluse

Why do you live by yourself, without a telephone, away from family and friends? Do you enjoy being reclusive?

reincarnation *n* ˌrē̩in-kär-'nā-shən	rebirth of the soul in another body after death, as in some religious beliefs; new embodiment

Some believers in reincarnation *think the soul passes into another human body after death; others say it is embodied in a nonhuman species.*

resuscitate *v* ri-'sə-sə-ˌtāt	revive from apparent death; restore to life

To resuscitate *a victim of cardiac arrest, emergency measures should begin without a second's delay.*

troglodyte *n* 'trä-glə̩dīt	(literally, *cavedweller*) person living in seclusion; recluse; also, anyone who behaves like a caveman

Sam stayed in a cabin in the woods by himself, emerging about once a week to do some shopping; he lived like a troglodyte.

WORD	MEANING
viable *adj* 'vī-ə-bəl	able to live; likely to survive; workable

If you think my reorganization plan will not work, can you suggest a viable *alternative?*

| **vita** *n*
'vē-tə | brief outline of one's life and
experience; short
autobiographical sketch;
résumé |

Applicants for the position were asked to submit a vita *and three letters of recommendation.*

| **viviparous** *adj*
vī-'vi-pə-rəs | giving birth to living offspring
from within the mother's body,
rather than from eggs |

Humans are viviparous: *they produce living young.*

C. Building Additional "Living" Words

Add the appropriate "living" root to complete each word defined below. Choose your roots from the following:

from Greek: *bio, bi,* or *be,* meaning "life."
from Latin: *vita, vit, vivi,* or *viv,* meaning "life," "living," or "alive."

1. The growth of living, disease-causing bacteria can usually be stopped or inhibited by anti_____tics.
2. A gifted teacher knows how to _____lize (instill life into) a lesson.
3. _____luminescence is light produced by living organisms, such as light from fireflies.
4. A good watering will re_____fy the plant and put new life into its drooping leaves.
5. The entombment of a dead Pharaoh was often accompanied by live burial, or _____sepulture, of his faithful servants.
6. In _____logical warfare, living microorganisms

are used to harm an enemy's population, livestock, and crops.

7. _____medicine investigates the capacity of humans to withstand the stresses of abnormal environments.

8. Anti_____sectionists maintain that surgical experiments on living animals are immoral.

9. An aero_____ is a microorganism that can live only in the presence of free oxygen.

10. Micro_____cides are preparations designed to destroy microbes.

11. James Boswell's *Life of Samuel Johnson* is a remarkable _____graphy.

12. Yesterday there was no liveliness in her manner, but today she is _____acious.

13. The _____sphere is the zone of planet Earth in which life can exist.

14. This plant is not likely to live; it lacks _____lity.

15. A micro_____ is a microscopic organism, or germ.

16. Research in biological science is called _____research.

17. Do you enjoy eating and drinking in good company, or are you not the con_____al type?

18. If you know the plant and animal life of a region, you are familiar with its _____ta.

19. It is a new presentation of an old play. The reviewers call it a re_____al.

20. The story of your life would be an auto_____graphy if you wrote it yourself.

21. The yucca plant and the yucca moth have a sym_____tic (mutually dependent, live-together) relationship.

22. Your _____l signs—such as your pulse rate, temperature, and breathing rate—show how effectively your body is functioning.

23. The city has set aside funds to re_____lize (restore to life) its downtown business district.

24. If you hold that life is not created spontaneously but origi-

nates from preexisting life, you believe in
_____genesis.

25. An area's _____mass is its total content of
living organisms.

26. _____satellites are recoverable spacecraft that
enable us to study the effects of weightlessness, cosmic
radiation, and other space phenomena on living organisms.

27. Red is a more _____d color than gray.

28. _____metry is the statistical calculation of the
probable duration of human life.

29. The specter of nuclear war jeopardizes the
sur_____al of humankind.

30. A de_____lized tooth is one from which the pulp
has been removed.

D. Thinking with Your New Words

Read all of the following statements. Then answer each
question below.

Statements

When Emily paid us a visit last April and caught her first sight
of the neighbors' cat Hansie, she exclaimed with excitement: "I
could swear that's the same cat we had when I was a child!"

Darryl was nearly asphyxiated; firefighters found him
unconscious, face down, on the living-room floor.

Though her husband urged her to include them, Dorothy
made no mention in her résumé of the awards she had won at
commencement.

With his heavy reading assignments, José had little time for
watching TV, but he managed to run about twenty-five miles a
week.

Cheryl decided to finish writing her paper somewhere else,
since there was so much coughing and sneezing in the library.

For eleven years, Anthony was the Rome correspondent of a
leading New York daily.

Charley's favorites were bacon for breakfast, hamburgers for lunch, and steak or poultry for dinner. They were Andrea's, too, before her changeover to fresh vegetables, fresh fruit, and whole-grain foods.

Wendy's excuse for eating by herself was that she had too much on her mind and no time for talk.

When he lived less than a mile from the station, Walter could walk to the train in good weather, but his new home is eight miles farther away.

What Sonia particularly enjoyed on holidays was inviting friends, or being invited by them, to dinner at her favorite restaurant.

Questions

1. Who seemed like a reincarnation? _____
2. Who lost a viable option? _____
3. Who was convivial? _____
4. Who required resuscitation? _____
5. Who was reclusive? _____
6. Who was an expatriate? _____
7. Who was partial to aerobics? _____
8. Who sought a relatively
   microbe-free environment? _____
9. Who had macrobiotic
   preferences? _____
10. Who prepared a vita? _____

E. Analogies

Write the *letter* of the pair of words related to each other in the same way as the words in the capitalized pair.

1. VIRUS : MICROORGANISM
a. rayon : clothing   d. antipyretic : fever
b. ant : insect   e. visibility : microscope
c. nucleus : cell   **Answer**_____

2. GLOWWORM : BIOLUMINESCENCE
a. wound : pain   d. rattlesnake : reptile
b. bee : hive   e. pyromaniac : conflagration
c. rose : fragrance   **Answer**_____

3. MICROBICIDE : MICROBES
a. pesticide : weeds   d. antibiotic : bacteria
b. parasite : host   e. herbicide : insects
c. fungicide : viruses   **Answer**_____

4. AEROBE : OXYGEN
a. cactus : moisture   d. vacuum : air
b. fish : water   e. photosynthesis : light
c. furnace : heat   **Answer**_____

5. COEVAL : PERIOD
a. semicolon : comma   d. exemplar : inspiration
b. forebear : posterity   e. bachelor : marriage
c. compatriot : country   **Answer**_____

Alpha-Privative Words

A, or alpha, is the first letter of the Greek alphabet. When used as a prefix, this *"a"* deprives a word or root of its positive force and gives it a negative meaning. That is why we call it *alpha privative* ('al-fə 'pri-və-tiv).

EXAMPLES:

a + social = asocial (not social; not considerate of others; selfish)
a + symmetrical = asymmetrical (lopsided; not symmetrical)

The prefix *an* is used, instead of *a*, when the root or word with which it is used begins with a vowel:

an + archy (root meaning *government*) = *anarchy* (absence of government; lawlessness; disorder)

There are, of course, other privative prefixes in our language, such as *un, in,* and *non*. This chapter, however, will deal only with words beginning with *alpha privative*.

A. Preview

Use each of the following alpha-privative words no more than once in completing the sentences below.

abiogenesis	amnesia	anaerobic	anodyne
abyss	amnesty	anemia	anomaly
agnostic	amorphous	anesthesia	anorexia
aphasia	asexual	asylum	atrophy
apolitical	asphyxiation	asymptomatic	atypical

1. An amoeba multiplies by
   _____ reproduction, splitting
   itself in two.
2. The theory of _____ was chal-
   lenged when several experiments showed that life can
   originate only from preexisting life.
3. An obsession with being as slim as possible may lead to
   _____, especially in young
   women.
4. There is no certainty that the victim of
   _____ will recover his memory.
5. Temporary muscular _____ is
   common when a limb is in a cast, as the muscles are not
   being used.
6. Do not run an automobile engine in a closed garage; the
   fumes can cause _____.
7. The average daily attendance has been about 100, so
   yesterday's turnout of more than 300 was
   _____.
8. The safe return of the missing children lifted the parents
   from an _____ of despair.
9. The _____ mass ahead as we
   approached cautiously in the fog was a stalled motorbus.
10. For a Republican to be elected mayor by an overwhelming
    majority in this traditionally Democratic city is indeed an
    _____.
11. One cause of _____ is a loss of
    blood.
12. The hijackers flew from country to country, vainly seeking
    _____.
13. Some bacteria do not require air or free oxygen; they are
    _____.
14. A relaxing afternoon at the beach on a midsummer day is
    an _____ for a troubled mind.
15. Though not denying that God may exist, as atheists do,
    _____s remain skeptical and
    unconvinced.
16. With the help of speech therapists, many victims of
    _____ have been able to regain
    the power of coherent speech.
17. Rebels who fled the country may return without being
    prosecuted for treason, now that
    _____ has been granted.

18. When guests quarrel over whether the views of the liberals are better than those of the conservatives, I try to introduce an _____ topic, like sports.

19. Usually, I have a filling done without _____. But if a tooth is extremely sensitive, I am given some novocaine.

20. My cold may be over because I no longer cough or sneeze or have fever. For the past two days, I have been _____.

B. Details About the New Words

WORD	MEANING
abiogenesis *n* ˌā-ˌbī-ō-ˈje-nə-səs	theory that life can originate from nonliving matter; spontaneous generation

The theory of abiogenesis *was challenged when several experiments showed that life can originate only from preexisting life.*

| **abyss** *n*
ə-ˈbis | (literally, "without bottom") seemingly bottomless pit or gulf; chasm; anything immeasurably deep |

The safe return of the missing children lifted their parents from an abyss *of despair.*

| **agnostic** *n*
ag-ˈnäs-tik | (literally, one who does "not know") person who is not committed to believing in either the existence or nonexistence of God or a god |

Though not denying that God may exist, as atheists do, agnostics *remain skeptical and unconvinced.*

| **amnesia** *n*
am-ˈnē-zhə | (literally, condition of "not remembering") loss of memory |

There is no certainty that the victim of amnesia *will recover his memory.*

WORD	MEANING

amnesty n
'am-nə-stē

general pardon for an offense, including a political offense against a government

Rebels who fled the country may return without being prosecuted for treason, now that amnesty *has been granted.*

---

amorphous adj
ə-'mȯr-fəs

without definite form; shapeless; vague

The amorphous *mass ahead as we approached cautiously in the fog was a stalled motorbus.*

---

anaerobic adj
ˌa-nə-'rō-bik

able to live or grow in the absence of oxygen

Some bacteria do not require air or free oxygen; they are anaerobic.

---

anemia n
ə-'nē-mē-ə

(literally, condition of being "without blood") red cell or hemoglobin deficiency in the circulating blood; paleness; lack of vigor

One cause of anemia *is a loss of blood.*

---

anesthesia n
ˌa-nəs-'thē-zhə

(literally, "without feeling") partial or complete loss of the sense of pain, with or without loss of consciousness, artificially induced by drugs

Usually, I have a filling done without anesthesia. *But if a tooth is extremely sensitive, I am given some novocaine.*

---

anodyne n
'a-nə-ˌdīn

(literally, "without pain") drug that relieves pain; anything that soothes or comforts

A relaxing afternoon at the beach is an anodyne *for a troubled mind.*

WORD	MEANING

anomaly *n*
ə-'nä-mə-lē

(literally, "not regular")
irregularity; departure from the
common rule; abnormality

*For a Republican to be elected mayor by an overwhelming
majority in this traditionally Democratic city is indeed an*
anomaly.

anorexia *n*
‚a-nə-'rek-sē-ə

(literally, "without longing")
of appetite, especially
when prolonged

An obsession with being as slim as possible may lead to
anorexia, *especially in young women.*

aphasia *n*
ə-'fā-zh(ē)ə

(literally, condition of "not
speaking") partial or complete
loss of the power to use and
understand words

With the help of speech therapists, many victims of aphasia
have been able to regain the power of coherent speech.

apolitical *adj*
‚ā-pə-'li-ti-kəl

not connected with political
matters; of no political
significance; uninterested in
politics

*When guests quarrel over whether the views of the liberals
are better than those of the conservatives, I try to introduce
an* apolitical *topic, like sports.*

asexual *adj*
‚ā-'sek-shə-wəl

occurring or produced without
sexual action; sexless

An amoeba multiplies by asexual *reproduction, splitting
itself in two.*

asphyxiation *n*
as-‚fik-sē-'ā-shən

(literally, condition of "no
throbbing" or pulsation) loss of
consciousness due to lack of
oxygen or presence of poisonous gases; suffocation

*Do not run an automobile engine in a closed garage; the
fumes can cause* asphyxiation.

WORD	MEANING
asylum *n* ə-'sī-ləm	(literally, "without right of seizure") inviolable place where one can be free from arrest; protection; sanctuary; shelter

The hijackers flew from country to country, vainly seeking asylum.

asymptomatic *adj* ˌā-ˌsimp-tə-'ma-tik	without evidence of disease; symptomless

My cold may be over because I no longer cough or sneeze or have fever. For the past two days, I have been asymptomatic.

atrophy *n* 'a-trə-fē	(literally, condition of being "without nourishment") wasting away or decrease in size of a body organ or tissue

Temporary muscular atrophy *is common when a limb is in a cast, as the muscles are not being used.*

atypical *adj* ˌā-'ti-pi-kəl	not typical; irregular; abnormal

The average daily attendance has been about 100, so yesterday's turnout of more than 300 was atypical.

C. Building Additional Alpha-Privative Words

Complete the spelling of each unfinished alpha-privative word by adding the appropriate root from the following list as in 1, below.

alg (pain)	ox (oxygen)	seism (shaking; earthquake)
archy (government)	pathy (feeling)	
bio (life)	phon (voice; sound)	sthen (strength)
bul (will; volition)	pnea (breathe)	the (God or gods)
hydr (water)	pter (wing)	tom (cut)
onym (name)		

1. The donor is nameless and wants us to preserve his an____onym____ity.
2. The a_____ on her face when I tell her of our victories or defeats shows she has no feeling about whether we win or lose.
3. The environment can be subdivided into the biotic (living) environment, and the a_____tic (nonliving) environment.
4. Those who believe in an_____ insist that the best government is no government at all.
5. As originally conceived, an a_____ was a particle of matter that could not be cut into anything smaller than itself.
6. Her physician recommended an over-the-counter an_____esic drug to relieve the pain.
7. An an_____ide is a chemical compound formed by removing water from another compound.
8. An a_____ous insect cannot fly.
9. A_____ia is an abnormal lack of will power or ability to make decisions.
10. The bedridden patients have not exercised in a long time. It is no wonder they are suffering from a_____ia.
11. Inhabitants of an a_____ic region are usually not subject to earthquakes.
12. A_____ is a temporary cessation of breathing, as in some adults during sleep, or in hibernating animals.
13. Overuse of the vocal cords may result in the loss of all but whispered speech, a condition known as a_____ia.
14. The convict had been an a_____ist, but in prison he turned to religion.
15. An _____ia is a condition in which there is an abnormally low level of oxygen in the body tissues.

D. Thinking with Your New Words

Read all of the following statements. Then answer each question below.

Statements

"You may be able to work in this place," Agnes told Morris,

"but I can't. There is no air here. Why don't you open a window?" She left the room.

Pasteur proved that bacteria originate from parent bacteria, rather than from nonliving matter.

The songs Gail sang and played on her guitar made Mario forget his pain, and he even joined in some of the sing-along numbers.

Richard, a volunteer, walked with a few of the elderly inmates of the nursing home, enabling them to get some exercise.

The foods Rosina used to like no longer appealed to her. She ate almost nothing, complaining of a poor appetite.

Manny was told that he would have to be careful not to overexert himself until his red-blood-cell count returned to normal.

After being turned away at every door because of his criminal record, Valjean was welcomed and given lodging by the Bishop of Digne.

When Charlene was using carbon tetrachloride indoors as a cleaning fluid, she lost consciousness from the fumes. Luckily, she was rushed out of the room and revived.

The dean was concerned that a low grade in the course would hurt Debra's chances of admission to graduate school, but Debra herself did not seem to care.

Harvey was so upset at the time of the accident that when he was asked for his address and telephone number, he couldn't remember them.

Questions

1. Who offered asylum?   _____
2. Who provided an anodyne?   _____
3. Who was afflicted with anorexia?   _____
4. Who showed apathy?   _____
5. Who was practically accused of
   being anaerobic?   _____
6. Who helped prevent asthenia?   _____
7. Who was almost asphyxiated?   _____

8. Who was apparently anemic? _____

9. Who had temporary amnesia? _____

10. Who found no support for
    abiogenesis? _____

E. Discussion with Your New Words

Answer each of the following in a brief paragraph.

1. You are a naturalized American citizen applying for
   admission to graduate school. A few years ago, in your
   native land, you were imprisoned on suspicion of being a
   rebel but were released during a general amnesty. Should
   you mention this episode in your vita? Explain.

   _____

   _____

   _____

   _____

2. In the anteroom of your oral surgeon, a fellow patient
   about to have a wisdom tooth extracted discusses the following matter with you: The surgeon has given her a
   choice of local anesthesia, which would temporarily
   desensitize the area of the wisdom tooth, or general anesthesia, which would render her unconscious during the
   surgery. Which choice would you make if you were the
   patient? Why?

   _____

   _____

   _____

   _____

3. As governor, you are about to fill a vacant judgeship. An
   impartial advisory board has recommended three apolitical
   individuals, of whom the best qualified is persona non
   grata to you because of a remark she made in the past.
   Would you appoint that individual? Why, or why not?

   _____

   _____

---

4. A customer is negotiating to purchase something which you feel will become a white elephant for him, though it will yield a handsome profit for you. The situation bothers you, so you discuss it with an associate. He advises you that business dealings are amoral—that is, outside the sphere where moral issues apply. Would you go through with the transaction? Explain.

---

5. Having taken a course in cardiopulmonary resuscitation, you know how to administer artificial respiration. One day, you happen to be passing when a neighbor is carried unconscious from his garage, apparently the victim of carbon monoxide asphyxiation. You also happen to be a lawyer, and you are afraid you may be sued if you go to the aid of the victim and he were subsequently to die. Would you administer artificial respiration? Why, or why not?

Words Dealing with Words

Shibboleth, like many of the other words about words in this chapter, is rich in meaning.

In Biblical times, the Ephraimites made war on the Gileadites but were beaten back. When they tried to escape over the Jordan River, they met Gileadites at the crossing places who asked them if they were Ephraimites. If they replied "no," they were asked to pronounce the test word *shibboleth*, meaning "stream" in Hebrew. Since the Ephraimites could not make an *sh* sound and said "sibboleth," they met a sad fate.

A *shibboleth*, then, is "any word, saying, or custom used to distinguish the members of one group from those of another."

But *shibboleth* has also taken on the meaning of an "empty slogan," or "discredited doctrine," as we see in the following example:

> If we allow notorious criminals to get rich at the expense of the public without going to jail, how can we teach that "crime does not pay"? Who will believe that *shibboleth*?

A. Preview

Use each of the following words no more than once in completing the sentences below.

abstract	concrete	logorrhea	pejorative
acronym	diatribe	maxim	pun
argot	epithet	metaphor	redundant
articulate	euphemism	metonymy	satire
blend	glib	oxymoron	shibboleth
cliché	irony	palindrome	understatement

1. Asked if she would stay for a second helping of pie, she said it would be a "delightful inconvenience." We were amused by the _____.

2. "Brunch" is a(n) _____: it is formed from "breakfast" and "lunch."

3. Avoid the _____ "last but not least." Just say "finally."

4. Each candidate violently attacked the record of the other. They exchanged _____s.

5. _____ words, like "honesty" and "wisdom," denote things that do not exist physically.

6. If you say "He was fired," you are using a(n) _____ expression.

7. A "hit man," in the _____ of the under-world, is a hired assassin.

8. The humorous spelling "Bored of Education" is one of the commonest _____s of schoolchildren.

9. When I arrived a half hour late, as usual, one of my impatient friends said with obvious _____, "Aren't you a bit early?"

10. I wanted Dexter to present our case, instead of Louise, because he is more _____.

11. "He flew around the bases" is a(n) _____ because it equates or identifies the baserunner with a bird.

12. One thing that "rotor," "level," and "gag" have in common is that they are all _____s.

13. One _____ heard in World War I was that it was "a war to end war." Another was that it was "a war to make the world safe for democracy."

14. _____ words denote things that have material existence, like "silk" and "door."

15. Would you like being called a "bookworm" or an "egghead"? I am sure you would not enjoy those _____s.

16. Marie often makes statements without bothering to check on the facts, and some people believe her. We must not let a(n) _____ talker mislead us.

17. "City Hall," in the sentence "City Hall will ask for a tax increase," is an example of _____ because it stands for "the mayor."

18. "Misery loves company" is a familiar _____.

19. NATO is a(n) _____ for North Atlantic Treaty Organization.
20. George Orwell's *Animal Farm* is apparently a(n) _____ on totalitarianism in the time of Stalin.
21. In the following, the last word should be removed because it is _____: "My opinion is the same as Ray's opinion."
22. "Passed away" is often used as a(n) _____ for "died."
23. Stella's remark that she was "slightly bruised" in the crash is an _____. She suffered two broken ribs.
24. It is hard to get a word in when you talk with anyone afflicted with _____.

B. Details About the New Words

WORD	MEANING
abstract *adj* 'ab-,strakt	considered apart from material or specific instances; existing as a concept; not concrete

Abstract *words, like "honesty" and "wisdom," denote things that do not exist physically.*

| **acronym** *n*
'a-krə-,nim | word formed from the first letter or letters of other words |

NATO is an acronym *for North Atlantic Treaty Organization.*

| **argot** *n*
'är-'gət | language peculiar to a particular group or class; slang |

A "hit man," in the argot *of the underworld, is a hired assassin.*

| **articulate** *adj*
är-'ti-kyə-lət | capable of speech; able to express oneself effectively |

I wanted Dexter to present our case, instead of Louise, because he is more articulate.

WORD	MEANING

blend *n*
'blend

word produced from parts of other words

"Brunch" is a blend: *it is formed from "breakfast" and "lunch."*

---

cliché *n*
klē-'shā

overused expression; trite phrase; platitude

Avoid the cliché *"last but not least." Just say "finally."*

---

concrete *adj*
kän-'krēt

having a material existence; not abstract; tangible

Concrete *words denote things that have material existence, like "silk" and "door."*

---

diatribe *n*
'dī-ə,trīb

bitter spoken or written attack; angry criticism; denunciation

Each candidate violently attacked the record of the other. They exchanged diatribes.

---

epithet *n*
'e-pə-,thet

word or phrase used to characterize a person or thing, often disparagingly

Would you like being called a "bookworm" or an "egghead"? I am sure you would not enjoy those epithets.

---

euphemism *n*
'yü-fə-,mi-zəm

mild expression substituted for one that may be harsh or unpleasant

"Passed away" is often used as a euphemism *for "died."*

---

glib *adj*
'glib

having a ready flow of words but lacking accuracy or understanding; superficial; shallow

Marie often makes statements without bothering to check on the facts, and some people believe her. We must not let a glib *talker mislead us.*

WORD	MEANING

irony *n*
'ī-rə-nē

humorous or sarcastic use of language, in which the intended meaning is the opposite of the words used

When I arrived a half hour late, as usual, one of my impatient friends said with obvious irony, *"Aren't you a bit early?"*

---

logorrhea *n*
ˌlò-gə-'rē-ə

excessive flow of words; talkativeness; prolixity

It is hard to get a word in when you talk with anyone afflicted with logorrhea.

---

maxim *n*
'mak-səm

concisely expressed statement of a general truth or rule of conduct; proverbial saying; adage

"Misery loves company" is a familiar maxim.

---

metaphor *n*
'me-tə-ˌfòr

implied comparison using a word or phrase with something or someone it does not ordinarily go with

"He flew around the bases" is a metaphor *because it equates or identifies the baserunner with a bird.*

CAUTION: Do not confuse metaphor with *simile.* A *simile* is a direct comparison containing "like" or "as." Example: "He whizzed around the bases *like a bird.*"

---

metonymy *n*
mə-'tä-nə-mē

(literally, "substitute naming") naming a thing or person by substituting an associated name

"City Hall," in the sentence "City Hall will ask for a tax increase," is an example of metonymy *because it stands for "the mayor."*

WORD	MEANING

oxymoron *n*
ˌäk-si-'mōr-än

figure of speech that combines contradictory terms

Asked if she would stay for a second helping of pie, she said it would be a "delightful inconvenience." We were amused by the oxymoron.

palindrome *n*
'pa-lən-ˌdrōm

any word, phrase, or sentence that reads the same backward or forward

One thing that "rotor," "level," and "gag" have in common is that they are all palindromes.

pejorative *adj*
pi-'jȯr-ə-tiv

having a derogatory meaning or effect; disparaging; downgrading

As for the reporter who once called us "mediocre," our team never forgave him for that pejorative *remark.*

pun *n*
'pən

play on words having the same sound but different meanings; play on different meanings of the same word

The humorous spelling "Bored of Education" is one of the commonest puns *of schoolchildren.*

redundant *adj*
ri-'dən-dənt

exceeding what is necessary or normal; superfluous; surplus

In the following, the last word should be removed because it is redundant: *"My opinion is the same as Ray's opinion."*

satire *n*
'sa-ˌtīr

use of ridicule to expose folly or abuse; literary work holding up human stupidity or wickedness to scorn

George Orwell's Animal Farm *is apparently a* satire *on totalitarianism in the time of Stalin.*

WORD	MEANING
shibboleth *n* 'shi-bə-ləth	password, saying, or custom distinguishing the members of one group from those of another; slogan, especially one that has lost its meaning; discredited doctrine

One shibboleth *heard in World War I was that it was "a war to end war." Another was that it was "a war to make the world safe for democracy."*

WORD	MEANING
understatement *n* ˌən-dər-'stāt-mənt	restrained statement in mocking contrast to what is warranted by the facts

Stella's remark that she was "slightly bruised" in the crash is an understatement. *She suffered two broken ribs.*

C. Building Additional *Onym* Words

Each incomplete word below consists of the root *onym*, meaning "word" or "name," plus an additional root. Select that additional root from the following list, and insert it as in 1, below.

ADDITIONAL ROOTS	MEANINGS
a *or* an	not *or* without
anti *or* ant	against *or* opposite
crypto *or* crypt	secret
epi *or* ep	for, upon
hetero *or* heter	different
homo *or* hom	same
patri *or* patr	father
poly	many
pseudo *or* pseud	false
syn	with *or* like

1. "Rich and "wealth" are _____syn____ **onym**s.
2. To conceal her identity in an age hostile to women authors, Charlotte Brontë wrote under the _____**onym** Currer Bell.

3. "Pale" and "pail" are _____**onym**s.

4. "Love" and "hate" are _____**onym**s.

5. Someone just called but would not give his name. Have you ever received _____**onym**ous phone calls?

6. Top-secret projects are code-named. For example, the test of the first atomic bomb in the New Mexico desert was assigned the _____**onym** "Trinity."

7. _____**onym**ics are names derived from the name of a father or paternal ancestor, like McDougal (son of Dougal), Fitzpatrick (son of Patrick), and Isaacson (son of Isaac).

8. _____**onym**s are words that have exactly the same spelling but different pronunciations and meanings, like *row* (to propel a boat by means of oars) and *row* (a noisy quarrel).

9. Zeus, the chief god of the Greeks, was _____**onym**ous: he had many names.

10. Andrew Jackson is the person for whom Jacksonville, Florida, is named, and Daniel Boone is the _____**onym** of Boonesboro, Kentucky.

D. Thinking with Your New Words

Read all of the following statements. Then answer each question below.

PART ONE

Statements

About all you could get from Paul was "yes," "no," and "maybe." He was not good at conversation.

In 1642, Abel Tasman, a Dutch navigator, discovered the island of Tasmania off the southeastern coast of Australia.

Mona advised replacing "first and foremost," an overused expression, but Brian could not see what was wrong with it.

The letter Carole received ended as follows:

Your loving enemy,
Charlotte

The pollution was heavy in the factory district. Andy called it smoke, Ruth thought it was fog, but their brother Alex said it was smog.

Reginald's angry denunciation of Violet's proposal to amend his resolution rallied considerable support to her side.

Cliff could have saved effort, time, and space by writing UNESCO, but he preferred "United National Educational, Scientific, and Cultural Organization."

The short-story writer O. Henry was William Sydney Porter in private life.

When Kathy said she liked art, Vincent asked what she meant. She replied by leading him to the reproductions of Picasso's "Guernica" and "The Three Musicians," which hung in her den.

Ann protested that we would be an hour late for the party, but Joyce said, "Better late than never."

Frank scolded Bernice for saying we stole out of the meeting. The fact is we made no effort to conceal our departure.

On returning from our lavish seven-course dinner, Gretta explained to our friends that she and I had stopped at the diner for a bite.

Questions

1. Who used an oxymoron? _____
2. Who had a pseudonym? _____
3. Who used a maxim? _____
4. Who spurned an acronym? _____
5. Who was inarticulate? _____
6. Who used a blend? _____
7. Who clung to a cliché? _____
8. Who became an eponym? _____
9. Who used a pejorative
   expression? _____
10. Who employed irony? _____
11. Who made an abstract term
    concrete? _____
12. Who unleashed a diatribe? _____

PART TWO

Statements

When the Smiths told Ed they are tired of quarreling over property lines and they want peace, he remarked to me that what they probably want is a "piece" of his property.

Uncle Ned called from Burlington to say that fresh snow has blanketed the town.

And Aunt Emma added that the wind is cutting like a knife.

Jim Burke's aliases included James Barclay and Ronald Matthewson.

Arthur has promised to give up the bottle, but Esther doubts he will keep his word.

Napoleon is reputed to have said, "Able was I ere I saw Elba." If you read that sentence backward, it says the same thing.

After his conquest of the English at the Battle of Hastings in 1066, the Norman Duke William was known as William the Conqueror.

Taking the customer's order, Dolores called in to the chef, "BLT to go; hold the mayo."

Henry was careless with his use of "always" and "never." As a result he made some misleading assertions.

The code name Ariel assigned to Parker was known only to two other agents.

When Swift poked fun at the cruel and greedy rulers of the imaginary kingdoms of Lilliput and Blefuscu, he was really ridiculing the English and French monarchs of his time.

Agatha contributed the funds for the new wing with the stipulation that her name should not be disclosed.

With the dollar losing value almost daily in inflationary times, Wesley scoffed at the proverb about "saving for a rainy day," and spent every penny as fast as he earned it.

Questions

13. Who was glib?   _____
14. Who used argot?   _____
15. Who requested anonymity?   _____
16. Who had a cryptonym?   _____
17. Who ignored a shibboleth?   _____
18. Who used a simile?   _____
19. Who earned an epithet?   _____
20. Who used a pun?   _____
21. Who used a metaphor?   _____
22. Who was credited with a
    palindrome?   _____
23. Who used satire?   _____
24. Who was known by a
    patronymic?   _____
25. Who used metonymy?   _____

E. Analogies

Write the *letter* of the pair of words related to each other in the same way as the words in the capitalized pair.

1. CARTOON : EXAGGERATION
a. diatribe : antipathy   *d.* title : rank
b. violinist : bow   *e.* cache : valuables
c. pun : homonyms   **Answer** _____

2. AMNESIA : MEMORY
a. humiliation : face   *d.* abyss : depth
b. anesthesia : relief   *e.* amnesty : prosecution
c. anonymity : privacy   **Answer** _____

3. MOTEL : BLEND
a. hotel : transient   *d.* garage : vehicle
b. madam : palindrome   *e.* proverb : maxim
c. cook : mixer   **Answer** _____

4. CLICHÉ : FRESHNESS
a. monologue : boredom   *d.* metaphor : comparison
b. anemia : pallor   *e.* shibboleth : credibility
c. glibness : misinformation   **Answer** _____

5. MEDICATION : RECOVERY

a. satire : reform
b. anodyne : suffering
c. biopsy : uncertainty
d. acronym : space
e. antipyretic : fever

Answer _____

6. CHATTERBOX : LOGORRHEA

a. superpatriot : chauvinism
b. tyro : know-how
c. bibliophobe : library
d. pollyanna : pessimism
e. prognosticator : future

Answer _____

7. UNDERSTATEMENT : HYPERBOLE

a. cerebrum : brain
b. exodus : influx
c. reclusiveness : seclusion
d. reincarnation : rebirth
e. amnesty : offense

Answer _____

8. REDUNDANT : CONCISENESS

a. amorphous : shape
b. cryptic : mystery
c. insidious : treachery
d. mendacious : deceit
e. enterprising : initiative

Answer _____

9. EUPHEMISM : UNPLEASANTNESS

a. diatribe : hostility
b. faux pas : tact
c. repetition : boredom
d. presentiment : foreboding
e. lubrication : friction

Answer _____

Allusions

Allusions are indirect references to real or fictional persons, places, or events. Here are two examples:

A *donnybrook* was sparked by the close decision at home plate.

Allusion: *donnybrook*
Source: *Donnybrook Fair,* dating from 1204, was held annually in Donnybrook, a suburb of Dublin, Ireland. Notorious for its brawling and rowdiness, the fair was discontinued in 1855.
Meaning: A *donnybrook* is an "uproarious brawl" or "free-for-all."

The candidate charges that the *Lilliputians* controlling the legislature are incapable of planning for the future.

Allusion: *Lilliputians*
Source: *Lilliput,* in Jonathan Swift's *Gulliver's Travels,* is an imaginary island, whose inhabitants are no more than six inches tall.
Meaning: *Lilliputians* are "petty, insignificant, narrow-minded people."

A. Preview

Use each of the following allusions no more than once in completing the sentences below.

Achilles' heel	carry coals to	cry wolf
Armageddon	Newcastle	dog in the manger
bell the cat	Catch-22	fifth column
between Scylla	crocodile tears	fourth estate
and Charybdis	cross the Rubicon	Freudian slip

Hobson's Choice	last straw	Pandora's box
hoist with one's	Midas touch	Parkinson's law
own petard	Murphy's law	Pyrrhic victory
juggernaut	open sesame	sour grapes

1. Few of my investments are doing well, but every one of hers shows a handsome profit. She has the
   _____.

2. The expressions of regret at the party for the retiring executive were _____. The staff was glad to be rid of him.

3. I was given _____: I could take the room offered, or none at all.

4. Most people hope nuclear war can be avoided, but some are sure _____ is at hand.

5. Her uncle and cousins are reporters, and she, too, hopes to join the _____.

6. A professional degree is regarded by many as the _____ to financial security.

7. The only department in which our team is vulnerable is relief pitching. It is our _____.

8. Despite _____, the clerical staff completed its work by 3:30, though they could easily have stretched it out to 5 P.M.

9. We have all the ingredients for a feast at our house, so please bring no food. Why _____?

10. When she didn't get the promotion, she said it would really have been a demotion for her. Is this the truth, or just _____?

11. Why not let one of the standees sit in the vacant seat next to you? Surely you don't want to be a(n) _____.

12. After sixteen consecutive victories, the Red Sox _____ ground to a halt as the Rovers scored twice in the bottom of the ninth for a 2–1 triumph.

13. The mayor's advisers opposed a public hearing, warning that it was a(n) _____, and the mayor later regretted that he had not listened to them.

14. The cook's fiery temper kept the sailors from complaining to him about the food. Not one of them dared to _____.

15. I had a flat tire on the way to work, and when I opened the trunk I found that my spare, too, was flat. The only explanation for such a coincidence is _____.

16. In accepting the Oscar, she made a(n) _____: instead of saying "I couldn't have done it all without you," she said "I could have done without all of you."

17. We won the game but lost our star quarterback for the rest of the season; it was a(n) _____.

18. The Nazis coordinated their surprise attack with acts of sabotage by a well-organized _____, so there was little effective resistance.

19. The Budget Fitting Room was closed, so we went to the other fitting room, where a sign said: "Closed. Use Budget Fitting Room." It was _____.

20. For several agonizing minutes before the helicopter rescue, the people trapped on the roof were _____: they could either leap or be devoured by the flames.

21. The probationer's tenth lateness was the _____; the next day the employer sent him a dismissal notice.

22. The signers of the Declaration of Independence knew they would be hanged if caught, but they nevertheless decided to _____.

23. The arsonist trapped by the flames had never expected that he might some day be _____.

24. Those who _____ may find that people will not come to their aid when they may truly be in trouble.

B. Details About the Allusions

ALLUSION	MEANING
Achilles' heel ə-ˌki-lēz	vulnerable spot or weak point (Thetis dipped her son Achilles in the river Styx, making him invulnerable, except in the heel by which she held on to him. That is the spot where he was mortally wounded by an arrow.)

The only department in which our team is vulnerable is relief pitching. It is our Achilles' heel.

Armageddon ˌär-mə-ˈge-dᵊn	vast, decisive battle (The Bible prophesies that the final battle between the forces of good and evil will take place before the end of the world at a place called Armageddon.)

Most people hope nuclear war can be averted, but some are sure Armageddon *is at hand.*

bell the cat	do a daring, risky deed for the sake of others (A wise mouse, according to a fable, suggested that a bell be hung around the cat's neck to warn of its approach, but none of the mice had the courage to do it.)

The cook's fiery temper kept the sailors from complaining to him about the food. Not one of them dared to bell the cat.

ALLUSION	**MEANING**
between Scylla and Charybdis 'si-lə kə-'rib-dəs	between two equally difficult alternatives, neither of which can be avoided without incurring the other (In Homer's *Odyssey*, Odysseus has to guide his ship between Scylla, a man-eating monster on the Italian side of the narrow Strait of Messina, and Charybdis, a whirlpool on the Sicilian side.)

For several agonizing minutes before the helicopter rescue, the people trapped on the roof were between Scylla and Charybdis: *they could either leap or be devoured by the flames.*

carry coals to Newcastle	take something to a place where it is plentiful and not needed; do something superfluous (Newcastle, an English seaport, is a coal center.)

We have all the ingredients for a feast at our house, so please bring no food. Why carry coals to Newcastle?

Catch-22	paradox (contradiction) in an order or regulation that makes people victims of its provisions, regardless of what they do (*Catch-22*, a novel by Joseph Heller, satirizes victimizing situations in the military.)

The Budget Fitting Room was closed, so we went to the other fitting room, where a sign said: "Closed. Use Budget Fitting Room." It was a Catch-22 *situation.*

ALLUSION	MEANING
crocodile tears 'krä-kə-,dīl	false tears; insincere show of grief (It used to be believed that crocodiles shed tears while devouring their victims.)

The expressions of regret at the party for the retiring executive were crocodile tears. *The staff was glad to be rid of him.*

cross the Rubicon 'rü-bi-'kän	take a decisive, irrevocable step (In 49 B.C., Caesar's enemies ordered him to return from his conquests without his army. Caesar knew that to cross the Rubicon River with his army would be to invade Roman soil and start a civil war—a step from which there was no going back, but he took that gamble.)

The Founding Fathers crossed the Rubicon *when they signed the Declaration of Independence.*

cry wolf	give alarm without occasion; give a false alarm (This is an allusion to the fable in which a shepherd boy cries the alarm "wolf" as a joke.)

Those who cry wolf *may find that people will not come to their aid when they may truly be in trouble.*

dog in the manger 'măn-jər	person who prevents others from using something he or she cannot use and does not need (A dog in one of Aesop's fables positioned himself in a manger [feed box for cattle] and prevented an ox from eating hay.)

Why not let one of the standees sit in the vacant seat next to you? Surely you don't want to be a dog in the manger.

ALLUSION	MEANING
fifth column	subversive group of civilians working secretly within their own country to turn it over to an invading enemy (General Mola, advancing on Madrid with four columns in 1936, said that he would be aided by a fifth column of sympathizers within the city.)

The Nazis coordinated their surprise attack with acts of sabotage by a well-organized fifth column, *so there was little effective resistance.*

| **fourth estate** | reporters; the press; journalism (Edmund Burke is alleged to have so designated the Reporters' Gallery. The traditional three estates [classes] were the clergy, the nobility, and the commons.) |

Her uncle and cousins are reporters, and she, too, hopes to join the fourth estate.

| **Freudian slip** 'fròi-dē-ən | slip of the tongue by which it is thought a person unintentionally reveals his or her true feelings |

In accepting the Oscar, she made a Freudian slip: *instead of saying "I couldn't have done it all without you," she said "I could have done without all of you."*

| **Hobson's choice** | choice of taking what is offered or nothing at all (Thomas Hobson, who ran a horse rental in the seventeenth century, required each customer to take the horse nearest the stable door.) |

I was given Hobson's choice: *I could take the room offered, or none at all.*

ALLUSION	MEANING
hoist with one's own petard pǝ-'tärd	blown up with one's own bomb; victimized by one's own schemes (Rosenkrantz and Guildenstern, Hamlet's false friends, accompany him to England with sealed instructions that he is to be murdered there, but Hamlet secretly alters the instructions so that they, not he, meet that fate. They are hoist with their own petard.)

The arsonist trapped in the flames had never expected that he might some day be hoist with his own petard.

juggernaut 'jǝ-gǝr-ˌnȯt	massive, irresistible force crushing everything in its path (*Juggernaut* is a name of the Hindu god Vishnu, and hence of his idol and the huge car on which it is annually hauled in a procession. Worshipers are alleged to have thrown themselves under its wheels to be crushed.)

After sixteen consecutive victories the Red Sox juggernaut *ground to a halt as the Rovers scored twice in the bottom of the ninth for a 2–1 triumph.*

last straw	final test of patience or endurance (The fabled last straw, when added, broke the camel's back because the animal had already been loaded to the limit.)

The probationer's tenth lateness was the last straw; *the next day the employer sent him a dismissal notice.*

ALLUSION	**MEANING**
Midas touch 'mī-dəs	talent for making money in any enterprise one engages in (Midas, mythical king of Phrygia, had the power of turning everything he touched into gold.)

Few of my investments are doing well, but every one of hers shows a handsome profit. She has the Midas touch.

| **Murphy's Law** | satirical maxim stating that if anything can go wrong, it will |

I had a flat tire on the way to work, and when I opened the trunk I found that my spare, too, was flat. Clearly, I was a victim of Murphy's Law.

| **open sesame**
'se-sə-mē | any means or formula that works like magic to help one achieve a desired end ("Open sesame" are the magic words that opened the door of the robbers' den in *Ali Baba and the Forty Thieves*.) |

A professional degree is regarded by many as the open sesame *to financial security.*

| **Pandora's box**
pan-'dōr-əz | source of extensive unforeseen troubles (Beautiful Pandora, the first mortal woman according to Greek mythology, received a box she was forbidden to open, but she did, releasing all the ills that have since plagued the world.) |

The mayor's advisers opposed a public hearing, warning that it could be a Pandora's box, *and the mayor later regretted that he had not listened to them.*

ALLUSION	MEANING
Parkinson's Law	satirical maxim about the lack of productivity, stating that work expands to fill the time available for its completion; also, that the number of subordinates increases regardless of the amount of work produced (The above are observations by the British economist C. Northcote Parkinson.)

Despite Parkinson's Law, *the clerical staff completed its work by 3:30, though they easily could have stretched it out to 5 P.M.*

| **Pyrrhic victory** 'pir-ik | victory achieved at ruinous cost (Pyrrhus, king of Epirus, sustained unacceptably high losses in defeating the Romans at Asculum in 279 B.C.) |

We won the game but lost our star quarterback for the rest of the season; it was a Pyrrhic *victory.*

| **sour grapes** | disparagement of something that one does not or cannot have (A fox in one of Aesop's fables, frustrated in his efforts to reach some grapes, tried to save face by saying they were sour.) |

When she didn't get the promotion, she said it would really have been a demotion for her. Is this the truth, or just sour grapes?

C. Thinking with Your New Allusions

Read all of the following statements. Then answer each question below.

PART ONE

Statements

If Gregory remained at his barren outpost, he might starve before help arrived. If he left to hunt, he might freeze to death before finding game.

Of course we thanked Chris for the bagful of homegrown tomatoes, but the truth is that if there was anything we didn't need, it was tomatoes. We had twenty plants of our own.

The Citizens' Advisory Committee that Liu had voluntarily instituted to improve relations with the community became a complaint bureau that threatened his political career.

Fortunately, Marcus dealt tactfully with the principal antagonists, or the meeting would have ended in a riot.

Lila was pleased that Jeffrey, a chainsmoker, was being transferred out of her office, but she told him she would miss him.

Lasker's neighbor sued him for $100,000, and would probably have settled out of court for about $10,000. Lasker fought the case and won, but spent $34,000 in legal fees.

Karim had to take the copy with the slightly worn cover, as it was the only one on the shelf and the bookseller refused to give him the one in the window.

The Russian counteroffensive at Stalingrad, led by General Zhukov, destroyed the myth of Nazi invincibility and snapped Hitler's string of military successes.

Besides writing fiction, Jack London was a seaman, a gold prospector, and a war correspondent.

Suleiman started with nothing and amassed a small fortune in fourteen months.

Questions

1. Who won a Pyrrhic victory? _____
2. Who shed crocodile tears? _____
3. Who belonged to the fourth estate? _____
4. Who opened a Pandora's box? _____
5. Who prevented a donnybrook? _____
6. Who was between Scylla and Charybdis? _____
7. Who halted a juggernaut? _____
8. Who carried coals to Newcastle? _____
9. Who had the Midas touch? _____
10. Who took Hobson's choice? _____

Part Two

Statements

Ruth's credit card got her courteous and preferred treatment at car rentals, shops, motels, and restaurants.

A scout for fourteen years, Hernandez had a talent for noting the techniques of rival ball clubs and the strengths and weaknesses of their players.

Cheri parked the car in such a way that the adjacent parking place could not be used by another driver. I urged her to repark, as the lot was filling, but she said she liked to have room.

Worried that the application hadn't come, Myron made a phone call and was told that it was "in the mail." It came on the last day for filing. He completed it and took it to the Commission in person, but the staff had left—it wasn't even 3 P.M.—so he slipped it under the door. When it was rejected and he complained, he was told no applications could be received after the deadline.

When Bruce, whom Pamela secretly dislikes, said he would not be at the meeting, Pamela remarked that she was "*heartily* sorry." Later she regretted not having said "*very* sorry," as "heartily" was an inadvertent clue to her true feeling.

After Dorothy was rejected by the school of her first choice, she told friends she had heard that its faculty was overrated.

Alarmed by the burdensome assignments, the students wanted to petition the instructor for relief. Darryl was proposed as spokesperson, but he declined, and so did others who were asked. Finally, Connie agreed to represent us, if I would accompany her.

Irma ran her bureau with one assistant, though she was authorized to hire up to four. The other director thought she was mad.

In Norway, Quisling, a former defense minister, organized a fascist party that facilitated Hitler's takeover of the country.

The vacuum cleaner was in a sealed carton and had been pretested at the factory. At Martha's request, it was unpacked and checked once more by the dealer. When she plugged it in at home, it would not start.

Questions

11. Who ignored Parkinson's Law? _____
12. Who had an eye for an Achilles' heel? _____
13. Who was a fifth columnist? _____
14. Who made a sour grapes remark? _____
15. Who had an open sesame? _____
16. Who was a dog in the manger? _____
17. Who was a Catch-22 victim? _____
18. Who made a Freudian slip? _____
19. Who refused to bell the cat? _____
20. Who apparently ran afoul of Murphy's Law? _____

D. Using Fewer Words

Replace the italicized words with an allusion discussed in this chapter.

1. I am not good at *putting on a false show of grief.* _____
2. The witness was *faced with two difficult alternatives, neither of which he could avoid without subjecting himself to the other.* _____

3. There were 48,000 Union and Confederate casualties in the *vast, decisive battle* at Gettysburg. _____

4. We have a very wide selection. You do not have to take *what is offered or nothing at all.* _____

5. My brother purposely extends his call when he sees me waiting for the phone. It is hard to live with a *person who prevents others from using what he does not need.* _____

6. Whenever I invest, I lose. I do not have the *talent for making money.* _____

7. In a democracy, the *members of the press* must have access to information. _____

8. Most of us are *petty, insignificant people* in comparison with such intellectual giants as Newton and Einstein. _____

9. Our excessive dependence on foreign oil is an alarming *area of weakness and vulnerability.* _____

10. Why are you buying Charley another set of tools? He already has a whole workshop full of them. You should not *do something that is totally superfluous.* _____

E. Discussion with Your New Vocabulary

Answer each of the following in a brief paragraph.

1. Despite your letter of protest to the company, its computer keeps dunning you for a bill already paid. What further steps would you take to resolve this Catch-22 predicament?

_____

_____

2. When, if ever, is it justifiable for a democracy to incarcerate potential fifth columnists? Explain.

3. As a public official, you have just called a press conference. You would like to bar a particularly captious member of the fourth estate from that conference. Should you do so? Why, or why not?

4. Give an example of someone's crossing or failing to cross the Rubicon.

5. Give an example of someone's being hoist with his or her own petard.

New Words from Commonsense Clues in the Context

The term "commonsense clue," as used in this book, is a context clue *other than an antonym or synonym* that helps us get the meaning of an unfamiliar word.

Question: What is the meaning of *gelid* in the following sentence?

> Minutes after the January plane crash into the Potomac, a passerby rescued a passenger from its *gelid* waters.

Procedure: Using common sense, we ask ourselves what the waters of the Potomac River would be like in January.
Answer: *Gelid* means "extremely cold" or "icy."

Question: What does *firmament* mean in the following?

> The moon at night is the brightest object in the *firmament*.

Answer: *Firmament* obviously means "heavens" or "sky."

Let us now consider additional possibly unfamiliar words, like *gelid* and *firmament,* in contexts containing commonsense clues.

A. Preview

Define the italicized words below with the help of the commonsense clues in the context.

1. By *extrapolating* from the current rate of population growth, we can tell the probable date by which the world's population will have doubled.

   Extrapolating means _____.

2. Dentists advise brushing your teeth after consuming sweets because sugar is *cariogenic.*

   Cariogenic means _____.

3. The fire started by accident. It was not the work of an *incendiary.*

   An *incendiary* is _____.

4. Two of the guests had antagonistic political views, so we spent a good part of the evening listening to *polemics.*

   Polemics are _____.

5. At the bell, the *pugilists* moved to the center of the ring and touched gloves.

   Pugilists are _____.

6. When a foreign nation took Americans hostage and refused to set them free, the *hawks* in Congress favored a military response.

   Hawks are _____.

7. Hector and Gladys are good friends, but it is unlikely that they will marry because he is a *misogamist.*

   A *misogamist* is _____.

8. The new employee failed to get enough sleep not because he was an *insomniac,* but because he had a second job.

   An *insomniac* is _____.

9. Adam's *telegenic* personality would make him an ideal host for a TV talk show.

   Telegenic means _____.

10. Pollution is *ubiquitous:* there seems to be no place on earth that is free of it.

    Ubiquitous means _____.

11. Most charities report a drop in the *eleemosynary* spirit. Contributions are down more than 20 percent.

    Eleemosynary means _____.

12. If you *gorge* yourselves on the appetizers, you will have no room for the rest of the meal.

    Gorge means _____.

13. I became suspicious when I saw the list again. A new name had been *interpolated*, and I was no longer fourth but fifth.

    Interpolated means _____.

14. The firm is still in business. Its "Going-out-of-Business Sale" last year was just promotional *hype*.

    Hype means _____.

15. April's record thirteen-inch *precipitation* has filled our reservoirs.

    Precipitation means _____.

16. You will *scorch* the material if your iron is too hot.

    Scorch means _____.

17. On hearing that we might be snowed in, I checked the *comestibles* in the refrigerator, breadbox, and pantry.

    Comestibles are _____.

18. Ann has not connected with the ball today, and it would *mortify* her to strike out again in full view of this crowd.

    Mortify means _____.

19. The pain was severe for the first minute or two and then, fortunately, began to *subside*.

    Subside means _____.

20. Since I had made the announcement twice, I saw no need for further *iteration*.

    Iteration means _____.

B. Details About the New Words

WORD	MEANING
cariogenic *adj* ˌka-rē-ə-'je-nik	causing the development of *caries* (tooth decay)

    Dentists advise brushing your teeth after consuming sweets because sugar is cariogenic.

WORD	MEANING
comestibles *n pl* kə-'mes-tə-bəlz	(literally, things that can be eaten up) edibles; food

On hearing that we might be snowed in, I checked the comestibles *in the refrigerator, breadbox, and pantry.*

eleemosynary *adj* ‚e-li-'mä-sᵊn-‚er-ē	of, relating to, or supported by alms; charitable; philanthropic

Most charities report a drop in the eleemosynary *spirit. Contributions are down more than 20 percent.*

extrapolate *v* ik-'stra-pə-‚lāt	estimate or infer unknown information by extending or projecting known information

By extrapolating *from the current rate of population growth, we can tell the probable date by which the world's population will have doubled.*

gorge *v* 'gȯrj	stuff (oneself); eat greedily

If you gorge *yourselves on the appetizers, you will have no room left for the rest of the meal.*

hawk *n* 'hȯk	person who advocates immediate firm action, including the use of force, to resolve international crises

When a foreign nation took Americans hostage and refused to set them free, the hawks *in Congress favored a military response.*

hype *n* 'hīp	exaggerated claims, especially in advertising; anything intended to mislead

The firm is still in business. Its "Going-out-of-Business Sale" last year was just promotional hype.

incendiary *n* in-'sen-dē-‚er-ē	person who maliciously sets fire to dwellings or other property; arsonist

The fire started by accident. It was not the work of an incendiary.

WORD	MEANING

insomniac *n*
in-'säm-nē-,ak

person suffering from *insomnia* (prolonged and abnormal inability to obtain sufficient sleep)

The new employee failed to get enough sleep not because he was an insomniac, *but because he had a second job.*

---

interpolate *v*
in-'tər-pə-,lāt

insert between other parts or things; introduce

I became suspicious when I saw the list again. A new name had been interpolated, *and I was no longer fourth but fifth.*

---

iteration *n*
,i-tə-'rā-shən

repetition; something *iterated* (repeated)

Since I had made the announcement twice, I saw no need for further iteration.

---

misogamist *n*
mi-'sä-gə-mist

person who hates marriage

Hector and Gladys are good friends, but it is unlikely that they will marry because he is a misogamist.

---

mortify *v*
'mor-tə-,fī

humiliate; subject to shame

Ann has not connected with the ball today, and it would mortify her to strike out again in full view of this crowd.

---

polemic *n*
pə-'le-mik

(from a Greek word meaning "war") attack on or refutation of another's opinions; controversial discussion

Two of the guests had antagonistic political views, so we spent a good part of the evening listening to polemics.

---

precipitation *n*
pri-,si-pə-'tā-shən

amount of rain, snow, sleet, hail, etc., falling on an area in a specified period

April's record thirteen-inch precipitation *has filled our reservoirs.*

WORD	MEANING

pugilist *n*
'pyü-jə-ləst

prizefighter; professional boxer

At the bell, the pugilists *moved to the center of the ring and touched gloves.*

---

scorch *v*
'skȯrch

burn slightly, discoloring the surface

You will scorch *the material if your iron is too hot.*

---

subside *v*
səb-'sīd

become less intense; abate; wane

The pain was severe for the first minute or two and then, fortunately, began to subside.

---

telegenic *adj*
,te-lə-'je-nik

making or likely to make a pleasing appearance on television; videogenic

Adam's telegenic *personality would make him an ideal host for a TV talk show.*

---

ubiquitous *adj*
yú-'bi-kwə-təs

existing or seeming to exist everywhere at the same time; omnipresent

Pollution is ubiquitous: *there seems to be no place on earth that is free of it.*

C. Building Additional *Genic* Words

The ending *-genic*, of Greek origin, appears in a growing number of scientific, medical, and technical words. Among its meanings are the following:

"Producing," "inducing," or "causing"
    Chimney soot and the hydrocarbons in cigarette smoke are *carcinogenic* (cancer-producing).

"Produced by" or "originating in"
    His illness had physical causes. It was not *psychogenic* (produced by mental factors).

"Suitable for production or reproduction" in photography, radio, TV, etc.

You are *photogenic* (suitable as a subject for photography; likely to look good in a photo).

Complete the spelling of each *-genic* word below by adding the correct root from the following list. Use no root more than once.

ROOT	MEANING	ROOT	MEANING
aero	air *or* gas	immuno	immunity
chromo	color	patho	suffering *or*
cryo	cold		disease
crypto	hidden *or*	pyo	pus
	invisible	pyro	fire *or* fever
gastro	stomach	sapro	rotten
hallucino	hallucination	socio	society
hepato	liver	thermo	heat
iatro	physician		

1. Not all bacteria cause disease; some are non_____genic.
2. Dried smallpox virus is _____genic. It protects us against smallpox.
3. _____genic bacteria produce gas.
4. The _____genic (rot-producing) bacteria in a compost pile hasten decay.
5. _____genic bacteria produce color.
6. A(n) _____genic disorder is hard to treat because its causes are unknown.
7. _____genic anemia is caused by bleeding in the stomach.
8. A suggestible patient who misinterprets a physician's words during diagnosis may develop _____genic (physician-induced) symptoms.
9. Ice, dry ice, and liquid air are _____genic substances.
10. When infectious bacteria attack us, the _____genic substances they manufacture induce fever.
11. Staph bacteria are responsible for _____genic (pus-producing) infections, like abscesses and boils.
12. _____genic physiological processes produce heat in the body.

13. Escapists who try _____genic drugs are not always aware of the risks involved.

14. Poor housing and high unemployment are sometimes cited as evidence for the view that a good deal of crime is _____genic.

15. Jaundice is usually _____genic; that is, it is produced by a disorder of the liver.

D. Thinking with Your New Words

Read all of the following statements. Then answer each question below.

PART ONE

Statements

The inscription "Kilroy was here" was encountered on walls all over the world during and after World War II.

Bruce was able to control his weight and reduce the number of cavities by giving up chocolate, cake, and ice cream.

Natalie gave half of the proceeds of her garage sale to the Salvation Army.

Ramon was the arts-and-crafts instructor, George taught swimming, and Kaori was the cook.

The cause of Lady Macbeth's illness, according to her physician, was a diseased mind.

Henry Clay urged war with England and was instrumental in bringing about the War of 1812.

Sir Alexander Fleming discovered the antibiotic penicillin.

"We won! We won!" Debra shouted triumphantly.

Yvette won out over a score of applicants for a role in a TV commercial.

In 1952, Floyd Patterson won the Olympic middleweight championship.

Formerly a jazz fan, Donald now prefers classical music.

When she was Commissioner of Consumer Affairs,

Genevieve gave most of her attention to combatting fraud in the marketplace.

Questions

1. Who seemed ubiquitous? _____
2. Who was in charge of comestibles? _____
3. Who was apparently telegenic? _____
4. Who was a hawk? _____
5. Who used iteration? _____
6. Who had a psychogenic malady? _____
7. Who aided an eleemosynary cause? _____
8. Who renounced cariogenic edibles? _____
9. Who was a pugilist? _____
10. Whose enthusiasm subsided? _____
11. Who dealt pathogenic bacteria a deadly blow? _____
12. Who exposed hype? _____

PART TWO

Statements

Ab Snopes, one of William Faulkner's characters, was a notorious horse thief and barn burner.

Insisting that she does not take a good picture, May wanted Fred not to waste any of his film on her.

In retyping her report, Adele inserted two new sentences in paragraph seven.

Because of the many unhappy marriages he knew about, Gary vowed not to marry.

Brooks calculated he would reach Exit 20 by 7:30 P.M. if he could keep up his 55-mile-an-hour speed.

Joanne was embarrassed when her brother accused her, in the presence of her friends, of stealing his postage stamps.

Jeff, a mechanical engineer, had specialized in refrigeration and air conditioning.

Because of her past ineptness as an ironer, Celina is grateful for the availability of permanent-press garments.

For some time, Aunt Susan had been having difficulty falling asleep; she was awake most of the night.

Eight of the girls brought home-baked pies and cakes. Eileen sampled the cheesecake, but Alton consumed lots of everything.

In her report, Selma explained that the inhalation of asbestos particles as much as thirty years ago by asbestos workers has resulted in numerous malignancies.

When one of Commissioner Blake's projects was attacked in the press, he wrote a reply but thought it would be better not to mail it.

Clay cleared seven inches of snow from his driveway.

Questions

13. Who claimed not to be photogenic? _____
14. Who made an extrapolation? _____
15. Who was an insomniac? _____
16. Who was a scorcher? _____
17. Who discussed a carcinogenic substance? _____
18. Who dealt personally with precipitation? _____
19. Who avoided polemics? _____
20. Who was an incendiary? _____
21. Who made an interpolation? _____
22. Who was familiar with cryogenic materials? _____
23. Who did some gorging? _____
24. Who was mortified? _____
25. Who was a misogamist? _____

E. Analogies

Write the *letter* of the pair of words related to each other in the same way as the words in the capitalized pair.

1. POLEMICIST : WORDS
a. motorist : tolls
b. recidivist : relapses
c. scofflaw : summonses
d. pugilist : fists
e. campaigner : votes

Answer _____

2. HAWK : AGGRESSION
a. vulture : carrion
b. dove : conciliation
c. whale : extinction
d. ox : intelligence
e. woodchuck : hibernation

Answer _____

3. CAULIFLOWER : COMESTIBLE
a. spinach : iron
b. thirst : beverage
c. penicillin : antibiotic
d. utensil : saucepan
e. lilac : fragrance

Answer _____

4. SCORCH : BURN
a. gorge : eat
b. soak : rinse
c. shout : speak
d. love : like
e. tap : strike

Answer _____

5. LIQUID AIR : CRYOGENIC
a. fever : antipyretic
b. boil : pyogenic
c. pain : analgesic
d. surgery : anesthetic
e. ugliness : photogenic

Answer _____

Expressions Adopted from Other Languages

There is an old legend that when the Countess of Salisbury lost a garter while dancing with Edward III, the gallant king picked it up, fastened it on his own leg, and said, *"Honi soit qui mal y pense"* ("Shame to anyone who thinks evil of this"). So much for the legend.

It is a fact that Edward III founded the Most Noble Order of the Garter, England's highest order of knighthood, in 1348, and that the motto of this order has always been *Honi soit qui mal y pense.* Though the words are French, English has incorporated this expression into its vocabulary.

Note, by the way, that Edward III, King of England, spoke French. It was his language—his mother was the daughter of Philip IV, King of France. We must not forget that from the Norman-French Conquest of England in 1066 to the end of the fourteenth century, though the Anglo-Saxon inhabitants continued to speak English, they were ruled by French-speaking monarchs.

A. Details About Some New Expressions

EXPRESSION	SOURCE AND MEANING
Caveat emptor. 'ka-vē-,ät-'em(p)-tər	Latin: "Let the buyer beware." The buyer is at risk and the seller cannot be held respon- sible (except when there is a warranty).

EXPRESSION	SOURCE AND MEANING
Cherchez la femme. 'sher-ˌshā-là-ˌfàm	French: "Look for the woman." This is a suggestion that the key to a particular problem or mystery is a woman, and that she need only be found for the matter to be solved.
Cogito, ergo sum. 'kō-gi-ˌtō-er-gō-'sùm	Latin: "I think, therefore I exist." The fact that one thinks is proof that one exists. So wrote French philosopher René Descartes (1596–1650).
De gustibus non est disputandum. dā-'gùs-tə-ˌbùs-ˌnōn-ˌest-ˌdis-pù-'tän-ˌdùm (also **De gustibus**)	Latin: "There is no disputing about tastes."
E pluribus unum. ˌē-ˌplùr-ə-bəs'-(y)ü-nəm	Latin: "Out of many, one." Motto of the United States, one nation composed by the uniting of many states.
Eureka. yú-'rē-kə	Greek: "I have found (it)." This expression of triumph was allegedly made by Archimedes (287–212 B.C.) when he discovered a method for determining the purity of gold.
Gaudeamus igitur. ˌgaù-dē-ä-mús-'i-gi-ˌtùr (also **Gaudeamus**)	Latin: "Then let us be merry (while we are young)." Title of a medieval Latin student song of German origin.

EXPRESSION	SOURCE AND MEANING
Habeas corpus. 'hā-bē-əs-'kȯr-pəs	Latin: "You shall have the body (in court)." First two words of a writ issued by a court, requiring a person detained against his or her will to be brought before the court to determine the lawfulness of that detention. A writ of *habeas corpus* is a citizen's protection against illegal imprisonment.
Honi soit qui mal y pense. ȯ-nē-swȧ-kē-mȧl-ē-päns	French: "Shame to anyone who thinks ill of this," or "Evil to anyone who evil thinks."
Laissez-faire. ˌle-ˌsā-'far	French: "Let (people) do (as they choose)." (*a*) Policy of non-interference in the affairs of others; (*b*) theory that government should interfere as little as possible in economic affairs.
Mens sana in corpore sano. māns-'sä-nä-in-ˌkȯr-pȯ-re-'sä-nō	Latin: "A sound mind in a sound body." These words of the Roman poet Juvenal (A.D. 55?–127?) are often used to describe the ideal that education should strive for.
O tempora! O mores! ō-'tem-pȯ-rä-ō-'mō-ˌräs	Latin: "Oh the times! Oh the customs!" So spoke the Roman orator Cicero (106–43 B.C.) when he complained that the times had changed for the worse and the morals of people had degenerated.
Tempus fugit. ˌtem-pəs-'fü-git	Latin: "Time flies."

EXPRESSION	SOURCE AND MEANING
Tout comprendre, c'est tout pardonner. 'tü-kōn-pràⁿ-drə- se'tü-pȧ-dȯ-nā	French: "To understand all is to forgive all."
Verbum sat sapienti est. wer-bům-'sät- ˌsä-pē-'en-tē-ˌest (also **Verbum sat** or **Verbum sap**)	Latin: "A word to the wise is sufficient."

B. Using Your New Expressions

Write the most appropriate of the above expressions, but use each of them only once. See 1, below.

1. If Nick likes to chew and swallow apple seeds, don't criticize him for it.
   De gustibus non est disputandum. (*or* De gustibus.)

2. Just before the road begins to wind, you will see a sign with the word "Caution!"

3. Parents who are too strict with their children may be just as remiss as parents who follow a policy of total

4. I thought I still had plenty of time, but the clock showed the test was nearly over.

5. In some shops, the policy is "All sales final. No refunds. No returns." Therefore,

6. A starving person should not be sent to jail for having stolen a loaf of bread.

7. During the War Between the States (1861–65), the unity implied in the expression

   was temporarily broken.

8. None of us suspected why Ted was paying more attention to his personal appearance until someone suggested

"   "

9. Defenders of Michelangelo's *David* do not agree that the statue is bad art because of its nudity; they say

"   "

10. Waking from a nightmare, I think I am dead, but

"   "

comes to mind to persuade me I am mistaken.

11. When we who are young hear of the aches and illnesses of old age, one message comes through loud and clear:

"   "

12. If the suspect, who as yet has not been charged, is not released from detention, his attorney will apply for a writ of

_____

13. Those of us who had joined in the search for the missing earring were about ready to admit failure when Andrea shouted

_____

14. Increasing drug abuse, violence, homelessness, and poverty have many alarmed citizens exclaiming

"   "

15. Fortunate are those who have

_____

Review of Chapters 21–26

I. Choose your answers from the following list:

a	archy	crypto	phon	seism
alg	bio	genic	pnea	the
an	chromo	patho	pseudo	viv

1. "Government" is the meaning conveyed by _____.

2. The suffix _____ means "producing" or "produced by."

3. A(n) _____ word deals with something hidden or unknown.

4. "False" is the meaning conveyed by _____.

5. A word containing _____ has something to do with disease.

6. The prefix _____ or _____ means "not" or "without."

7. A(n) _____ word deals with color.

8. A word containing _____ or _____ has something to do with life or living.

9. A word containing _____ has something to do with pain.

10. A word containing _____ has something to do with God or gods.

11. _____ology is the science that deals with earthquakes.

12. The medical term for labored or difficult respiration is dys_____.

13. Eu_____ious sounds are pleasing to the ear.

II. For each italicized word or expression in the sentences below, enter *two* synonyms from the following list as in 1, below.

abate	edibles	proverb	superfluous
abnormality	food	reiteration	surplus
adage	irregularity	repetition	talkativeness
charitable	journalism	reporters	vague
disparaging	philanthropic	shapeless	wane
downgrading	prolixity	superficial	

1. "Look before you leap" is a familiar *maxim.*
   <u>adage   proverb</u>

2. If your binoculars are out of focus, the object you are viewing will appear *amorphous.*
   _____

3. The strike created a shortage of *comestibles.*
   _____

4. At first it may be difficult to tell whether a speaker is well informed or just *glib.*
   _____

5. Ordinary, everyday happenings are not a principal concern of *the fourth estate.*
   _____

6. We can do without the *iteration.*
   _____

7. A three-legged chicken would be a(n) *anomaly.*
   _____

8. We waited for the force of the storm to *subside.*
   _____

9. Obviously, the guest was embarrassed by your *pejorative* remarks.
   _____

10. What, if anything, can you set aside for *eleemosynary* purposes?
    _____

11. Jack is known for *logorrhea;* he monopolizes conversations.
    _____

12. Did you remove all *redundant* words from your composition?
    _____

III. Complete each sentence below by inserting the most appropriate allusion or expression from the following list:

Achilles' heel	between Scylla and Charybdis
Armageddon	carry coals to Newcastle

dog in the manger   last straw
Eureka   Midas touch
habeas corpus   open sesame
Hobson's choice   Pandora's box
hoist with one's own petard   Pyrrhic victory
laissez-faire

1. The company is vulnerable because it has no understudies for its key managerial posts. What is it going to do about this _____
   _____?

2. The only potatoes on the menu were French fries, though I would have preferred a baked potato or even mashed potatoes; so I took _____
   _____

3. If the President signs the bill, he will incur the wrath of farmers; if he vetoes it, he will infuriate consumers. He is
   _____

4. It would have been cheaper to pay the fine. I succeeded in getting it revoked, but at such cost in time and money that I scored a(n) _____

5. I have lost money in every investment I have ever made. Evidently I do not have the _____
   _____

6. Some of the scientists who helped to develop nuclear weapons came to fear that their work might lead to _____
   _____

7. Our customers keep returning because we treat them well. Courteous service has been the _____
   _____
   of our success.

8. If the hotel provides towels, why do you bring your own? It is useless to _____
   _____.

9. Others are waiting to use this reference book, so if you have finished with it, relinquish it. Do not be a(n) _____
   _____

10. Making a special exception for one person is like opening a(n) _____
    _____

11. Dr. Grimesby Roylott, in Arthur Conan Doyle's "The Adventure of the Speckled Band," was _____

_____.
He tried to murder his stepdaughter with the bite of a poisonous snake, but it bit him instead.

12. We put up with Ron's practical jokes until he interrupted an important meeting by squirting us with a water gun; that was the _____
_____

13. A policy of _____
_____ in
the disposal of toxic wastes could lead to very serious consequences.

14. I heard you cry "_____
_____ !"
Tell me what you discovered.

15. _____
_____
protects Americans against illegal imprisonment.

IV. Complete the spelling of the word hinted at. Each blank stands for one missing letter.

1. Our reservoirs are overflowing; we do not need more
   pre __ __ pitation.
2. What good is a spokesperson who is not ar __ __ culate?
3. __ __ robic exercise conditions the heart and lungs.
4. "Delmarva" is a(n) __ __ end of *Delaware, Maryland,* and
   Virginia.
5. Without __ __ esthesia, most operations would be unbearably painful.
6. To update my report, I had to in __ __ rpolate two sentences between my opening and second paragraphs.
7. UNICEF is an a __ __ onym for United Nations International Children's Emergency Fund.
8. Reduced consumption of __ __ riogenic foods leads to fewer cavities.
9. "Madam" is a pa __ __ ndrome; it reads the same forward and backward.
10. __ __ emia is a red-blood cell deficiency.
11. Toxic wastes are bio __ __ dal.
12. When in London, I asked an American who lives there how it feels to be an ex __ __ triate.
13. "Painful joy" is an o __ __ moron.

14. Before stalling in Russia, the Napoleonic __ __ ggernaut had rolled through country after country.

15. Rose was opposed to my views, and when she got the floor I knew I would be the target of a(n) __ __ lemic.

16. Long John Silver liked to describe himself as a gentleman of fortune, a euph __ mism for "pirate."

17. People suffering from ab __ lia are unable to make decisions or to act.

18. Lice are __ pterous, but mosquitoes have wings.

V. Two words have been omitted from each sentence below. Find those words in the following list, and insert them.

abyss	deception	omnipresent	solitary
argot	denunciation	platitude	stuff
arsonist	diatribe	prizefighter	tangible
chasm	humiliate	pugilist	telegenic
cliché	hype	reclusive	ubiquitous
coeval	gorge	résumé	videogenic
concrete	incendiary	slang	vita
contemporary	mortify		

1. If you had lived at the time of Cleopatra, you would have been her _____ or
_____.

2. In describing the singer's debut on TV, the critics hailed her as "_____" and
"_____."

3. The celebrity encounters reporters wherever he goes; they are _____ or
_____.

4. What is a(n) _____ if not an overused expression or _____?

5. No one should enter professional boxing without carefully weighing the risks and rewards of being a(n) _____ or
_____.

6. Anyone who maliciously sets fire to a building or other property is considered a(n)
_____ or
_____.

7. You may be asked for a brief autobiographical sketch, so

    prepare a(n) _____ or
_____ for your interview.

8. Almost every trade and profession has a language peculiar to itself, its own _____ or
_____.

9. Animals, as a rule, do not eat greedily, so why do so many humans _____ and
_____ themselves?

10. Yesterday's bitter editorial on the Governor's policies is not the first _____ or
_____ he has had to reply to.

11. Some advertising is misleading. The consumer must be on guard against _____ and
_____ in the media.

12. The differences between the two are immeasurably deep. There is a(n) _____, a(n)
_____, between them.

13. Very few live apart from the rest of society because there is little joy in a(n) _____,
_____ life.

14. Unlike "imagination," which is abstract, "earring" has material existence; it is _____
and _____.

15. Publication of the names of the suspects will subject them to shame. It will _____ and
_____ them.

Answer Key

Chapter 1: Number Words

A. Preview (pages 2–3)

1. two
2. seven
3. twenty-seven
4. 1636
5. 1926, 1976
6. 1984
7. 1930, 1940, 1950, 1960
8. one
9. thirty-one
10. four
11. five
12. one
13. thirty
14. one
15. nineteen
16. two
17. two
18. five
19. five
20. fifteen

C. Thinking with Your New Words (pages 6–7)

1. May 15
2. 7
3. $3.75
4. twenty-one
5. none
6. 1776
7. five
8. 600
9. two
10. 2066

D. Concise Writing (page 7)

2. When is Nevada's sesquicentennial?
3. Are your neighbors octogenarians?
4. Donald's plurality was four.
5. Most septuagenarians are retired.

E. Analogies (pages 7–9)

4. *b* 5. *a* 6. *c* 7. *d* 8. *b*
9. *b* 10. *b*

Chapter 2: *Phobia, Mania,* and *Phile* Words

Preview (*pages 10–12*)

1. photophilic
2. xenophobia
3. dipsomaniac
4. audiophile
5. acrophobia
6. phobia
7. bibliomania
8. bibliophile
9. photophobic
10. agoraphobia
11. megalomania
12. claustrophobia
13. photophobia
14. monomania
15. pyromaniac
16. balletomania
17. mania
18. hemophiliac
19. kleptomaniac
20. bibliophobia

C. Building Additional Words (*pages 14–15*)

1. monomaniac
2. Sinophile
3. pyrophobia
4. Francophobia
5. Hispanophile
6. Anglophilic
7. megalomaniacs
8. Germanophore
9. kleptomania
10. xenophile
11. claustrophobic
12. dipsomania
13. Hemophilic
14. Russophobia
15. Italiophiles

D. Thinking with Your New Words (*pages 15–16*)

2. *b*   3. *a*   4. *c*   5. *c*   6. *b*
7. *c*   8. *b*   9. *c*   10. *b*

E. Analogies (*pages 16–17*)

3. *c*   4. *d*   5. *c*   6. *d*
7. *a*   8. *a*

Chapter 3: "One" and "Many" Words

A. Preview (*pages 18–19*)

1. polygamist
2. monosyllabic
3. multinational
4. monotonous
5. polymath
6. uniform
7. multimedia
8. polylateral
9. polytheistic
10. monograph
11. unilateral
12. monologue
13. Polytechnic
14. polyglot
15. unicameral
16. multifaceted
17. Unisex
18. monorail
19. unanimous
20. unique

C. Building Additional Words (*pages 22–23*)

1. unison
2. multimillionaire
3. polyclinic
4. monolingual
5. polychromatic
6. multiracial
7. Polygamy
8. unicycle
9. Monotheism
10. monocle

D. Thinking with Your New Words (*pages 23–24*)

2. Louise
3. Koji
4. Smith
5. Edna
6. Constantine
7. Mitchell
8. Henrietta
9. Mario
10. Davis

E. Analogies (*pages 24–25*)

3. *d* 4. *e* 5. *c* 6. *a* 7. *a*
8. *c*

Chapter 4: "Over" and "Under" Words

A. Preview (*pages 26–27*)

1. hypersensitive
2. hypertension

3. subservient
4. supersonic
5. hypotension
6. superficial
7. hyperacidity
8. hypercritical
9. sublethal
10. hypothermia
11. subaqueous
12. hypodermic
13. supernatural
14. supererogatory
15. subcutaneous
16. supernumerary
17. hypoglycemic
18. hyperactive
19. submarginal
20. hyposensitize

C. Building Additional Words (*pages 30–31*)

1. suboceanic
2. superstructure
3. hypertensive
4. hypothyroidism
5. supertanker
6. Hypoallergenic
7. Submicroscopic
8. hypervitaminosis
9. subaudible
10. hyperbole

D. Thinking with Your New Words (*pages 31–32*)

1. Helen
2. Edith
3. Hamlet
4. Bill
5. Andy
6. Fred

7. Kathy
8. Pearson
9. Ralph
10. Richard

10. Henry
11. Steve
12. Shelly

E. Analogies (*pages 32–34*)

1. *e* 2. *b* 3. *b* 4. *e*
5. *d* 6. *a* 7. *a* 8. *d*

Chapter 5: New Words from Opposites in the Context

A. Preview (*pages 35–37*)

1. talkative
2. truthfulness
3. disobedient
4. worsened
5. patience
6. in agreement
7. forgivable
8. sloppy
9. importance
10. liking

C. Thinking with Your New Words (*pages 39–40*)

1. Charlotte
2. Joyce
3. Charlotte
4. Emma
5. Patricia
6. Ben
7. Anne
8. Walt
9. Myo

D. Concise Writing (*page 40*)

2. Sometimes crowds are refractory.
3. Cy's blunders are venial.
4. My despair was transitory.
5. Nobody questioned Sandy's veracity.

E. Analogies (*page 41*)

1. *a* 2. *c* 3. *e* 4. *b* 5. *c*

Review of Chapters 1–5

I. (*page 42*)

1. mono, uni
2. Phile
3. Pent
4. Quadr
5. hyper, super
6. Phobia
7. hypo, sub
8. Mania
9. multi, poly
10. Deca

II. (*pages 43–44*)

1. bagatelle
2. quadrennially
3. superficial
4. megalomania

5. sublethal
6. Francophile
7. hypothermia
8. decade
9. acrophobia
10. unique
11. submarginal
12. kleptomaniac
13. monosyllabic
14. garrulous
15. bicentennial
16. exacerbate
17. decimate
18. reconcile
19. Polytheism
20. triumvirate

III. *(pages 44–45)*

1. dichotomy
2. uniform
3. dipsomaniac
4. brace
5. treble
6. monologue
7. penchant
8. veracity
9. aspect
10. millennium
11. moment
12. slatternly
13. forbearance
14. photophilic
15. supererogatory

IV. *(pages 46–47)*

1. unilateral
2. bibliophile
3. mania
4. multifaceted
5. phobia
6. venial

7. hyposensitize
8. subaqueous
9. hypercritical
10. pyrophobia
11. supernumerary
12. tithe
13. monogamist
14. transitory
15. subservient
16. monotonous
17. xenophile
18. unisex
19. submicroscopic
20. subcutaneous

V. *(page 47)*

1. Chinese
2. high
3. ten
4. seventy
5. French
6. two
7. 2045
8. low
9. 300
10. 2017
11. hemophiliac
12. Agoraphobia
13. multicultural
14. septuagenarian
15. one

Chapter 6: Words of Concealment and Deception

A. Preview *(pages 48–49)*

1. subterfuge
2. alias

3. con
4. cache
5. seclusion
6. latent
7. facade
8. suborn
9. impersonate
10. covert
11. malinger
12. canard
13. abscond
14. cryptic
15. feign
16. insidious
17. collusion
18. duplicity
19. anonymous
20. connive

C. Thinking with Your New Words (pages 52–53)

1. Lucille
2. Regina
3. Anderson
4. Watkins
5. Simmons
6. Mrs. Jackson
7. Peters
8. Simpson
9. Coretta
10. Jones

D. Concise Writing (pages 53–54)

2. The charges were anonymous. *Also correct:* Anonymous persons made charges.
3. Who suborned the witness?

4. Nobody discovered our cache. *Also correct:* Our cache remained undiscovered.
5. A hermit enjoys seclusion.

E. Analogies (pages 54–55)

1. *a* 2. *a* 3. *e* 4. *b* 5. *a*
6. *c*

Chapter 7: Medical Vocabulary

A. Preview (pages 56–57)

1. gastritis
2. arthritis
3. encephalitis
4. gingivitis
5. neuritis
6. appendicitis
7. dermatitis
8. hepatitis
9. laryngitis
10. colitis
11. peritonitis
12. nephritis
13. bronchitis
14. sinusitis
15. carditis
16. phlebitis
17. cystitis
18. bursitis
19. otitis

C. Building Additional Words

I. (pages 59–60)

2. ear
3. vein
4. skin
5. brain
6. stomach
7. gum
8. liver
9. kidney
10. nerve
11. bladder
12. heart

II. (pages 60–61)

1. cystoscope
2. otology
3. neurosurgeon
4. cardiologist
5. Neurology
6. cardiac
7. hepatoma
8. cardiogram
9. encephalogram
10. gingival
11. nephrologist
12. gastrointestinal
13. gastrectomy
14. hepatectomy
15. Phlebotomy
16. arthralgia
17. Gastric
18. dermatologist

D. Using Medical Terms (pages 61–62)

1. cardiologist
2. gingivitis
3. phlebotomy
4. gastrectomy
5. laryngitis
6. cardiac
7. neuritis
8. sinusitis
9. peritonitis
10. hepatitis

E. Analogies (pages 62–63)

1. d   2. b   3. a   4. b   5. e

Chapter 8: Words of Beginning and Ending

A. Preview (pages 64–65)

1. debut
2. ultimate
3. initiative
4. ultimatum
5. genesis
6. rudiment
7. demise
8. swan song
9. premiere
10. finale
11. penultimate
12. inchoate
13. terminal
14. lapse
15. antepenultimate
16. maiden
17. preamble
18. infinite
19. tyro
20. coup de grace

C. Thinking with Your New Words (*pages 68–69*)

1. Audrey
2. Village Motors
3. Gina
4. Jack
5. Adele
6. Eva
7. Comstock
8. Thomas E. Dewey
9. Lee
10. Helen

D. Concise Writing (*pages 69–70*)

2. Space is infinite.
3. His debut was unforgettable.
4. Your ultimatum disappointed us.
5. It was May 29.
6. Her preamble was indispensable (*or* essential).
7. Danny's insurance has lapsed.
8. My plan is inchoate.
9. They were tyros.
10. We attended his debut.

E. Analogies (*pages 70–71*)

1. *c* 2. *a* 3. *c* 4. *b* 5. *c*

Chapter 9: *Extra, Intra,* and *Inter* Words

A. Preview (*pages 72–73*)

1. intravenous
2. interracial
3. extraneous
4. Intracoastal
5. intracity
6. intermarriage
7. interregional
8. extraterrestrial
9. intramural
10. interpersonal
11. extrasensory
12. interdenominational
13. extralegal
14. interdependent
15. intraorganizational
16. extramarital
17. interurban
18. extramural
19. interlinear
20. intradepartmental

C. Building Additional Words (*pages 76–77*)

1. interdisciplinary
2. interservice
3. extracurricular
4. Intercity
5. intraspinal
6. extrajudicial
7. interhemispheric
8. extraterritorial
9. interlining
10. Intramuscular
11. intercoastal
12. Interstellar

13. extravehicular
14. interoceanic
15. extrasolar

D. Thinking with Your New Words (pages 77-78)

1. Auland
2. Nadia Comaneci
3. Harriet
4. Cheryl
5. Desdemona
6. Dr. Arno
7. Collins
8. Cynthia
9. Dan
10. Cartier

E. Analogies (page 79)

1. *b* 2. *d* 3. *a* 4. *b* 5. *e*

Chapter 10: Loanwords

A. Preview (pages 80-82)

1. alfresco
2. persona non grata
3. honcho, kudos
4. arrivederci, auf Wiedersehen, au revoir, sayonara
5. Shalom
6. brouhaha
7. de rigueur
8. ad nauseam
9. hoi polloi
10. ersatz
11. non compos mentis
12. chutzpah

13. ad infinitum
14. salaam
15. faux pas
16. entre nous
17. in medias res
18. ad hominem
19. postmortem
20. non sequitur

C. Thinking with Your New Vocabulary (pages 85-86)

1. Frank
2. Andy
3. Carl
4. Ruth
5. Terry
6. Mona
7. Phil
8. Camille
9. Tony
10. Dr. Pell

D. Using Loanwords (page 87)

1. entre nous
2. de rigueur
3. ad nauseam
4. in medias res
5. ad infinitum
6. non sequitur
7. postmortem
8, 9, 10. *Any three of the following may be used in order:* Au revoir; auf Wiedersehen; arrivederci; sayonara; *and* shalom

E. Analogies *(page 88)*

1. *b* 2. *a* 3. *c* 4. *c* 5. *e*

Review of Chapters 6–10

I. *(pages 89–90)*

1. encephal
2. phleb
3. Extra
4. Itis
5. gingiv
6. gastr
7. cardi
8. Intra
9. arthr
10. Dermat
11. hepat
12. nephr
13. Neur
14. Inter

II. *(pages 90–92)*

1. ultimate
2. laryngitis
3. alias
4. postmortem
5. interdependent
6. coup de grace
7. abscond
8. faux pas
9. facade
10. hepatitis
11. cache
12. ad nauseam
13. non compos mentis
14. connive
15. penultimate
16. malinger
17. latent
18. lapse
19. anonymous
20. arthritis
21. debut
22. canard
23. swan song
24. intradepartmental
25. duplicity

III. *(page 92)*

1. subterfuge, stratagem
2. kudos, fame
3. tyro, neophyte
4. covert, surreptitious
5. ad infinitum, endlessly
6. counterfeit, feign
7. finale, end
8. chutzpah, brazenness
9. infinite, limitless
10. hoi polloi, commoners
11. ersatz, synthetic
12. honcho, chief
13. brouhaha, commotion
14. sayonara, au revoir

IV. *(page 93)*

1. preamble
2. demise
3. genesis
4. de rigueur
5. collusion
6. seclusion
7. alfresco
8. extraneous
9. insidious
10. initiative

V. *(pages 93–94)*

1. rudiments
2. cryptic
3. Shalom
4. extraterrestrial
5. sinus
6. inchoate
7. persona non grata
8. interurban
9. suborn
10. in medias res

Chapter 11: *Anti Words*

A. Preview *(pages 95–96)*

1. antidote
2. anticorrosive
3. antibodies
4. antiviral
5. antibiotic
6. antithesis
7. antipyretic
8. antipathy
9. antiseptic
10. Antihypertensive
11. anticoagulant
12. antiestablishment
13. antiscorbutic
14. antipodes
15. Antimacassar
16. antitrust
17. antihistamine
18. anticlimax
19. antipersonnel
20. Antioxidant

C. Building Additional Words *(pages 100–101)*

1. antinoise
2. antipatriotic
3. antilabor
4. antisocial
5. antivivisectionist
6. antiperspirant
7. antifreeze
8. antimalarial
9. Antiaircraft
10. antimissile
11. antilitter
12. antifeminist
13. antipoverty
14. antitank
15. antitoxin

D. Thinking with Your New Words *(pages 101–102)*

1. Paula
2. Sidney
3. Basil
4. Ernie
5. Joyce
6. Dr. Evans
7. Alice
8. Juana
9. Yoko
10. Vasco da Gama's crew

E. Discussion with Your New Words *(pages 102–103)*

1, 3, 4. *Answers will vary.*
2. To achieve the humorous effect of anticlimax, I should have said that the winner would get a new car, a trip to Hawaii, and

a year's supply of facial tissues.

5. The contributions of Alexander Fleming and Jonas Salk have saved, and will continue to save, millions of lives. Anyone who can do this deserves the highest kudos.

Chapter 12: "Cutting" Words

A. Preview (pages 104–105)

1. vivisection
2. excise
3. intersect
4. incision
5. tome
6. anatomy
7. fraticidal
8. herbicide
9. laparotomy
10. conciseness
11. rescission
12. gingivectomy
13. sectionalism
14. entomology
15. homicidal
16. incisive
17. lobotomy
18. dissect
19. trisect
20. suicidal

C. Building Additional Words (pages 109–110)

1. splenectomy
2. laryngectomy
3. neurectomy
4. tracheotomy
5. mastectomy
6. arteriotomy
7. thyroidectomy
8. hysterotomy
9. hepatectomy
10. cholecystetomy
11. nephrotomy
12. neurotomy
13. parathyroidectomy
14. hysterectomy
15. mastoidectomy
16. pneumonectomy
17. osteotomy
18. prostatectomy

D. Thinking with Your New Words (pages 110–111)

1. Aunt Susan
2. Senator Berg
3. Marva
4. Andy
5. Brian
6. Donna
7. Israel
8. Macduff
9. Thorndike
10. Jackie

E. Analogies (pages 111–112)

1. *a* 2. *d* 3. *b* 4. *e* 5. *b*

Chapter 13: "Before" and "After" Words

A. Preview (pages 113–114)

1. prerecord
2. metaphysics
3. metempsychosis
4. prophesy
5. posthumous
6. antediluvian
7. presentiment
8. posterity
9. metastasis
10. antecedent
11. predecease
12. anterior
13. prescient
14. prognosis
15. antemeridian
16. postprandial
17. prophylaxis
18. antepenult
19. metacarpal
20. posterior

C. Building Additional Words (pages 118–119)

1. preselected
2. postatomic
3. preelection
4. proposition
5. postgraduate
6. predated
7. prologue
8. metamorphosis
9. postdated
10. preadolescent
11. prognosticate
12. prepaid
13. anteroom
14. predesignated
15. unpremeditated

D. Thinking with Your New Words (pages 119–120)

1. Herman
2. Patricia
3. Rip Van Winkle
4. Salk
5. Martha
6. Adrienne
7. Valdine
8. Roberto
9. Delwyn
10. Leila

E. Discussion with Your New Words (pages 120–121)

(Answers will vary.)

1. The Tories were *ante*-revolutionary because they had settled in the colonies *before* the American Revolution. They were *anti*revolutionary because they opposed that revolution.

2. Since the wrist and fingers are involved in writing and typing, a meta*carpal* injury would be more serious for a writer.

3. Because the proboscis is the long flexible tube with which the elephant picks up food and sucks

up water to convey to its mouth, it is an anterior organ.

4. Yes. Snacking between three full meals is generally inadvisable because serious weight and health problems may result.

5. Yes. Since several nations have nuclear arsenals, the fallout from a nuclear war could endanger the lives of all of Earth's inhabitants.

Chapter 14: "People" Words

A. Preview (*pages 122–124*)

1. mesmerize
2. gargantuan
3. stentorian
4. Machiavellian
5. John Hancock
6. atlas
7. mentor
8. sadistic
9. odyssey
10. Adonis
11. Damoclean
12. quisling
13. Baedeker
14. malapropism
15. boycott
16. quixotic
17. chauvinist
18. philippic
19. cicerone
20. bowdlerize

C. Using "People" Words (*pages 128–129*)

1. sadistic
2. draconian
3. quixotic
4. boycott
5. cicerone
6. chauvinist
7. bowdlerize
8. mesmerize
9. Pollyanna
10. Adonis

D. Thinking with Your New Words (*pages 129–130*)

1. Audrey
2. Pierre Laval
3. Bruce's
4. Kegel
5. Walter
6. Toshi
7. Joan
8. Paul Bunyan
9. Hobart
10. Caroline

E. Analogies (*page 131*)

1. *b*   2. *a*   3. *d*   4. *a*   5. *e*

Chapter 15: New Words from Similar Words in the Context

A. Preview (pages 132–134)

1. magic
2. uncommunicative
3. amusing
4. objected to
5. pick out
6. be ambiguous
7. lavish tributes
8. untruthful
9. demands for payment
10. light meal
11. disuse
12. neatening one's appearance
13. finding fault
14. suppositional
15. naïve
16. tip
17. cowardly
18. difficult situation
19. unscientific
20. regret

C. Thinking with Your New Words (pages 138–139)

1. William Shakespeare
2. Carmelita West's
3. Amos Parker
2. Lou Marquez
5. Jennifer Gale
6. Mildred Jones
7. Dr. Josephs
8. Olga Evans
9. Evelyn Tarrant
10. Sandra McCloud
11. Jean Stanowski
12. Jonathan Kaplan

D. Concise Writing (page 140)

2. He likes to equivocate.
3. Her claims are mendacious.
4. We're in a quagmire.
5. Who is dunning you?
6. Jim's conclusion is hypothetical.
7. His carping irritates people
8. They rue their mistakes.
9. Roberta is taciturn.
10. Many panegyrics are boring.

E. Discussion with Your New Words (pages 140–141)

1, 2, 4. *Answers will vary.*
3. I would demur. I could not endorse anyone who uses deceit and cunning for selfish ends.
4. To disarm unilaterally is naïve. It would invite attack by other nuclear powers.

Review of Chapters 11–15

I. (page 142)

1. crani
2. meta, post

3. mast
4. cid, cis, sect, tom
5. hyster
6. trache
7. Splen; cholecyst; hepat
8. anti
9. ante, pre, pro
10. pneumon

II. *(page 143)*

1. ti 2. ci 3. te 4. is
5. ch 6. me 7. di 8. ty
9. qu 10. pr

III. *(pages 143–144)*

1. gargantuan, prodigious
2. forecast, prognosis
3. Baedeker, handbook
4. bellicose, warlike
5. imprimatur, sanction
6. cunning, Machiavellian
7. cancelation, recission
8. eulogy, panegyric
9. pusillanimous, timid
10. cull, select

IV. *(pages 144–145)*

1. metastasis
2. antiestablishment
3. vivisection
4. rue
5. antipyretic
6. predecease
7. carp
8. Adonis
9. intersect
10. equivocate
11. anticoagulant
12. odyssey
13. sectionalism

14. collation
15. mentor
16. posterity
17. antithesis
18. boycott
19. antediluvian
20. herbicide

V. *(page 146)*

1. alchemy
2. postprandial
3. hypothetical
4. antigen
5. incision
6. tirade
7. aversion
8. demur
9. coagulation
10. morphology

Chapter 16: "Going" Words

A. Preview *(pages 147–148)*

1. exodus
2. obsolescent
3. amble
4. peripatetic
5. retrogress
6. somnambulist
7. founder
8. transition
9. concomitant
10. labyrinth
11. meanders
12. wanderlust
13. obituary
14. safari

15. yaw
16. congregate
17. flounder
18. peregrinations
19. itinerary
20. incursion

C. Building Additional "Going" Words (pages 151–153)

1. circuitous
2. curriculum
3. preamble
4. incur
5. ingress
6. progress
7. ambulatory
8. excursion
9. transgressor
10. precursor
11. transitory
12. digress
13. perambulation
14. gradual
15. initiation
16. concurred
17. biodegradable
18. current
19. ambulation
20. upgraded

D. Thinking with Your New Words (pages 153–154)

1. Ralph
2. Harold II
3. Rupert
4. Rebecca
5. Bernard
6. Dorothy
7. Agnes Latham
8. Nathaniel Canterbury
9. Dan
10. Felicia

E. Analogies (pages 154–155)

1. b 2. b 3. a 4. a 5. c

Chapter 17: Words of Crime and Punishment

A. Preview (pages 156–158)

1. inculpate
2. venue
3. incarceration
4. poacher
5. culpability
6. misdemeanor
7. extradition
8. felony
9. larceny
10. recidivist
11. vandals
12. capital
13. accessory
14. plagiarism
15. exculpate
16. charlatan
17. embezzlement
18. penal
19. contraband
20. subpoena

C. Thinking with Your New Words (*pages 161–164*)

1. Joe G.
2. Joshua B.
3. Warden Alderman
4. Hobart G.
5. Phil E.
6. William T.
7. Pamela E.
8. Andrea O.
9. Marisa W.
10. Elizabeth S.
11. Bill L.
12. Doc B.
13. Sally O.
14. Henry T.
15. Sanford M.
16. Helene Q.
17. Ruth V.
18. Dudley M.
19. Marcia B.
20. Fred G.

D. Concise Writing (*page 164*)

2. Do vandals deserve incarceration?
3. Her testimony inculpated others.
4. Littering is a misdemeanor.
5. Many people trust charlatans.
6. His confession exculpated us.
7. Were any felonies reported?
8. Contraband may be confiscated.
9. A poacher was arrested.
10. Recidivists deserve no leniency.

E. Discussion with Your New Words (*pages 165–166*)

1–4. *Answers will vary.*
5. Deborah helped the car thief by leaving her car unlocked and the keys in the ignition. She has therefore been an accessory in the theft of her car.

Chapter 18: Character and Personality Words

A. Preview (*pages 167–169*)

1. altruistic
2. skeptical
3. gullible
4. sanguine
5. vindictive
6. impetuous
7. diffident
8. obstreperous
9. intrepid
10. irrational
11. biased
12. contrite
13. indolent
14. obsequious
15. opinionated
16. impassive
17. gregarious
18. captious

19. parisimonious
20. supercilious

C. Thinking with Your New Words (*pages 171–173*)

1. Burton
2. Gladys
3. Sonia
4. Baxter
5. Jane
6. Brenda
7. Stanley
8. Jennifer
9. Santia
10. Gloria
11. Otis
12. Neighbor Jones
13. Campbell
14. Audrey
15. Philip

D. Concise Writing (*pages 173–174*)

2. Are our rulers altruistic?
3. Sometimes we are skeptical.
4. Michael is obsequious.
5. Most teenagers are gregarious.
6. The vandals seem contrite.
7. Many victims are vindictive.
8. Our opponents are opinionated.
9. Occasionally, everyone is indolent.
10. Our fans remain sanguine.

E. Analogies (*pages 174–175*)

1. *b*   2. *c*   3. *a*   4. *c*   5. *e*

Chapter 19: Body Vocabulary

A. Preview (*pages 176–177*)

1. digital
2. manual
3. lachrymose
4. visceral
5. supine, prone
6. genuflect
7. olfactory, tactile
8. cervical
9. carpal
10. labial, lingual
11. subcutaneous
12. Corporal
13. spleen, vascular
14. eviscerate
15. pulmonary
16. cerebral
17. guttural
18. sanguinary
19. gustatory
20. plantar

C. Building Additional Body Words (*pages 181–183*)

1. manipulate
2. metacarpal
3. splenectomy
4. intact
5. monolingual, bilingual

6. contact
7. Linguistics
8. manual
9. corpse
10. tangible
11. intangible
12. tactful, tactless
13. sublingual
14. incorporated
15. corps
16. manicurist
17. linguist
18. corpuscles
19. mandate
20. manuscript
21. multilingual
22. emancipator
23. corporation
24. manacles
25. splenetic

D. Thinking with Your New Words (*pages 183–185*)

1. John
2. Angelina
3. Marcia
4. Carol
5. Alphonse
6. Olga
7. Rupert Brooke
8. Erica
9. Hanlon
10. Philip
11. Sir Walter
12. Fowler
13. Chester
14. Magdalena
15. Kit
16. Jason
17. Amy
18. Agnes

19. Billings
20. Caesar

E. Discussion with Your New Words (*pages 185–186*)

1, 2, 4, 5. *Answers will vary.*
3. An impetuous person acts suddenly without forethought. Such behavior in a driver is likely to cause accidents.

Chapter 20: Figurative Expressions

A. Preview (*pages 187–189*)

1. roll out the red carpet
2. come home to roost
3. has an ax to grind
4. stick to one's last
5. pay the piper
6. busman's holiday
7. play possum
8. hold water
9. play the devil's advocate
10. white elephant
11. hold a candle to
12. fish or cut bait
13. Dutch treat
14. stick in his craw
15. red herring
16. French leave
17. poker face
18. eat crow
19. whistling in the dark
20. lame duck

C. Thinking with Your New Vocabulary (*pages 192–194*)

1. Judge Smith
2. Lorber
3. Freida
4. Compton
5. The Queen
6. Agnes
7. Schultz
8. Lydia
9. Chuck
10. Belle

D. Using Figurative Language (*pages 194–195*)

1. red herring
2. play possum
3. come home to roost
4. French leave
5. whistle in the dark
6. poker face
7. hold water
8. stick to your last
9. stick in his craw
10. hold a candle to

E. Using Some Additional Figurative Expressions (*pages 195–196*)

1. have a bone to pick
2. go begging
3. bury the hatchet
4. has a chip on his shoulder
5. burn the midnight oil

E. Discussion with Figurative Language (*pages 196–197*)

Answers will vary.

Review of Chapters 16–20

I. (*page 198*)

1. manu
2. viscer
3. lingu
4. digit
5. cerebr
6. Tact
7. sangu
8. corpor
9. labi
10. Gust

II. (*pages 198–200*)

1. recidivist
2. flounder
3. obsolescent
4. contrite
5. congregate
6. exodus
7. itinerary
8. labyrinth
9. altruistic
10. contraband
11. meander
12. vandal
13. transition
14. accessory
15. captious

III. (*page 200*)

1. incarceration, jailing
2. illogical, irrational
3. calm, impassive
4. bloody, sanguinary
5. miserly, parsimonious
6. guttural, rasping

7. unforgiving, vindictive
8. dauntless, intrepid
9. collapse, sink
10. disembowel, eviscerate
11. disbelieving, skeptical
12. obstreperous, unruly
13. diffident, timid
14. charlatan, imposter
15. incursion, inroad

IV. (pages 200–201)

1. hold water
2. pay the piper
3. a bone to pick
4. poker face
5. red herring
6. white elephant
7. ax to grind
8. hold a candle to
9. come home to roost
10. roll out the red carpet

V. (pages 201–202)

1. plantar
2. corporal
3. olfactory
4. gustatory
5. tactile
6. cervical
7. Pulmonary
8. supine
9. prone
10. subcutaneous
11. capital
12. genuflect
13. sanguinary
14. guttural
15. manual

VI. Concise Writing
(page 202)

1. Lachrymose people are hypersensitive.
2. Expensive imports went begging.
3. They buried the hatchet.
4. Her remarks were splenetic.
5. Lame ducks feel unimportant.

Chapter 21: "Living" Words

A. Preview (pages 203–205)

1. biocidal
2. macrobiotic
3. ecology
4. exurbanite
5. coevals
6. resuscitate
7. viable
8. aerobic
9. microorganisms
10. extant
11. troglodyte
12. animated
13. viviparous
14. expatriates
15. vita
16. biodegradable
17. reincarnation
18. biopsy
19. reclusive
20. amphibian

C. Building Additional "Living" Words (*pages 208–210*)

1. antibiotics
2. vitalize
3. Bioluminescence
4. revivify
5. vivisepulture
6. biological
7. Biomedicine
8. Antivivisectionists
9. aerobe
10. Microbicides
11. biography
12. vivacious
13. biosphere
14. vitality
15. microbe
16. bioresearch
17. convivial
18. biota
19. revival
20. autobiography
21. symbiotic
22. vital
23. revitalize
24. biogenesis
25. biomass
26. Biosatellites
27. vivid
28. Biometry
29. survival
30. devitalized

D. Thinking with Your New Words (*pages 210–211*)

1. Hansie
2. Walter
3. Sonia
4. Darryl
5. Wendy
6. Anthony
7. José
8. Cheryl
9. Andrea
10. Dorothy

E. Analogies (*pages 211–212*)

1. *b*   2. *c*   3. *d*   4. *b*   5. *c*

Chapter 22: Alpha-Privative Words

A. Preview (*pages 213–215*)

1. asexual
2. abiogenesis
3. anorexia
4. amnesia
5. atrophy
6. asphyxiation
7. atypical
8. abyss
9. amorphous
10. anomaly
11. anemia
12. asylum
13. anaerobic
14. anodyne
15. agnostics
16. aphasia
17. amnesty
18. apolitical
19. anesthesia
20. asymptomatic

C. Building Additional Alpha-Privative Words (*pages 218–219*)

1. anonymity
2. apathy
3. abiotic
4. anarchy
5. atom
6. analgesic
7. anhydride
8. apterous
9. Abulia
10. asthenia
11. aseismic
12. Apnea
13. aphonia
14. atheist
15. anoxia

D. Thinking with Your New Words (*pages 219–221*)

1. the Bishop of Digne
2. Gail
3. Rosina
4. Debra
5. Morris
6. Richard
7. Charlene
8. Manny
9. Harvey
10. Pasteur

E. Discussion with Your New Words (*pages 221–222*)

Answers will vary.

Chapter 23: Words Dealing with Words

A. Preview (*pages 223–225*)

1. oxymoron
2. blend
3. cliché
4. diatribes
5. Abstract
6. pejorative
7. argot
8. puns
9. irony
10. articulate
11. metaphor
12. palindromes
13. shibboleth
14. Concrete
15. epithets
16. glib
17. metonymy
18. maxim
19. acronym
20. satire
21. redundant
22. euphemism
23. understatement
24. logorrhea

C. Building Additional *Onym* Words (*pages 229–230*)

1. synonyms
2. pseudonym
3. homonyms
4. antonyms
5. anonymous
6. cryptonym
7. Patronymics

8. Heteronyms
9. polyonymous
10. eponym

D. Thinking with Your New Words (*pages 230–233*)

1. Charlotte
2. William Sydney Porter
3. Joyce
4. Cliff
5. Paul
6. Alex
7. Brian
8. Abel Tasman
9. Bernice
10. Gretta
11. Kathy
12. Reginald
13. Henry
14. Dolores
15. Agatha
16. Parker
17. Wesley
18. Aunt Emma
19. Duke William
20. Ed
21. Uncle Ned
22. Napoleon
23. Swift
24. Jim Burke
25. Arthur

E. Analogies (*pages 233–234*)

1. *c*   2. *a*   3. *b*   4. *e*   5. *a*
6. *a*   7. *b*   8. *a*   9. *e*

Chapter 24: Allusions

A. Preview (*pages 235–237*)

1. Midas touch
2. crocodile tears
3. Hobson's choice
4. Armageddon
5. fourth estate
6. open sesame
7. Achilles' heel
8. Parkinson's Law
9. carry coals to Newcastle
10. sour grapes
11. dog in the manger
12. juggernaut
13. Pandora's box
14. bell the cat
15. Murphy's Law
16. Freudian slip
17. Pyrrhic victory
18. fifth column
19. Catch-22
20. between Scylla and Charybdis
21. last straw
22. cross the Rubicon
23. hoist with his own petard
24. cry wolf

C. Thinking with Your New Allusions (*pages 245–247*)

1. Lasker
2. Lila
3. Jack London
4. Liu
5. Marcus
6. Gregory

7. General Zhukov
8. Chris
9. Suleiman
10. Karim
11. Irma
12. Hernandez
13. Quisling
14. Dorothy
15. Ruth
16. Cheri
17. Myron
18. Pamela
19. Darryl
20. Martha

D. Using Fewer Words
(pages 247–248)

1. crocodile tears
2. between Scylla and Charybdis
3. Armageddon
4. Hobson's choice
5. dog in the manger
6. Midas touch
7. fourth estate
8. Lilliputians
9. Achilles' heel
10. carry coals to Newcastle

E. Discussion with Your New Vocabulary *(pages 248–249)*

Answers will vary.

Chapter 25: New Words from Commonsense Clues in the Context

A. Preview *(pages 250–252)*

1. projecting
2. *caries* (tooth-decay) causing
3. a person who set fires
4. controversial discussions
5. prizefighters
6. persons advocating bold action
7. one who dislikes marriage
8. unable to obtain sufficient sleep
9. pleasing-on-television
10. found everywhere
11. charitable
12. stuff
13. inserted
14. deceptive advertising
15. amount of rain and/or snow
16. burn
17. food
18. humiliate
19. wane
20. repetition

C. Building Additional *Genic* Words *(pages 255–256)*

1. nonpathogenic
2. immunogenic
3. saprogenic
4. Aerogenic

5. Chromogenic
6. cryptogenic
7. Gastrogenic
8. iatrogenic
9. cryogenic
10. pyrogenic
11. pyogenic
12. Thermogenic
13. hallucinogenic
14. sociogenic
15. hepatogenic

D. Thinking with Your New Words (*pages 257–259*)

1. Kilroy
2. Kaori
3. Yvette
4. Henry Clay
5. Debra
6. Lady Macbeth
7. Natalie
8. Bruce
9. Floyd Patterson
10. Donald's
11. Sir Alexander Fleming
12. Genevieve
13. May
14. Brooks
15. Aunt Susan
16. Celina
17. Selma
18. Clay
19. Commissioner Blake
20. Ab Snopes
21. Adele
22. Jeff
23. Alton
24. Joanne
25. Gary

E. Analogies (*pages 259–260*)

1. *c* 2. *b* 3. *d* 4. *e* 5. *b*

Chapter 26: Expressions Adopted from Other Languages

B. Using Your New Expressions (*pages 264–265*)

2. Verbum sat sapienti est. *Also correct:* Verbum sat *or* Verbum sap
3. laissez-faire
4. Tempus fugit.
5. Caveat emptor.
6. Tout comprende, c'est tout pardonner.
7. e pluribus unum
8. Cherchez la femme.
9. Honi soit qui mal y pense.
10. cogito ergo sum
11. Gaudeamus igitur. *Also correct:* Gaudeamus.
12. habeas corpus
13. Eureka!
14. O tempora! O mores!
15. Mens sana in corpore sano.

Review of Chapters 21–26

I. (*page 266*)

1. archy
2. genic

3. crypto
4. pseudo
5. patho
6. a, an
7. chromo
8. bio, viv
9. alg
10. the
11. Seismology
12. dysapnea
13. Euphonious

II. *(pages 266–267)*

2. shapeless, vague
3. edibles, food
4. shallow, superficial
5. journalism, reporters
6. reiteration, repetition
7. abnormality, irregularity
8. abate, wane
9. disparaging, downgrading
10. charitable, philanthropic
11. talkativeness, prolixity
12. superfluous, surplus

III. *(pages 267–269)*

1. Achilles' heel
2. Hobson's choice
3. between Scylla and Charybdis
4. Pyrrhic victory
5. Midas touch
6. Armageddon
7. open sesame
8. carry coals to Newcastle
9. dog in the manger
10. Pandora's box
11. hoist with his own petard
12. last straw
13. laissez-faire

14. Eureka
15. habeas corpus

IV. *(pages 269–270)*

1. precipitation
2. articulate
3. Aerobic
4. blend
5. anesthesia
6. interpolate
7. acronym
8. cariogenic
9. palindrome
10. Anemia
11. biocidal
12. expatriate
13. oxymoron
14. juggernaut
15. polemic
16. euphemism
17. abulia
18. apterous

V. *(pages 270–271)*

1. coeval, contemporary
2. telegenic, videogenic
3. omnipresent, ubiquitous
4. cliché, platitude
5. prizefighter, pugilist
6. arsonist, incendiary
7. résumé, vita
8. argot, slang
9. gorge, stuff
10. denunciation, diatribe
11. deception, hype
12. abyss, chasm
13. reclusive, solitary
14. concrete, tangible
15. humiliate, mortify

Dictionary of Words and Expressions

abate   become less intense; subside   255

abiogenesis   theory that life can originate from nonliving matter; spontaneous generation   215

abiotic   nonliving   219

abscond   depart secretly and hide, especially to avoid prosecution   50

abstract   considered apart from material or specific instances; existing as a concept, not concrete   225

absurd   irrational; senseless   170

abulia   inability to make decisions or to act   219

abyss   seemingly bottomless pit or gulf; chasm; anything immeasurably deep   215

accessory   person who, though not present at the time of a crime, aids in its commission or helps the perpetrator to escape; accomplice   158

Achilles' heel   weak point   238

acronym   word formed from the first letter or letters of other words   229

acrophobia   abnormal fear of being in high places   10, 12

adage   proverbial statement; maxim   227

ad hominem   appealing to a listener's or reader's prejudices, rather than to reason   82

ad infinitum   endlessly; forever; without limit   82

ad nauseam   to a sickening degree; to the point of nausea or disgust   82

Adonis   very handsome man   124

adulterous   extramarital   74

aerobe   microorganism that can live only in the presence of free oxygen   209

aerobic   (1) able to live or grow only in the presence of oxygen; (2) having to do with exercise that increases oxygen intake and conditions the heart and lungs   205

aerogenic   gas-producing   256

aggravate   make more severe; exacerbate   37

agoraphobia   abnormal fear of being in crowds, public places, or open areas   12

agnostic   person who believes humans cannot know anything beyond material phenomena, including whether God exists, or how the universe was created   213

alchemy   medieval chemistry concerned with finding a way to change base metals into gold and a single cure for all diseases; hence, magic, or magic power   135

alfresco   in the open air; outdoors   82

alias   assumed name   50

altruistic   unselfishly concerned for the welfare of others; unselfish   169

amble   walk unhurriedly; saunter   149

ambulation   walking   152

ambulatory   able to walk   152

amnesia   loss of memory   215

amnesty   general pardon for political offenses against a government   216

amoral   outside the sphere where moral issues apply   222

amorphous   without definite form; shapeless; vague   216

amphibian   any animal or plant that can live both on land and in water   205

anaerobic   able to live or grow in the absence of oxygen   216

analgesic   pain-relieving   219

anarchy   absence of government   213, 219

anatomy   "cutting apart" or dissection of body or organism to determine the location, structure, and interrelationships of its parts; science of structure; morphology   106

anemia   hemoglobin deficiency in the circulating blood; paleness; lack of vigor   216

anesthesia   partial or complete loss of the sense of pain, with or without loss of consciousness, artificially induced by drugs   216

Anglomania   exaggerated devotion to the English   10

Anglomaniac   person imbued with Anglomania   10

Anglophile   admirer of the English   10

Anglophilic   showing partiality to the English   15

Anglophobe   person imbued with Anglophobia   10

Anglophobia   abnormal dislike of the English   10

anhydride   chemical compound formed by removing water from another compound   219

animated   alive; lively; spirited   205

anodyne   drug that relieves pain; anything that soothes or comforts   216

anomaly   irregularity; departure from the common rule; abnormality   217

anonymity   condition of being nameless   219

anonymous   supplied by one whose name is withheld or not known   230

anorexia   loss of appetite, especially when prolonged   217

anoxia   abnormally low level of oxygen in body tissues   219

antecedent   word that a pronoun refers to   115

antedate   assign an earlier date than the true one   118

antediluvian   very old; primitive   115

antemeridian   occurring before noon   115

antepenult   syllable before the penult; third syllable from the end of a word   115

antepenultimate   coming immediately before the next to the last   65

anterevolutionary   before the revolution   114

anterior   situated before or toward the front   115

anteroom   room leading into a more important one; waiting room   119

antiaircraft   used for defense against hostile planes   101

antibiotic   substance that inhibits the growth of or destroys harmful bacteria and other microorganisms   97

antibody   immunizing substance formed in the body to counteract an invading antigen (foreign body)   97

anticlimax   sudden drop in importance or dignity, either in writing or speaking, creating a humorous effect   97

anticoagulant   substance that delays or prevents coagulation (clotting of blood)   97

anticorrosive   counteracting or preventing corrosion   97

antidote   remedy that counteracts a poison   97

antiestablishment   opposed to the principles of a ruling class or inner circle   98

antifeminist   opposed to the equality of the sexes   101

antifreeze   substance added to water to lower its freezing point   100

antigen   foreign body   97

antihistamine   drug that helps prevent histamine from causing allergic reactions or cold symptoms   98

antihypertensive effective in reducing high blood pressure 98

antilabor opposed to the interests of workers 100

antilitter intended to reduce littering 101

antimacassar small cover for arms or backs of sofas or chairs, either as a decoration or a protection from soiling 98

antimalarial designed to combat malaria 100

antimissile intended for defense against missiles 101

antinoise intended to reduce noise 100

antioxidant chemical compound that slows down oxidation and checks deterioration 98

antipathy strong feeling against someone or something; dislike; aversion 98

antipatriotic having the effect of undermining patriotism 100

antipersonnel designed for use against an enemy nation's military personnel or civilians, rather than its equipment 99

antiperspirant cosmetic used to check excessive perspiration 95, 100

antipodes parts of the earth, or their inhabitants, directly opposite one another on globe 95, 99

antipollution intended to reduce or eliminate pollution 100

antipoverty intended to combat poverty 101

antipyretic substance that reduces fever 99

antirevolutionary opposed to revolution 120

antiscorbutic preventing or relieving scurvy 99

antiseptic substance that kills or inhibits growth of microorganisms 99

antisocial averse to being with others; hostile to society 100

antitank designed for defense against enemy tanks 101

antithesis exact opposite; contrast 99

antitoxin substance that counteracts a disease-causing agent 101

antitrust opposing, or intended to oppose, trust 100

antiviral acting to make viruses ineffective 100

antivivsectionist person opposed to medical experimentation on living animals 100, 209

antonym word of opposite meaning 230

apathy lack of feeling or interest; indifference 219

aphasia partial or complete loss of the power to use and understand words 217

aphonia   loss of voice and of all but whispered speech   219
apnea   cessation of breathing   219
apolitical   not connected with political matters; uninterested in politics   217
appendectomy   surgical removal of the appendix   104
appendicitis   inflammation of the appendix   57
apterous   lacking wings   270
argot   language peculiar to a particular group or class; slang   225
Armageddon   vast decisive battle   238
arrivederci   till we see each other again; good-bye   82
arsonist   one who maliciously sets fires; incendiary   253
arteriotomy   opening of an artery   109
arthralgia   pain in a joint   61
arthritis   inflammation of the joints   57
articulate   capable of speech; able to express oneself effectively   225
aseismic   free of earthquakes   219
asexual   occurring or produced without sexual action; sexless   217
asocial   not social; not considerate of others; selfish   213
asphyxiation   loss of consciousness due to lack of oxygen or presence of poisonous gases; suffocation   217
asthenia   loss or lack of strength   219
asylum   inviolable place where one can be free from arrest; protection; sanctuary; shelter   218
asymmetrical   lopsided; not symmetrical   213
asymptomatic   without subjective evidence of disease; symptomless   218
atheist   person who does not believe in God   219
atlas   book of maps   124
atom   tiny indivisible particle   219
atrophy   wasting away or decrease in size of a body organ or tissue   218
atypical   not typical, irregular, abnormal   218
audiophile   one especially interested in high-fidelity sound reproduction   10, 12
auditory   pertaining to hearing   176
auf Wiedersehen   till we see each other again; good-bye   83
au revoir   till we see each other again; good-bye   83
autobiography   story of one's life written by oneself   209
aversion   dislike; antipathy   98

Baedeker guidebook; handbook 124

bagatelle trifle; something of little value or importance 35, 37

baker's dozen thirteen 3

baksheesh gift of money; tip; gratuity 135

balletomania extreme enthusiasm for the ballet 12

Beatlemania exaggerated adoration of the Beatles 10

bellicose inclined to fight or quarrel; pugnacious; warlike 132, 135

bell the cat do a daring, risky deed for the sake of others 238

between Scylla and Charybdis between two equally difficult alternatives, neither of which can be avoided without incurring the other 239

biased prejudiced; unduly or unfairly influenced 169

bibliomania craze for acquiring books 12

bibliophile lover of books 12

bibliophobe one who has a strong dislike for books 13

bibliophobia strong dislike of books 13

bicentennial 200th anniversary 3

bilingual using or able to use two languages 182

biocidal destructive to living organisms 205

biodegradable capable of being readily decomposed by living microorganisms 205

biogenesis belief that life originates from preexisting life 210

biography story of a person's life 209

biological involving the use of living organisms 208

bioluminescence light produced by living organisms 208

biomass total content of living organisms in an area 210

biomedicine branch of medicine dealing with capacity of humans to withstand abnormal environments 209

biometry statistical calculation of probable human life span 210

biopsy removal and diagnostic examination of bits of tissues, cells, or fluids from the living body 206

bioresearch research in biological science 209

biosatellite recoverable spacecraft for studying the effects of space on human, animal, and plant life 210

biosphere zone in which life can exist 209

biota plant and animal life of a region 209

bisect cut into two equal sections 104

blend word produced from parts of other words 226

boisterous   excessively noisy; obstreperous   146
boomerang   have disagreeable repercussions   189
bowdlerize   expurgate; clear of objectionable words or passages   124
boycott   join with others to refuse to use, buy, or deal with   125
brace   two of a kind; pair; couple   3
brazenness   nerve; chutzpah   83
bronchitis   inflammation of the lining of the bronchial tubes, which convey air into the lungs   57
brouhaha   noisy stir; hubbub; uproar   83
burn the midnight oil   work or study far into the night   195
bursitis   inflammaton of a sac, especially of the shoulder or elbow   57
bury the hatchet   settle a disagreement; make peace   195
busman's holiday   holiday spent in an activity the same as, or similar to, one's occupation, as a bus driver who takes his family for a Sunday drive   189

cache   safe place for hiding and storing treasure, supplies, etc.   50
canard   false, deliberately made-up report or story   50
capital   involving or punishable by the death penalty   158
captious   quick to find fault, especially over petty matters; carping   169
carcinogenic   cancer-causing   255
cardiac   person with a heart ailment   61
cardiogram   tracing showing force and form of heart movements   61
cardiologist   heart specialist   60
carditis   inflammation of the heart   57
cariogenic   causing the development of caries (tooth decay)   252
carp   find fault unreasonably; complain in a nagging way   135
carpal   having to do with the wrist   178
carpus   wrist   115, 178
carry coals to Newcastle   take something to a place where it is plentiful and not needed; do something superfluous   239
Catch-22   paradox (contradiction) in an order or regulation that makes people victims of its provisions, regardless of what they do   239
caveat emptor   let the buyer beware   261
centenarian   one who is 100 or older   3

centennial 100th anniversary 3

cerebral having to do with the cerebrum (brain); intellectual 178

cerebrum brain 178

cervical pertaining to a cervix (neck) 178

cervix neck 178

charlatan person who fradulently claims to have expert skill or knowledge; fake; quack; impostor 158

chasm deep crack in earth's surface; abyss 215

chauvinist fanatical patriot; jingoist 125

cherchez la femme look for the woman 262

cholecystectomy excision of the gallbladder 110

chromogenic color-producing 256

chutzpah supreme self-confidence; shameless audacity; nerve; brazenness 83

cicerone guide who explains to tourists the history and special features of a place 125

circuitous going round and round 152

claustrophobia dread of being in closed or narrow spaces 13

claustrophobic suggesting claustrophobia; confining 15

cliché overused expression; trite phrase; platitude 226

coagulation clotting of the blood 97

coeval contemporary; person of the same period or age 206

cogito ergo sum I think; therefore I exist 262

colitis inflammation of the colon 58

collation light meal 135

collusion secret agreement for a deceitful purpose; conspiracy 50

come home to roost having disagreeable repercussions; boomerang 189

comestibles (literally, things that can be eaten up) edibles; food 252

compassionate sympathetic awareness of the sufferings of others 167

con swindle, after first gaining the confidence of the victim; trick; hoax 50

concise free of needless words; brief and to the point 104

conciseness brevity and compactness in expression resulting from the avoidance of needless words and elaborate detail 106

concomitant accompanying; concurrent 149

concrete   having a material existence; not abstract; tangible   226

concur   come to an agreement; agree   152

concurrent   accompanying; concomitant   149

confidentially   privately; entre nous   83

congregate   gather into a crowd; assemble   149

connive   cooperate secretly with someone for a deceitful purpose; conspire   51

contact   meeting; association   182

contemporary   person of the same period or age; coeval   206

contraband   goods illegally imported or exported; smuggled merchandise   158

contrite   sorrowful for a misdeed that one has committed; deeply repentant   169

convivial   fond of dining in good company   209

corporal   having to do with or inflicted on the body; bodily   178

corporation   body legally authorized to function as a single individual   183

corps   group of persons associated or acting together   182

corpse   dead body   182

corpuscle   minute particle (tiny body), as a blood cell   182

corrosion   gradual wearing away, especially of metals   97

coup de grace   decisive finishing blow   66

covert   covered over; secret; surreptitious   51

craniotomy   surgical opening of the skull   109

credulous   easily deceived; gullible   170

crocodile tears   false tears; insincere show of grief   240

cross the Rubicon   take a decisive, irrevocable step   240

cryogenic   producing very cold temperatures   256

cryptic   having or appearing to have a hidden meaning; baffling; mysterious   51

cryptogenic   produced by hidden or unknown factors   256

cryptonym   secret or code name   229

cry wolf   give a false alarm   240

cull   select; pick out; choose   135

culpability   quality or state of being culpable (deserving blame or censure); blameworthiness   159

culpable   deserving blame or censure   159

current   now going on; present   152

curriculum   courses of study offered in a school or college   152

cystitis   inflammation of the urinary bladder   58

cystoscope   instrument for examining the interior of the urinary bladder   60

Damoclean   involving imminent disaster   125

dauntless   not afraid; intrepid   170

debut   first public appearance   66

decade   period of ten years   4

decathlon   track-and-field contest consisting of ten events   4

decimate   destroy ten or more percent, or a large portion of   4

de gustibus non est disputandum   (or **de gustibus**) there is no disputing about tastes   262

demise   cessation of existence; death   66

demur   object; take exception   136

denomination   religion; sect   74

de rigueur   socially obligatory; required by custom, etiquette, or fashion; proper   83

dermatitis   inflammation of the skin   58

dermatologist   skin specialist   61

desuetude   condition of no longer being used; disuse   136

devitalize   deprive of vitality; make lifeless   210

diatribe   bitter spoken or written attack; angry criticism; denunciation   226

dichotomy   division in two; split   4

diffident   lacking confidence; timid; shy   169

digital   (1) involving a finger or fingers; (2) involving digits (the numbers one through nine and the zero)   178

digits   the numbers one through nine and zero   178

digress   depart from the topic   152

dipsomania   abnormal craving for alcoholic drink   15

dipsomaniac   person with an uncontrollable craving for alcoholic beverages   13

disparaging   downgrading; pejorative   228

dissect   cut apart piece by piece for study; analyze closely   106

divert   amuse; entertain; give pleasure to   136

dog in the manger   person who prevents others from using something he cannot use and does not need   240

donnybrook   uproarious brawl   235

draconian   extremely harsh or severe   122

dun   make repeated, insistent demands for payment   136

duplicity   double-dealing; hypocritical deception   49

Dutch treat   meal or entertainment for which each participant pays his or her own share   189

dyspnea   labored or difficult breathing   266

eat crow   be forced into a humiliating or extremely disagreeable situation   189

ecology   interrelationship between living organisms and their environment   206

egress   exit   147

eleemosynary   of, relating to, or supported by alms; charitable; philanthropic   252

emancipator   one who frees others from the power (hand) of an overlord   183

embezzlement   stealing of money, securities, etc., entrusted to one's care   159

empirical   relying solely on observation or experience   136

encephalitis   inflammation of the brain   58

encephalogram   tracing showing changes in electric potential in the brain   61

enterprise   initiative   66

enthrall   hypnotize; mesmerize   127

entomology   branch of zoology dealing with insects, so named for their "cut in," notched, segmented bodies   106

entre nous   between us, confidentially   83

epithet   word or phrase used to characterize a person or thing, often disparagingly   226

e pluribus unum   one out of many   262

eponym   person for whom a place is named   230

equivocate   be deliberately ambiguous; use misleading terms so as not to commit oneself   136

ersatz   being an inferior substitute; synethetic; artificial   83

esprit de corps   common spirit in a group, inspiring enthusiasm, devotion, etc.   182

eulogy   high praise; panegyric   137

euphemism   mild expression substituted for one that may be harsh or unpleasant   226

euphonious   pleasing to the ear   266

eureka   I have found it   262

eviscerate   remove the viscera (entrails, intestines, guts) from; disembowel; gut   178

exacerbate   make more severe or violent; aggravate   37

excise   remove by cutting out   106

excursion   trip; expedition   152

exculpate   free from blame or fault; prove guiltless; exonerate   159

exodus   going out; mass departure   149

exonerate   free from blame; exculpate   159

expatriate   one who lives in a foreign country   206

expurgate   clear of objectionable passages; bowdlerize   124

extant   still in existence; not lost or destroyed   206

extracurricular   outside the curriculum   76

extradition   surrender of an alleged criminal by one state or country to the jurisdiction of another for trial   159

extrajudicial   outside of court   77

extralegal   beyond the jurisdiction of the law; not regulated by law   72, 74

extramarital   involving a sexual relationship outside one's marriage; adulterous   74

extramural   outside the walls or boundaries of a school, university, etc.   74

extraneous   coming from the outside; not an essential part; irrelevant   74

extraordinary   beyond what is visual, customary, or ordinary   72

extrapolate   estimate or infer unknown information by extending or projecting known information   253

extrasensory   outside the ordinary senses; not limited to sight, hearing, touch, taste, and smell   74

extrasolar   originating outside the solar system   77

extraterrestrial   originating or existing outside the earth or its atmosphere   74

extraterritorial   outside the territorial limits or jurisdiction of the country   77

extravehicular   taking place outside a vehicle (as a spacecraft)   77

exurbanite   former citydweller who lives in an exurb (region beyond the suburbs) but continues to earn a living in the city   206

facade   false front; artificial or superficial appearance   51

fathom   measure of water depth equaling six feet   4

faux pas   error; social blunder; tactless act   84

fawning   excessively submissive; obsequious   170

feign make a false show of; pretend; simulate; counterfeit 51

felony major crime, such as murder, rape, arson, or burglary, for which the penalty ranges from execution to imprisonment of more than a year 159

fifth column subversive group of civilians working secretly within their own country to turn it over to an invading enemy 203

finale last scene or act; conclusion; end 66

firmament heavens; sky 250

fish or cut bait proceed wholeheartedly or drop out altogether; stop procrastinating or temporizing 190

flounder struggle awkwardly to move or obtain a footing; proceed clumsily with frequent mistakes 149

forbearance self-control; patience 37

foreboding presentiment 117

fortnight two weeks 1, 4

fortnightly published every two weeks 6

founder come to grief; go to the bottom; sink; collapse 149

fourth estate reporters; the press; journalism 203

Francophile one who admires the French 43

Francophobe one who dislikes the French 15

fratricidal of or relating to fratricide (act of killing one's brother, sister, or fellow citizen) 107

fratricide killing one's brother, sister, or fellow citizen 107

French leave unauthorized, hasty, or secret departure 190

Freudian slip slip of the tongue by which it is thought a person unintentionally reveals his or her true feelings 241

fugitive one who flees or tries to escape 54

gargantuan enormous; gigantic; prodigious 126

garrulous talking too much about unimportant things; loquacious, talkative 37

gastrectomy surgical removal of all or part of the stomach 61

gastric having to do with the stomach 61

gastritis inflammation of the stomach 58

gastrogenic originating in the stomach 256

gastrointestinal having to do with both the stomach and the intestines 61

gastrotomy surgical opening of the stomach 109

gaudeamus igitur (or **gaudeamus**) then let us be merry (while we are young) 262

gelid extremely cold; icy 250

genesis origin; coming into being 66

genuflect bend the knee, as in reverence or worship; kneel 179

Germanophobe person who intensely fears or dislikes Germany or the Germans 15

gingival involving the gums 61

gingivectomy surgical excision of gum tissue 107

gingivitis inflammation of the gums 58

glib having a ready flow of words but lacking accuracy or understanding; superficial; shallow 226

gorge stuff (oneself); eat greedily 253

go begging be in little demand 195

gradual proceeding by steps or degrees 152

gratuity tip; gift of money 135

gregarious seeking or enjoying the company of others; sociable 169

gullible easily deceived or tricked; credulous 170

gustatory having to do with the sense of taste or tasting 179

guttural produced in the throat; harsh; rasping; throaty 179

habeas corpus you shall have the body (in court); citizen's protection against illegal detention 263

hallucinogenic producing hallucinations 256

have a bone to pick have something to argue or complain about 195

have a chip on one's shoulder have a disposition to quarrel 195

have an ax to grind have a selfish motive or ulterior purpose to promote 190

hawk person who advocates immediate firm action to resolve international crises 253

hemophilia inherited tendency to uncontrollable bleeding 13

hemophiliac person afflicted with hemophilia 13

hemophilic developing best in blood 15

hepatectomy surgical removal of all or part of the liver 61, 110

hepatitis inflammation of the liver 58

hepatogenic   produced in the liver   256

hepatoma   tumor of the liver   61

herbicide   chemical for destroying or inhibiting plant growth; weed killer   107

heteronym   word that has the same spelling as another, but a different pronunciation and meaning   230

Hispanophile   admirer of things Spanish   15

Hobson's choice   choice of taking what is offered or nothing at all   241

hoi polloi   masses; common people   84

hoist with one's own petard   blown up with one's own bomb; vicitimized by one's own schemes   242

hold a candle to   compare favorably with   190

hold water   remain sound, logical, or consistent; stand up   190

homicidal   having a tendency toward homicide; murderous   104, 107

homicide   killing of one person by another   104

homonym   word having the same pronunciation as another but a different meaning and spelling   230

honcho   person in charge; leader; boss; chief   84

honi soit qui mal y pense   shame to anyone who thinks ill of this   263

humiliate   subject to shame; mortify   254

hype   anything intended to mislead; questionable, deceptive advertising; deception   253

hyperacid   producing too much acid   26

hyperacidity   excessive acidity, especially in the stomach   28

hyperactive   excessively active   28

hyperbole   overstatement   31

hypercritical   excessively fault-finding; captious   28

hypersensitive   abnormally sensitive   28

hypertension   abnormally high blood pressure   28

hypertensive   afflicted with abnormally high blood pressure   31

hypervitaminosis   disorder resulting from excessive intake of one or more vitamins   31

hypoacid   producing too little acid   26

hypoallergenic   having a relatively low capacity to induce allergic reactions   31

hypodermic   small syringe with a hollow needle for making injection beneath the skin   28

hypoglycemia abnormally low concentration of sugar in the blood 28

hypoglycemic afflicted with hypoglycemia 28

hyposensitize make less sensitive 29

hypotension abnormally low blood pressure 29

hypotensive having abnormally low blood pressure 47

hypothermia subnormal body temperature 29

hypothesis supposition 136

hypothetical based on or involving a hypothesis (supposition); conjectural 136

hypothyroidism deficient production of hormones by the thyroid gland 31

hysterectomy surgical removal of the uterus 110

hysterotomy incision of the uterus 110

iatrogenic caused inadvertently by a physician 256

immunogenic producing immunity 256

impassive feeling or revealing no emotion; calm; unmoved 170

impersonate pretend to be some other person; assume the character of 51

impetuous acting suddenly without forethought; rash, impulsive 170

impostor quack; charlatan 158

imprimatur authorization; sanction; approval 132, 137

incarceration imprisonment; jailing; confinement 159

incendiary person who maliciously sets fire to dwellings or other property; arsonist 253

inchoate just begun; only partly in existence; incomplete 66

incision cut, especially for surgical purposes; gash 107

incisive sharp; keen; penetrating 107

incorporate unite so as to form one body 182

inculpate incriminate; make appear guilty 160

incur run into; become subject to 152

incursion sudden, brief invasion; inroad; raid 149

indolent inclined to avoid work; lazy; idle 170

infinite endless; without boundaries or limits; exceedingly great 66

ingenuous innocent and simple; artless; naïve 137

ingress entrance 152

initiation "going-in" or induction ceremony for new members 152

initiative ability to begin and follow through without being urged; enterprise 66

in medias res in the middle of things, rather than at the beginning 84

insidious lying in wait to entrap; crafty; treacherous 51

insomnia abnormal inability to sleep 253

insomniac person suffering from insomnia 253

intact untouched; entire 182

intangible incapable of being perceived by the sense of touch; immaterial 182

intercity between cities 76

intercoastal between coasts 77

interdenominational between, among, or shared by different denominations (religions) 74

interdependent dependent on one another; mutually dependent 75

interdisciplinary involving two or more branches of learning 76

interhemispheric between hemispheres 77

interlinear inserted between lines already written or printed 75

interlining lining between the outer fabric and the ordinary lining 77

intermarriage marriage between persons of different religions, races, castes, etc. 75

interpersonal between persons 75

interoceanic existing or extending between oceans 77

interpolate insert between other parts or things; introduce 254

interracial between, among, or involving people of different races 75

interregional between regions 75

intersect cut across each other; cross 107

interservice between two or more of the armed services 76

intersession period between two academic terms or sessions 72

interstellar between stars 66

interurban between cities or towns 75

intracity within a city 75

intracoastal within and close to the coast 76

intradepartmental within a department 76

intramural within the walls or boundaries of a school, university, etc. 76

intramuscular   within a muscle   77
intraorganizational   within an organization   76
intraparty   within a party   72
intraspinal   within or going into the spine   77
intravenous   within or entering by way of the veins   76
intrepid   not afraid; bold; dauntless   170
irony   humorous or sarcastic use of language, in which the intended meaning is the opposite of the words used   227
irrational   not rational (capable of reasoning); illogical; absurd; senseless   170
irrelevant   not relating to the subject; extraneous   74
iteration   repetition; something iterated (repeated)   254
Italophile   admirer of the Italians   15
itinerant   walking about from place to place; peripatetic   150
itinerary   route of a journey   150

jeremiad   bitter denunciatory speech; tirade; philippic   127
jingoist   fanatical patriot; chauvinist   125
John Hancock   person's signature   126
juggernaut   massive, irresistible force crushing everything in its path; anything that exacts blind, destructive devotion   242

kleptomania   persistent neurotic impulse to steal   10
kleptomaniac   one who has a persistent neurotic impulse to steal, though not in need   13
kudos   praise for an achievement; glory; fame   84

labial   involving the lips   179
labyrinth   place full of confusing interconnecting passageways and blind alleys; maze; anything extremely intricate and perplexing   150
lachrymose   given to shedding or causing tears; tearful; mournful   179
laissez-faire   let (people) do (as they choose); noninterference in the affairs of others; minimal government interference in economic affairs   263
lame duck   elected official who remains in office for a brief period after a successor has been elected   190
laparotomy   surgical incision into the abdominal cavity   107
lapse   come to an end; become void   67

larceny unlawful taking away of another's property, with intent to defraud the owner; theft 160

laryngectomy surgical removal of the larynx 109

laryngitis inflammation of the larynx, or voice box 58

larynx voice box 58

last form on which a shoe is made or repaired 192

last straw final test of patience or endurance 242

latent present though invisible and inactive; potential 52

lethal death-causing 29

Lilliputian petty, insignificant, narrowminded person 235

lingual having to do with the tongue, language, or languages; pronounced with aid of the tongue 179

linguist one who speaks several languages; polyglot 182

linguistics science of language 182

lobotomy surgical operation on a lobe of the brain 108

logorrhea excessive flow of words; talkativeness; prolixity 227

loqacious talkative; garrulous 37

Machiavellian crafty; deceitful; cunning 126

macrobiotic having to do with or consisting mainly of whole grain and vegetables, whose consumption is thought to promote health and long life 207

maiden first; earliest 67

malapropism humorous misuse of words by a person unaware of the error 126

malinger pretend to be ill or incapacitated so as to avoid work or duty 52

manger feed box for cattle 240

manacles handcuffs 183

mandate authorization (given into the hand of someone) to act 182

mania exaggerated enthusiasm; craze; mad impulse 10, 13

manicurist specialist in the care of the hands and fingernails 182

manipulate handle 182

manual having to do with a hand or the hands; worked by hand 179

manual small helpful book that can be carried in the hand 182

manuscript book, letter, or document written by hand 183

mastectomy surgical removal of a breast 109

mastoidectomy surgical removal of the mastoid (bone behind the ear) 110

maxim concisely expressed statement of a general truth or rule of conduct; proverbial saying; adage 227

maze place full of interconnecting, confusing passageways; labyrinth 150

meander follow a winding intricate course 150

megalomania mental disorder characterized fantasies of grandeur, power, wealth, etc. 13

megalomaniac one who has fantasies of grandeur, power, wealth, etc. 15

mendacious lying; untrue; deceitful 137

mentor wise, trusted adviser or teacher 127

mens sana in corpore sano a sound mind in a sound body 263

mesmerize hypnotize; spellbind; enthrall 127

metacarpal having to do with any of the five long bones after the carpus (wrist) and before the fingers 115, 182

metamorphosis transformation; changeover 118

metaphor implied comparison using a word or phrase with something or someone it does not ordinarily go with 227

metaphysics branch of philosophy dealing with the nature of existence 116

metastasis spread of a malignancy from its original site to other parts of the body 116

metatarsal between the ankle and the toes 114

metempsychosis supposed afterexistence, or passing of the soul at death into another body, either human or animal; transmigration of souls 116

metonymy naming a thing or person by substituting an associated name 227

microbe microscopic organism or germ 209

microbicide preparation designed to kill microbes 209

microorganism any microscopic or ultramicroscopic living animal or plant 207

Midas touch talent for making money in any enterprise one engages in 243

millennium period of 1,000 years 4

misdemeanor minor offense punishable by fine or imprisonment of usually less than a year; misdeed 160

misogamist person who hates marriage 254

moment importance; consequence 38

momentous important 40

monocle eyeglass for one eye 23

monoculture use of land for the growing of only one crop 18

monogamy practice of being married to only one person at a time 23

monograph learned treatise on a particular subject; scholarly article 20

monolingual speaking or using only one language 23, 182

monologue lengthy talk by one person 20

monomania derangement of the mind on one subject only 14

monomaniac person deranged on one subject only 15

monorail railway with cars on a single-rail track 20

monosyllabic having only one syllable 20

monotheism belief in one god 23

monotonous tiresome because of lack of variety 20

morphology anatomy; structure 106

mortify humiliate; subject to shame 254

multicultural reflecting many different cultures 20

multifaceted having many facets or aspects 20

multilateral having many sides; participated in by more than two participants 21

multilingual using several languages 183

multimedia involving the use of two or more media, such as slides, films, tape recordings, flashing colored lights, etc. 21

multimillionaire person having several million dollars 23

multinational having subsidiaries or operations in several countries 21

multinuclear containing many nuclei 18

multiracial representing or inhabited by many races 23

Murphy's Law satirical maxim, stating that if anything can go wrong, it will 243

naïve innocent and simple; ingenuous 137, 139

neophyte novice; tyro 68

nephritis inflammation of the kidneys 59

nephrologist kidney specialist 61

nephrotomy incision of a kidney 110

neural having to do with a nerve or the nervous system 60

neuralgia pain along the course of one or more nerves 61

neurectomy excision of a nerve 110

neuritis inflammation of a nerve 59

neurology scientific study of the nervous system 60

neurosurgeon specialist in surgery involving the nerves, brain, and spine 60

neurotomy cutting of a nerve 110

nonagenarian one who is at least ninety but less than a hundred 4

non compos mentis not of sound mind; not mentally competent to handle one's affairs 84

nonpathogenic not disease-causing 256

non sequitur comment bearing no relevance to what has just been said 84

obituary published notice of death ("going") including a short biographical account 150

obsequious much too attentive (to a superior); excessively submissive; servile; fawning 170

obsolescent going out of use; becoming obsolete (outmoded) 150

obsolete outmoded 150

obstreperous excessively noisy; boisterous, unruly 170

octogenarian one who is at least eighty but less than ninety 4

odyssey long, wandering journey 127

olfactory concerned with the sense of smell 179

omnipresent ubiquitous 255

open sesame any means or formula that works like magic to help one achieve a desired end 243

opinionated holding obstinately to one's own opinion 171

osteotomy surgical dividing of a bone 110

o tempora! o mores! oh the times! oh the customs! 263

otitis inflammation of the ear 59

otology science of the ear and its diseases 60

oxidation changes produced by oxygen 98

oxymoron figure of speech that combines contradictory terms 228

palindrome any word, phrase, or sentence that reads the same backward or forward 228

Pandora's box source of extensive unforeseen troubles 243

panegyric high praise, either written or spoken; eulogy; tribute 137

paradox contradiction 239

parathyroidectomy excision of the parathyroid 109

Parkinson's Law satirical maxim about the lack of productivity, stating that work expands to fill the time available for its completion; also, that the number of subordinates increases regardless of the amount of work produced 244

parsimonious extremely frugal; miserly; stingy 171

pathogenic disease-causing 256

patronymic name derived from that of a father 230

pay the piper suffer the unavoidable consequences of one's actions 190

pejorative having a derogatory meaning or effect; disparaging; downgrading 228

penal involving punishment; having to do with penalties or correctional institutions 160

penchant strong learning; fondness; liking 38

pentagon plane figure of five sides and five angles 5

penult next-to-last syllable of a word 115

penultimate next to the last 67

perambulation walk 152

peregrination travel; journey 150

peripatetic walking about from place to place; itinerant 150

peritoneum membrane lining the abdominal cavity 59

peritonitis inflammation of the peritoneum, the membrane lining the abdominal cavity 59

persona non grata person who is unwelcome; unacceptable person 85

philanthropic charitable; eleemosynary 252

philippic bitter denunciatory speech; tirade 127

phlebitis inflammation of a vein 59

phlebotomy surgical opening of a vein to draw blood 61

phobia abnormal and persistent fear, dislike, or hatred 14

photogenic likely to look good in a photo 255

photophilic light-loving; requiring abundant light 10, 14

photophobia painful sensitivity to light 14

photophobic shunning light; light-hating 10, 14

plagiarism act of plagiarizing (stealing the writing of another and passing it off as one's own) 160

plagiarize commit plagiarism 160

plantar having to do with the sole of the foot 179

platitude overused expression; cliché 224

play possum pretend to be dead or asleep; dissemble 191

play the devil's advocate uphold the wrong side of a cause for the sake of argument 191

plurality number of votes by which a winning candidate exceeds that of the runner-up 5

pneumonectomy excision of a lung 110

poach hunt or fish illegally 160

poacher one who hunts or fishes illegally 160

poker face expressionless face, as that of an experienced poker player 191

polemic attack on, or refutation of, another's opinions; controversial discussion 254

polemicist person skilled in refuting arguments 259

pollyanna one who is excessively and persistently optimistic 122

polychromatic using various or changing colors 23

polyclinic clinic or hospital treating many diseases 23

polygamist person married to two or more mates at the same time 21

polygamy practice of being married to two or more mates at the same time 23

polyglot person who speaks or writes several languages 21, 182

polymath person of great and diversified learning 21

polyonymous having many names 230

polysyllabic consisting of many syllables 18

polytechnic providing instruction in many technical arts and applied sciences 21

polytheism worship of more than one god 44

polytheistic believing in more than one god 22

postatomic after the explosion of the first atomic bomb 118

postdated marked with a later date than the true one 118

posterior coming after; situated behind or toward the back 116

posterity those born after a person; descendants; future generations 116

postgraduate occurring after graduation 118

posthumous born after the death of one's father; published or occurring after one's death 116

postmortem detailed evaluation of some event just completed 85

postoperative following a surgical operation 114

postprandial   occurring after a meal; after dinner   117
potential   present though invisible and inactive; latent   52
preadolescent   child between nine and twelve   118
preamble   preliminary statement or event; introduction   67, 152
precipitation   amount of rain, snow, sleet, hail, etc., falling on an area in a specified period   254
pre-Columbian   before the coming of Columbus   114
precursor   forerunner   152
predecease   die before another person   117
predesignate   indicate in advance   119
preelection   preceding an election   118
preen   dress up; make oneself trim; neaten up; fuss in dressing   137
premiere   first performance   67
prepaid   paid in advance   119
prerecord   record in advance   117
prescient   seeming to have knowledge of events before they occur; gifted with foresight   117
preselect   select beforehand   118
presentiment   feeling that something unfortunate is about to happen before that event occurs; foreboding   117
prodigious   gigantic; gargantuan   126
prognosis   forecast; prediction of the probable course of an illness; prognostication   117
prognosticate   foretell   119
prognostication   prediction   117
progress   move or go forward   152
prolixity   talkativeness; excessive flow of words   227
prologue   introduction; foreword   118
prone   (1) lying face downward; (2) having a bent or inclination; predisposed   180
prophesy   foretell; indicate beforehand; predict   117
prophylaxis   preventive treatment against disease   118
proposition   something offered (put forth) for consideration   118
proscenium   part of stage in front of the curtain   114
prostatectomy   surgical removal of the prostate   110
pseudonym   fictitious name; pen name   229
psyche   soul   116
psychogenic   produced by mental factors   256
pugilist   prizefighter; professional boxer   254
pugnacious   inclined to fight; bellicose   135

pulmonary having to do with the lungs 180

pun play on words having the same sound but different meanings; play on different meanings of the same word 228

pusillanimous lacking in courage; cowardly; timid 137

pyogenic pus-producing 256

pyrogenic fever-producing 256

pyromaniac person having an insane impulse to start fires 14

pyrophobia unreasoning fear of fire 15

Pyrrhic victory victory achieved at ruinous cost 244

quack impostor; charlatan 158

quadrennial occurring or being done every four years 5

quadrennially every four years 43

quadruped four-footed animal 5

quagmire wet, boggy ground that gives way under the foot; difficult situation 137

quisling traitor; collaborator 127

quixotic impractically idealistic; visionary 128

rash impulsive; impetuous 170

rational capable of reasoning 170

recidivist person with a tendency to relapse; chronic offender; habitual criminal 160

reclusive solitary; living in seclusion, apart from others; like a recluse 207

reconcile (1) make friendly again; (2) settle; adjust 38

red herring something used to distract attention from the real issue 191

redundant exceeding what is necessary; superfluous 228

refractory hard to control; resisting authority; unruly 38

reincarnation rebirth of the soul in another body after death, as in some religious beliefs; new embodiment 207

repentant sorrowful for a misdeed 169

rescission act of rescinding; cancelation; annulment 108

résumé short autobiographical sketch; vita 208

resuscitate revive from apparent death; restore to life 207

retrogress move backward to an earlier or worse condition; degenerate 151

revitalize restore to life 209

revival new presentation of something old 209

revivify put new life into; revitalize 208

roll out the red carpet show impressive courtesy and ceremonial hospitality 191

rudiment first principle that must be learned; fundamental (usually plural) 67

rue feel remorse for; wish undone; regret 128

Russophobia abnormal dislike of Russia or the Russians 15

sadistic deriving pleasure by inflicting pain on others; deliberately cruel 128

safari hunting expedition, especially in Africa; any lengthy adventurous expedition 151

salaam bow very low, placing the right palm on the forehead 85

sanctuary shelter; asylum 218

sanguinary bloody; having to do with bloodshed; bloodthirsty 180

sanguine confidently optimistic; hopeful 171

saprogenic rot-producing 256

satire use of ridicule to expose folly or abuse; literary work holding up human stupidity or wickedness to scorn 228

saunter walk unhurriedly; amble 149

sayonara farewell; good-bye 85

scorch burn slightly, discoloring the surface 254

score group of twenty; twenty 5

seclusion condition of being withdrawn in a place hard to reach; solitude 52

section cut 104

sectionalism exaggerated devotion to the interests of one section; regional prejudice 108

seismology scientific study of earthquakes 266

sepsis disease; decay 99

septuagenarian one who is at least seventy but less than eighty 5

servile excessively submissive; obsequious 170

sesquicentennial 150th anniversary 5

sexagenarian one who is at least sixty but less than seventy 5

shallow superficial; glib 226

shalom term of greeting or farewell 85

shibboleth password, saying, or custom distinguishing the members of one group from those of another; slogan, especially one that has lost its meaning; discredited doctrine   223, 229

simile   direct comparison containing "like" or "as"   227

simulate   pretend; feign   51

Sinophile   admirer of the Chinese   15

sinuses   hollow cavities connected by passageways to the nose   59

sinusitis   inflammation of the sinuses   59

skeptical   disbelieving; doubting; not easily convinced   171

slatternly   dirty; untidy; slovenly   38

slovenly   untidy, slatternly   38

sociogenic   caused by society   256

somnambulist   person who walks in his or her sleep; sleepwalker   151

sour grapes   disparagement of something that one does not or cannot have   244

spellbind   hypnotize; mesmerize   127

spleen   (1) ductless organ, near the stomach; (2) malice; anger; bad temper   180

splenectomy   surgical removal of the spleen   109, 182

splenetic   bad-tempered; spiteful   183

stentorian   very loud   128

stick in one's craw   be intolerable or unacceptable   192

stick to one's last   keep to one's own trade or field   192

stratagem   trick; subterfuge   52

subaqueous   underwater   29

subaudible   not quite audible   31

subcutaneous   being, living, or introduced beneath the skin   29, 180

sublethal   not quite lethal (death-causing); insufficient to cause death   29

sublingual   situated under the tongue   182

submarginal   below minimum standards; inadequate for some end; unproductive   29

submicroscopic   too tiny to be seen with a microscope   31

suboceanic   situated beneath the ocean   31

suborn   induce someone to testify falsely   52

subpoena   order summoning a person to testify in court under a penalty for failure to appear   161

subservient   useful in an "under," or subordinate, capacity; excessively submissive   30

subside   become less intense; abate; wane   255
substructure   foundation of a building   26
subterfuge   plan or trick to conceal one's true objective; stratagem; deception   52
suffocation   loss of consciousness due to oxygen deprivation   217
suicidal   tending toward suicide (act of voluntarily taking one's life); self-destructive; destructive of one's own interests   108
suicide   act of voluntarily taking one's life   108
supercilious   showing haughty contempt; disdainful; full of pride and scorn   171
supererogatory   beyond the requirements of duty; performed to an extent not demanded   30
superficial   over or on the surface only; not profound or thorough   30
supernatural   beyond what is natural or observable; not explainable by the laws of nature   30
supernumerary   exceeding the standard or prescribed number; extra   30
superpower   extremely powerful nation   31
supersonic   having a speed beyond that of sound   30
superstructure   all of a building above the foundation   26
supertanker   tanker with an extremely large capacity   31
supine   (1) lying on the back, face upward; (2) mentally or morally inactive; lethargic; listless   181
surreptitious   secret; covert   51
survival   continuation of life   210
swan song   farewell appearance; final creative work or performance   67
symbiotic   mutually dependent   209
synonym   word of the same or similar meaning   229

taciturn   habitually disinclined to talk; silent; uncommunicative   128
tact   skill in dealing with difficult or delicate situations   182
tactful   possessing tact   182
tactless   lacking tact; undiplomatic   182
tactile   having to do with the sense of touch   181
tangible   having material existence; concrete   182, 226
teetotaler   one who totally abstains from alcoholic drink   17
telegenic   making, or likely to make, a pleasing appearance on television; videogenic   255

tempus fugit   time flies   263

tercentennial   300th anniversary   5

terminal   coming at the end; ending in death   67

thermogenic   heat-producing   256

thyroidectomy   surgical removal of the thyroid   110

tirade   bitter denunciatory speech   127

tithe   one tenth, or tenth part, of something paid as a contribution or tax to support a religious establishment   6

tome   one volume, or "cut," of a work of two or more volumes; any large, scholarly book   108

tonsillectomy   removal of the tonsils   109

tonsillitis   inflammation of the tonsils   56

tout comprendre, c'est tout pardonner   to understand all is to forgive all   263

tracheotomy   surgical cutting into the windpipe   109

transgressor   one who goes beyond the bounds of law or morality   152

transition   process or period of passing from one condition, place, or action to another; change   151

transitory   lasting a short time only; temporary; short-lived   38, 152

treble   multiply by three; triple   6

trisect   cut into three parts   108

triumvirate   ruling body of three; troika   6

troglodyte   person living in seclusion; recluse; also, anyone who behaves like a caveman   205, 207

troika   ruling body of three   6

tyro   beginner in learning something; novice; neophyte   68

ubiquitous   existing or seeming to exist everywhere; omnipresent   255

ultimate   last in a progression; final; highest possible   68

ultimatum   final, uncompromising demand or offer, leading to serious consequences if rejected   68

unanimous   being of one and the same opinion; showing complete agreement   22

understatement   restrained statement in contrast to what is warranted by the facts   229

unicameral   consisting of or having one legislative chamber   22

unicorn   mythical animal with the body of a horse and a single horn in the middle of its forehead   18

unicycle   one-wheeled vehicle   23

unidirectional going in one direction only 18

uniform always the same; not varying in form, degree, or manner 22

unilateral involving or affecting one side only; one-sided 21

unique being the only one of its kind; highly unusual 22

unisex not distinguishable as male or female; designed for both sexes 22

unison harmony 23

unpremeditated not premeditated (thought about beforehand) 119

unruly hard to control; refractory 38

upgrade advance; step up in rank 153

vandal person who maliciously defaces, spoils, or destroys public or private property 161

vascular having to do with vessels that convey blood or lymph 181

venial forgivable; pardonable; excusable 38

venue locality in which a crime or cause of a legal action occurs and where the trial must be held 161

veracity truthfulness; honesty 38

verbum sat sapienti est (or **verbum sat**, or **verbum sap**) a word to the wise is sufficient 264

viable able to live; likely to survive; workable 208

videogenic telegenic 255

vindictive inclined to seek vengeance; unforgiving; spiteful 171

viscera entrails; intestines; guts 178

visceral having to do with or occurring in the viscera 181

visionary impractically idealistic 128

visual pertaining to seeing or sight 176

vita brief outline of one's life and experience; short autobiographical sketch; résumé 208

vitality capacity to live and develop 209

vitalize instill life into 208

vital signs signs of life, as pulse and breathing rates, body temperature, etc. 209

vivacious full of liveliness 209

vivid lively 210

viviparous giving birth to living offspring rather than eggs 208

vivisection   practice of subjecting living animals to surgical experimentation to advance medical knowledge   108
vivisepulture   live burial   208

wanderlust   restless longing to travel   151
whistle in the dark   put on a show of confidence in the face of impending danger or defeat; try to keep up one's courage   192
white elephant   possession entailing expense and trouble far greater than its usefulness to the owner   192

xenophile   admirer of foreigners   15
xenophobe   one who dislikes foreigners   15
xenophobia   fear or hatred of foreigners   14
xenophobic   showing dislike of foreigners   196

yaw   deviate abruptly from a straight course; swerve; veer   151

Pronunciation Symbols

ə ... banana, collide, abut

'ə, ˌə ... humdrum, abut

ə ... immediately preceding \l\, \n\, \m\, \ŋ\, as in battle, mitten, eaten, and sometimes open \'ō-p°n\, lock and key \-°ŋ-\; immediately following \l\, \m\, \r\, as often in French table, prisme, titre

ər
'ər-
'ə-r ... as in two different pronunciations of hurry \'hər-ē, 'hə-rē\

a ... mat, map, mad, gag, snap, patch

ā ... day, fade, date, aorta, drape, cape

ä ... bother, cot, and, with most American speakers, father, cart

à ... father as pronounced by speakers who do not rhyme it with bother, French patte

aù ... now, loud, out

b ... baby, rib

ch ... chin, nature \'nā-chər\

d ... did, adder

e ... bet, bed, peck

'ē, ˌē ... beat, nosebleed, evenly, easy

ē ... easy, mealy

f ... fifty, cuff

g ... go, big, gift

h ... hat, ahead

hw ... whale as pronounced by those who do not have the same pronunciation for both whale and wail

i ... tip, banish, active

ī ... site, side, buy, tripe

j ... job, gem, edge, join, judge

k ... kin, cook, ache

k̲ ... German ich, Buch; one pronunciation of loch

l ... lily, pool

m ... murmur, dim, nymph

n ... no, own

ⁿ ... indicates that a preceding vowel or diphthong is pronounced with the nasal passages open, as in French un bon vin blanc \œⁿ-bōⁿ-vaⁿ-bläⁿ\

ŋ ... sing \'siŋ\, singer \'siŋ-ər\, finger \'fiŋ-gər\, ink \'iŋk\

ō ... bone, know, beau

ò ... saw, all, gnaw, caught

œ ... French boeuf, German Hölle

œ̄ ... French feu, German Höhle

oi ... c**oi**n, destr**oy**
p ... **p**epper, li**p**
r ... **r**ed, ca**r**, **r**a**r**ity
s ... **s**ource, le**ss**
sh ... as in **sh**y, mi**ss**ion, ma**ch**ine, spe**ci**al (actually, this is a single sound, not two); with a hyphen between, two sounds as in gras**sh**opper \'gras-,hä-pər\
t ... **t**ie, a**tt**ack, la**t**e, la**t**er, la**tt**er
th ... as in **th**in, e**th**er (actually, this is a single sound, not two); with a hyphen between, two sounds as in knig**h**t**h**ood \'nīt-,hüd\
t̲h̲ ... **th**en, ei**th**er, **th**is (actually, this is a single sound, not two)
ü ... r**u**le, y**ou**th, un**io**n \'yün-yən\, few \'fyü\
u̇ ... p**u**ll, w**oo**d, b**oo**k, c**u**rable \'kyu̇r-ə-bəl\, f**u**ry \'fyu̇r-ē\
ue ... German f**ü**llen, h**ü**bsch
ū̲e̲ ... French r**u**e, German f**ü**hlen
v ... **v**i**v**id, gi**v**e
w ... **w**e, a**w**ay
y ... **y**ard, **y**oung, cue \'ky**ü**\, mute \'my**ü**t\, un**io**n \'y**ü**n-yən\

y ... indicates that during the articulation of the sound represented by the preceding character the front of the tongue has substantially the position it has for the articulation of the first sound of *yard*, as in French *digne* \dēny\
z ... **z**one, rai**s**e
zh ... as in vi**si**on, a**z**ure \'a-zhər\ (actually, this is a single sound, not two); with a hyphen between, two sounds as in *hogshead* \'hȯgz-,hed, 'hägz-\
\ ... slant line used in pairs to mark the beginning and end of a transcription: \pen\
' ... mark preceding a syllable with primary (strongest) stress: \'pen-mən-,ship\
, ... mark preceding a syllable with secondary (medium) stress: \'pen-mən-,ship\
- ... mark of syllable division
() ... indicates that what is symbolized between is present in some utterances but not in others: *factory* \'fak-t(ə-)rē\
÷ ... indicates that many regard as unacceptable the pronunciation variant immediately following: *cupola* \'kyü-pə-lə, ÷-,lō\

The system of indicating pronunciation is used by permission. From Merriam-Webster's Collegiate® Dictionary, Tenth Edition © 1996 by Merriam-Webster Inc.

Penguin Group (USA) Online

What will you be reading tomorrow?

Tom Clancy, Patricia Cornwell, W.E.B. Griffin,
Nora Roberts, William Gibson, Robin Cook,
Brian Jacques, Catherine Coulter, Stephen King,
Dean Koontz, Ken Follett, Clive Cussler,
Eric Jerome Dickey, John Sandford,
Terry McMillan, Sue Monk Kidd, Amy Tan,
John Berendt...

You'll find them all at
penguin.com

*Read excerpts and newsletters,
find tour schedules and reading group guides,
and enter contests.*

Subscribe to Penguin Group (USA) newsletters
and get an exclusive inside look
at exciting new titles and the authors you love
long before everyone else does.

PENGUIN GROUP (USA)
us.penguingroup.com